Lovemaps

Clinical Concepts of Sexual/Erotic Health and Pathology, Paraphilia, and Gender Transposition in Childhood, Adolescence, and Maturity

ALSO BY JOHN MONEY

Hermaphroditism: An Inquiry into the Nature of a Human Paradox, 1952
The Psychologic Study of Man 1957
A Standardized Road-Map Test of Direction Sense (with D. Alexander and H.T. Walker, Jr.), 1965
Sex Errors of the Body: Dilemmas, Education and Counseling, 1968
Man and Woman, Boy and Girl: The Differentiation and Dimorphism of Gender Identity from Conception to Maturity (with A.A. Ehrhardt), 1972
Sexual Signatures (with Patricia Tucker), 1975
Love and Love Sickness: The Science of Sex, Gender Difference, and Pairbonding, 1980
The Destroying Angel: Sex, Fitness, and Food in the Legacy of Degeneracy Theory, Graham Crackers, Kellogg's Corn Flakes, and American Health History, 1985
Venuses Penuses: Sexology, Sexosophy, and Exigency Theory, 1986

EDITED BY JOHN MONEY

Reading Disability: Progress and Research Needs in Dyslexia, 1962
Sex Research: New Developments, 1965
The Disabled Reader: Education of the Dyslexic Child, 1966
Transsexualism and Sex Reassignment (with R. Green), 1969
Contemporary Sexual Behavior: Critical Issues in the 1970's (with J. Zubin), 1973
Developmental Human Behavior Genetics (with W.K. Schaie, E. Anderson and G. McClearn), 1975
Handbook of Sexology (with H. Musaph), 1977
Traumatic Abuse and Neglect of Children at Home (with G. Williams), 1980
Handbook Human Sexuality (with B.B. Wolman), 1980

Lovemaps

*Clinical Concepts of Sexual/Erotic Health
and Pathology, Paraphilia, and Gender
Transposition in Childhood, Adolescence,
and Maturity*

John Money, Ph.D.

*Professor of Medical Psychology and Pediatrics
The Johns Hopkins University and Hospital
Baltimore, Maryland 21205*

Irvington Publishers, Inc.
New York

PROMETHEUS BOOKS
Buffalo, New York

APR 2 2 1991 $\bigwedge\bigwedge\times 3\,2\,4\,/$

First paperback edition copublished 1988 by
Prometheus Books and Irvington Publishers, Inc.

Copyright © 1986 by Irvington Publishers, Inc.

First published in hardcover by Irvington Publishers Inc.

Money, John, 1921-
Lovemaps: clinical concepts of sexual/erotic health and pathology, paraphilia,
and gender transposition in childhood, adolescence, and maturity.
Bibliography: pp. 299-306
Includes indexes.
1. Psychosexual disorders. 2. Sexual disorders.
[DNLM: 1. Identification (Psychology). 2. Paraphilias.
3. Sex Characteristics. WM 610 M742l]
RC556.M66 1985   155.3   85-24153
ISBN 0-87975-456-7

Printed in the United States of America

DEDICATION

To the members, past and present,
of the Psychohormonal Research Unit

Contents

Acknowledgments

During the period when this book was written, the author's Psychohormonal Research Unit at the Johns Hopkins University and Hospital was supported by USPHS Grant HD00325 and Grant 83086900 from the William T. Grant Foundation. The manuscript was typed by the late Mrs. Helen Cutler, Dr. Hap Morrow, Ms. Roberta Boyce, and Ms. Sion Kim. Indexing and tabulation of biographical data were done with the assistance of Margaret Lamacz (Chapters 21 and 22) and Frank Tedesco (Chapter 25). Together with Gregory K. Lehne, they were responsible also for some of the paraphilic follow-up interviews. Earlier interviews were, over the years, done by many different staff and trainee members of the Psychohormonal Research Unit. Susan and Dennis Danielson and Carol and Gerald Dusick are the parents who, because of the deaths of their sons from the syndrome of asphyxiophilia, have embarked on a program of public education and prevention of autoerotic death. Material from Chapter 15 has appeared also in the *Journal of Sex and Marital Therapy,* 10:75–82, 1984; from Chaptert 21 in the *International Journal of Family Psychiatry,* in press; and from Chapter 22 in *Comprehensive Psychiatry,* 25:392–403, 1984. Chapter 16 was dedicated to my friend and colleague, Herman Musaph, on the occasion of his retirement.

Introduction and Synopsis

Lovemaps! They're as common as faces, bodies and brains. Each of us has one. Without it there would be no falling in love, no mating, and no breeding of the species. Lacking a name, however, the lovemap has existed in a conceptually unexplored territory of the mind, unknown to science and scholarly inquiry.

By searching through my file of manuscripts, I found that I first wrote the word *lovemap* in 1980. It was in an article titled "Pairbonding and Limerence," published in 1983 in the *International Encyclopedia of Psychiatry, Psychology, Psychoanalysis and Neurology, Progress Volume 1* (New York, Aesculapius Publishers).

Before I wrote that article, I had already begun to talk about lovemaps in my lectures to students whose textbook was *Love and Lovesickness: The Science of Sex, Gender Difference and Pairbonding* which the Johns Hopkins University Press had published for me in 1980. In that book I had written (p. 65):

> There is a rather sophisticated riddle about what a boyfriend (or girlfriend) and a Rorschach inkblot have in common. The answer is that you project an image of your own onto each. In many instances, a person does not fall in love with a partner, per se, but with a partner as a Rorschach love-blot. That is to say, the person projects onto the partner an idealized and highly idiosyncratic image that diverges from the image of that partner as perceived by other people. Hence the popular idiom that love is blind, for a lover projects onto a partner, or love-blot, his/her unique love image, as unique as his/her own face or finger print.

To communicate fluently with students, I found it extremely awkward to have only the expression, *an idealized and highly idiosyncratic image*. Therefore, I began substituting the single term, *lovemap*. Everyone knew immediately exactly what I was talking about. The word became part of my vocabulary not only with students but also with patients. Patients also knew, without hesitation, the meaning of the word. They were adept also at deciphering their own personal lovemaps and the errors, if any, in them.

People who have heard the title of this book, or who have read it in typescript, now include the word *lovemap* in their everyday vocabulary. Sooner or later, therefore, *lovemap* will find its way into the standard dictionaries of the English language, and in translations. For those who will need a definition: a lovemap is not present at birth. Like a native language, it differentiates within a few years thereafter. It is a developmental representation or template in your mind/brain, and is dependent on input through the special senses. It depicts your idealized lover and what, as a pair, you do together in the idealized, romantic, erotic, and sexualized relationship. A lovemap exists in mental imagery first, in dreams and fantasies, and then maybe translated into action with a partner or partners.

Under optimum conditions, prenatally and postnatally, a lovemap differentiates as heterosexual without complexities. Age-concordant, gender-different, sexuoerotic rehearsal play in infancy and childhood is prerequisite to healthy heterosexual lovemap formation. Deprivation and neglect of such play may induce pathology of lovemap formation, as also may prohibition, prevention, and abusive punishment and discipline. Conversely, exposure too abruptly to socially tabooed expressions of sexuoeroticism may traumatize lovemap formation.

Lovemap pathology, whereas it has its genesis early in life, manifests itself in full after puberty. The three categories of pathology are hypophilia (also referred to as sexual dysfunction), hyperphilia (erotomania), and paraphilia (legally known as perversion). In all three, there is a cleavage between love and lust in the design of the lovemap. In hypophilia, the cleavage is such that lust is dysfunctional and infrequently used, whereas love and lovebonding are intact. In hyperphilia, lust displaces love and lovebonding, and the genitalia function in the service of lust alone, typically with a plurality of partners, and with compulsive frequency. In paraphilia, love and lovebonding are compromised because the genitalia continue to function in the service of lust, but according to the specifications of a vandalized and redesigned lovemap, and often with compulsive frequency, also. The redesigned lovemap manifests itself in fantasy, and in the staging of that fantasy in an actual performance.

A paraphilia typically has a dual existence, one in fantasy, and one as fantasy carried out in practice. On the criterion of its mental imagery, a paraphilia is a mental template or lovemap that, in response to the neglect, suppression, or traumatization of its normophilic formation, has developed with distortions, namely, omissions, displacements, and inclusions that would otherwise have no place in it. A paraphilia permits sexuoerotic arousal, genital performance, and orgasm to take place, but only under the aegis, in fantasy or live performance, of the special substitute imagery of the paraphilia.

A paraphilia is a strategy for turning tragedy into triumph according to the principles of opponent-process theory. This strategy preserves sinful lust in the lovemap by dissociating it from saintly love.

Sexosophy, the philosophy of sex characteristic of each major religion, influences the childhood development of lovemaps and their paraphilias. The definitive characteristic of the sexosophy of Christendom is the doctrine of the split between saintly love and sinful lust. This doctrine is all-pervasive. It penetrates all the institutions of contemporary Christendom. One way or another, usually quite deviously, it penetrates all of our child-rearing practices. Inevitably, therefore, it penetrates the formation of lovemaps in the early years of childhood. That is why, in this book, the pathological lovemaps of the paraphilias are developmentally explained in saint and sinner terms.

The idea that religious parables, strategies, or formulas undergo transformation so as to be scarcely recognizable in their new guise, as in paraphilia, has not hitherto been recognized. It defines a new universe of discourse in the etiology, treatment, and prevention of sexological as well as other disorders. It has ready applicability in pastoral counseling, and in designing sexual learning programs for parents intent on rearing their children so as to maximize the developmental healthiness of their lovemaps.

Paraphilias are not generated at random. They belong to one of six categories: sacrificial/expiatory; marauding/predatory; mercantile/venal; fetishistic/talismanic; stigmatic/eligibilic; and solicitational/allurative (Chapters 6-11).

The forty or so paraphilas distributed among these six categories have not only an individual or ontogenetic history, but also have a species or phylogenetic history. There are specific phylogenetic components or phylisms which, should they become ontogenetically entrained or recruited into the lovemap, change its childhood development from normophilic into paraphilic (Chapters 12-13).

Apart from its paraphilic quality, a lovemap may or may not be gender transposed. The different degrees and types of gender transposition include the bisexual, homosexual, transexual, and transvestite phenomena.

The paraphilias range from those that are playful and harmless, to those that are bizarre and deadly. The law permits some manifestations of paraphilic behavior to be a matter of mutual consent, whereas others are criminalized. It is a basic principle of the law that paraphilic behavior is engaged in by voluntary choice and can be controlled by will power or, failing that, by punishment. Biomedically, by contrast, it is a basic principle that a paraphilia is a syndrome that is not subject to voluntary control any more than is the syndrome of psychomotor epilepsy. In some cases, paraphilia coexists with clinical epilepsy. In others it is associated with an altered state of consciousness, or paraphilic fugue state.

The first use of the hormone MPA (medroxyprogesterone acetate), trade named Depo-Provera (Upjohn) in the treatment of a paraphilic sex offender was in December 1966, by Money, Migeon and Rivarola, in the psychohormonal unit at Johns Hopkins. The hormonal treatment was combined with individual counseling and family therapy.

MPA is a synthetic progestinic steroid related to progesterone which itself is the body's own precursor of testosterone. MPA is able to deceive testosterone-using cells into accepting it in place of testosterone. Whereas testosterone has high power as a hormonal fuel that induces the subjective feeling of sexual drive, MPA does not. Thus MPA enables an adolescent or adult male to return temporarily, for as long as weekly injections are given, to the hormonal state of prepuberty. His paraphilically obsessive sex drive goes on vacation, so to speak, and he is better able to undergo, with counseling, a realignment of his sex life in both practice and imagery.

New developments in medicine and science often create a storm of moral controversy which has, indeed, been the case with MPA for paraphilic sex offenders. Some critics claim that paraphilic sex offenders lose their power of informed consent and will sign for any form of treatment in order to escape arrest or imprisonment. Others maintain that sex offenders are degenerate heretics who deserve only punishment and death, not treatment.

New legislation has created a new profession of victimology. In many instances, the practitioners of victimology are caught in the dilemma of reporting to the police their clients or patients whose confidentiality is not accorded the legal status of privileged communication. Victimologists themselves, as a group, are oblivious to their own vulnerability, namely, to the fake accusation of having made an indecent sexual advance toward a patient. Many victimologists claim that they always believe the statements of the victim, especially one under the age of eighteen, the new legal limit of childhood in the United States.

Paraphilias are not socially contagious, though they are popularly believed to be so on the basis of 18th century medical degeneracy theory, now obsolete. According to this obsolete doctrine, paraphilic stories, pictures, films, and videotapes lure new recruits and convert them into paraphiles. The faulty logic of this doctrine is the underpinning of society's combined ambivalence and panic regarding pornography which is defined to include all sexually explicit material, even that portraying normal, healthy, heterosexuality. It is extremely difficult to counteract faulty dogma regarding pornography with impartial science, because society withholds funding for research on the genesis, prevention, and cure of paraphilia.

In addition to *lovemap*, *phylism* is another new and original term used in this book. A phylism is a unit or building block of individual existence that is species-determined. Phylism theory has some affinity with sociobiology insofar as it links phylogeny to social behavior; but it diverges from sociobiology insofar as phylisms may become ontogenetically enlisted or recruited from their primary behavioral context to a secondary one—for example, a sexual one. The transfer from primary to secondary context constitutes the ontogenetic strategy of a paraphilia.

Technical and uncommon terms used in this book are defined in Chapter 26 and in the Glossary, thus making the book eminently readable, as well as interesting to the nonspecialist in science, medicine, and the law, as well as to the literate readership at large. I have deliberately pitched the writing to appeal to such a readership, rather than making it a technical monograph for specialists. Nonetheless, it can perfectly well serve the specialist, and is quite suitable for use as a textbook in sexual medicine, human sexuality, sex education, and child development. The range of its appeal and applicability will be measured by specialists in not only sexology, but also psychology, psychiatry, social work, criminology, police policy, law, ethics, religion, and pedogogy.

Historically, this is the first book about lovemaps. As of now, it is the only one.

1

Human Sexual Rights

Interference versus Treatment

Kinky and bizarre are the popular words for paraphilic sexual fantasies and practices. Legally, they are called perverted and deviant. Medicine and science only recently gave up using the legal terms and adopted for full-time use the formerly neglected biomedical term, paraphilic, and its noun paraphilia. The person with a paraphilia is a paraphiliac, or a paraphile.

The word, paraphilia, is constructed from two Greek roots. *Philia* means love, as in Philadelphia, the city of brotherly love. *Para-*, the prefix that precedes it, means that the love goes beyond what is ordinarily expected or is apart from it. Thus, in medical usage it also means abnormal. Paranoid, by analogy, refers to abnormal thinking that goes beyond, or is apart from the usual by being delusional.

Calling a person paranoid may be not a diagnosis, but an insult. The same applies to paraphilic. Where does an insult end and a diagnosis begin? There is no clear dividing line. Indeed, there are some critics who protest that a paraphilic diagnosis is always stigmatizing. They protest also that biomedical personnel should quit meddling with other people's love lives, and let them do, sexually, as they please. More precisely, their protest is that, two by two, couples should be allowed to do as they please, provided both give their consent and agreement.

This argument appears to give fair-minded respect to human sexual rights. Its weakness is that it makes no provision for what should be done when there is not mutual consent, but when one of the partners is imposed upon, coerced, or violated. The outcome, then, is that the police may be called in. If the police define what happened as a crime, they arrest and prosecute the one partner as a criminal. If the verdict is guilty, then punishment is the treatment handed out. Especially if imprisoned, the offender's sexual and other human rights are taken away from him/her. With this outcome, the villain is not the distrusted biomedical system, but the revered criminal-justice system.

Most citizens raise no argument about depriving paraphilic sex offenders of their human rights, including their right to clinical treatment of their paraphilia, especially if they have been found guilty of violent and assaultive rape, forced child molestation, or lust murder. The public at large is out to get an eye for an eye, and a tooth for a tooth. Its first thought is to catch each degenerate bastard (the public wrongly expects every sex offender to be male), and put him behind bars, or on death row. Execution, insofar as it prevents sex offending, does it only one person at a time, and never for all the society, completely. Killing the offender has not been an effective method of eradicating sex offending. Other forms of punishment have done no better. Every generation produces a new crop of sex offending paraphiliacs.

Until very recently every generation produced a new crop of contagious carriers of smallpox. Many died. The way of prevention was not to punish, imprison, or exile people with smallpox. No. The way of prevention was the way of science. It required research to find out the cause of smallpox, then to control it with vaccination, and finally, by 1979, to wipe it out altogether (Breman and Arita, 1980). The way of science is the way that is needed also for the prevention of paraphilic sex offending, so that it will not be exponentially proliferated, generation upon future generation, as it has been for hundreds, if not thousands of years past. Just as poverty breeds poverty, so also malnutrition breeds malnutrition, cholera breeds cholera, and paraphilia breeds paraphilia. That is why it is imperative to learn how to perfect the technique of prevention.

There never was a popular referendum to decide whether or not to wipe out smallpox. Had there been one, there surely would have been some protestors. Just as Hitler thought it was a good idea to wipe out millions of people in his Holocaust, so also they would have thought it a good idea to keep smallpox as a means of population control. They would have assumed, of course, that they themselves, blessed with the privilege of vaccination, would be spared.

There are some people who are against the idea of preventing dental decay by fluoridization of the water supply. Likewise, some are against the idea of prevention as applied to paraphilic sex offending. It is not because they condone sex offending. Rather they favor the idea of punishing the offenders, or executing them. Some think that the law is too lenient, and that not enough forms of sexual expression are classified as sex offenses. Some fundamentalist preachers of the new right, for example, have publicly advocated the death penalty for homosexuals—that is, for an estimated ten million Americans. This figure would in all probability prove to be too low, should these preachers ever have power to begin a new Holocaust, and to round up homosexuals for their gas chambers and their intravenous cyanide drips.

Many, of course, are appalled by the threat of such a renewal of religious intolerance in a country officially dedicated to political democracy and human rights. Their response is to demand sexual democracy and sexual rights. They argue that no one group of people should have the authority to dictate what goes on sexually in the intimacy of the bedroom. They are able to make a mockery of sexual legislation by pointing to archaic laws (Bruno, 1984), for example in the State of Maryland, and in Washington, D.C., which make it a crime for anyone, husband and wife included, to have oral sex. Prosecution for this crime in Maryland could lead to ten years in prison and a $1000 fine, or both. The fact that the crimes of cunnilingus and fellatio are committed nightly by hundreds of thousands of people who are not prosecuted simply exposes the law to contempt. It proves the point that the law is not able to dictate arbitrary standards of what is sexually permissible, and then to enforce them.

Natural Law and Normality

The secular law, following the precedent of the medieval canonical law, has a long history of equating what it permits, sexually, with what it defines as natural. Natural means being in conformity with so-called natural law, and being, therefore, normal (Boswell, 1980).

Normal has two meanings. There is statistical or mathematical normality, and ideological normality. Statistical normality means what average people do or are like. In adulthood, average people are not giants over seven feet tall; nor are they dwarfs under four feet tall. They are somewhere in between. People of average height consider it ideal to be average. Thus their ideal or ideological definition of normality agrees with their statistical definition.

The two definitions do not always agree. These same average people usually get cavities in their teeth, sooner or later, and have to go to the dentist. Thus it is normal, in the statistical sense of being average, to have fillings in your teeth, but it is not normal in the ideological sense. Most people would say that it is ideal to have no cavities, and no fillings.

When the law defines normal sex on the basis of natural law, the definition is ideological, not statistical. In other words, normal does not mean what people do, on the average, but what they ought to do. Natural law is not statistically or mathematically based. It is theologically based. It is what the Church, and in particular St. Thomas Aquinas, declared as its ideological standard of normality (Bullough, 1976).

There is a deceptive plausibility in the sexual application of natural law. It declares that sexual intercourse is essential for procreation. Therefore, it is natural to have sexual intercourse only for procreation. Anything else is proscribed as unnatural. In former times, the Church decreed that there must be no romantic passion, no lust, no uncontrolled concupiscence, and no wasting of fluids, except to beget a child. The quicker and quieter, the better; and the less frequent, better still. Indeed, the Church spelled out, in its confessors' manuals and penitentials in the early centuries of Christendom, that marital sexual connection be performed in only one position (her lying under him), and not at all during penance, and not on Sundays, Wednesdays, and Fridays; and not for forty days before and after Easter, and the same at Christmas (Hunt, 1959).

The Church used its concept of natural law to create an ideological norm of sexual abstinence, and to impose an ecclesiastic dictatorship of antisexualism that, in the centuries of the Inquisition, rivaled Hitler's Holocaust. The antithesis of a dictatorship of antisexualism is a pluralistic democracy of sexualism. Sexual democracy, however, is not synonymous with sexual licentiousness whereby anything goes, lust violence and lust murder included.

Sexual democracy, just like political democracy, always confronts the inherent quandary of pluralism—the quandary of whether your sexual emancipation is gained at the cost of my sexual enslavement. It is the quandary of how to tolerate the maximal amount of social diversity and individual eccentricity, while guaranteeing human sexual rights equally to all.

Personal Inviolacy

As a principle that guarantees equal sexual rights for all, while safeguarding societal rights in a sexual democracy, I have formulated the principle of personal sexual inviolacy (Money,1979). According to this principle, no one has the right to infringe upon someone else's personal sexual inviolacy by imposing his/her own version of what is or is not erotic and sexual, without the other person's informed consent. It is possible to give informed consent, and to enter into a consensual contract, only if the terms of the contract are known in full, and not taken for granted. They can be known in full only if the end is predicated by the beginning. In a sexual engagement, that means no unexpected ending, unilaterally imposed on one partner by the other.

Whereas leaving a singles bar in the company of a pickup ordinarily predicates participation in lust, it does not predicate a lust death by strangulation. That outcome would be unpredictable to the intended victim so long as the other person's proclivity as a lust murderer remained undisclosed. Without the murderer's advance warning of this proclivity, the targeted victim would have no possibility of giving informed consent, nor of refusing to give it.

The hypothetical test case is one in which a masochist with a paraphilic fantasy of stage-managing his own lust murder meets a sadist with a paraphilic fantasy of lust murdering. A minutely planned and flawlessly executed lust-death pact could succeed so well as to be undetectable. Society would then not be confronted with adjudicating the human right to make an erotic death pact.

It is only if the murderer succeeds, and is then detected, that he has to face the societal consequences of having wrongly predicated nondetection as the conclusion of the pact. He might then go on trial not for a sexual act, but for murder—just as a mercy killer, so called, might go on trial not for an act of mercy, but for murder.

A lust-death pact outranks other extremes of mutual sadomasochistic pacts between consenting adults. There are also extremes of bondage and discipline, dominance and submission, or slave and master pacts. The agreed-upon activities in the pacts may include amateur surgery, tortures, abuse, and flagellation, with infliction of serious bodily injury. Society has a long history of leniency toward lust pacts of this type, perhaps because of its history of condoning violence more readily than lust. Our society has always been one that tolerates, if not glorifies, aggression. Its verdict on sadomasochism is determined more by the aggression than the lust in the sadomasochistic pact.

The verdict is quite different when sadomasochism is not consensual, but unilaterally coerced on one person by another. Society is ferociously intolerant also of nonsadomasochistic forms of coercion. It categorizes coercion, regardless of degree, as rape, exhibitionism, voyeurism, incest, and child molestation or abuse. There is no societal tolerance of sexual human rights for people whose sexual proclivity places them in one of these categories of sex offending.

It is on behalf of these people, in particular, that science and medicine have recently staked out a research claim. The goal is to discover the extent to which sex offenders may have an option to self-govern their sexual behavior, and thus to retrieve their human sexual rights to the fullest possible extent. The benefits of research success will not be restricted, however. They will be extended to others with a kinky sexual fixation or paraphilia that does not offend the law, but offends only themselves or their partners. On the basis of their informed consent, they will be entitled to receive help toward attaining an alternative to paraphilia.

2

Species Diversity of Sex and Mating

Nature's Diversity: Fish, Reptiles, Birds.

"Normal sex," a student[1] once said, "is what you do for fun. Abnormal sex is what other people do that you wouldn't enjoy." There is an aphoristic kind of truth to this statement. For the majority of people, their own sexuality belongs to them as profoundly, intimately, and personally as does their native language. Without it, the self does not exist. Those who criticize it, or disapprove of it, annihilate one's selfhood. Hence the extraordinary resistance that a paraphile encounters within himself/herself when confronted with the condemnation of other people who are intolerant of his/her difference. Their condemnation is mirrored back. Those who condemn are the ones whom the paraphile holds in contempt and, in turn, condemns for their lack of tolerance of his/her own small stanza of diversity in the wide-ranging epic of sexual and erotic expression in the human species.

Diversity applies sexually not only to the human species, but throughout the animal kingdom. It applies in the most basic sense not only to sexuality, but to the design of procreation itself (Crews, 1984). Procreation by the union of male and female is not a universal and eternal verity. There are microscopic creatures that bypass sexual union and reproduce by dividing. There are creatures, like oysters, snails, and worms, that are hermaphroditic, and fulfill the function of both male and female in reproduction, either simultaneously or on different occasions. Hermaphroditic fish, of which there are many species, actually change

7

their sex (Chan, 1977). They spend part of their lives breeding as female, and part as male, or as male and then female. Some change more than once, back and forth.

In the reptilian kingdom there are some species that are parthenogenic. One of these is a species of whiptail lizard found in Arizona and New Mexico (Crews, 1982). In the human species, the most famous claim of parthenogenesis is that of the Virgin Mary. Whereas no one doubts that Mary was a female, when an entire species is parthenogenic there are neither females nor males, but only unisexed parthenones. Each parthenone is capable of breeding which, in the case of the whiptail lizards, means laying eggs that are buried in sand and sun-hatched. That is not the full story, however. While its eggs are growing before being laid, the lizard seeks a nonovulating mate and the two of them go through a mating ritual, as if they were members of a species that has two sexes.

The function of this ritual is not to join egg and sperm, for there are no sperms. Apparently, however, the activity releases hormones from the pituitary gland that expedite egg formation and increase the size of the clutch. No one knows which came first in the history of life on earth, lizards with two sexes, or those with only one. What is known is that parthenones have all their chromosomes in sets of three, whereas the two-sexed species have them in pairs only.

There are no known parthenogenic birds and mammals, but there is an extraordinary diversity of mating patterns. Birds of most species mate for a lifetime. If birds were religious, they would be the ideal Christians! The female, of course, always lays the egg. In several species, the male shares other duties of parenthood. Male and female ring doves, for example, both engage in nest building, incubating the eggs, and brooding the young. The male has a fixed interval of six daylight hours on the nest. If he begins late, he cannot leave early, but attacks the returning female instead, and beats her off, until his time is up (Wallman, Grabon and Silver, 1979; Silver, 1983).

In other avian species, incubation is the duty of either the female (domestic fowl, for example) or the male (kiwi), with the other partner possibly providing food. In yet other species, such as the cuckoo and the cowbird, the female stealthily lays her egg in the nest of a foster mother, and leaves her to incubate it and rear the hatchling.

Species that mate seasonally, and not for a lifetime, differ as to how they conduct their courtship. In some species, the male bird puts on a display in a specially constructed parade ground or bower (the Australian bower bird) and waits for a female to respond. Males of other species display in groups, at a lekking ground (American sage grouse) and take their chances as to whether a visiting female will copulate with them or not.

In the courtship of many other birds, mate selection is mutual. The couple must together play their preordained parts like the dancer and the ballerina in a pas de deux. Otherwise they lose their cues and fail to copulate.

Man's Animal Nature: The Barnyard

No one ever compares man's bird nature with man's spiritual nature. The spiritual comparison is always with man's animal nature. Mythically, animal nature is personified in satyrs and Minotaurs. The animals of the barnyard are its prototype. Ever since the far distant age of the domestication of farm animals, the mating habits of barnyard species have been far better known than those of animals in the wild.

The barnyard species are those in which males engage in mating rivalry, and serve more than one female. In the herding species, a dominant male defends his position as the herd's breeding stud. He provides stud service to the female only when she is in heat, and does not participate in parental care. Dogs and cats of the barnyard also breed only when the female is in estrus, or heat, and gives off a vaginal odor or pheromone that is a male attractant. Rival dogs congregate around the estrous bitch, but it is she that signals her receptivity to a particular male. He completes the courtship ritual by copulating with her. Tomcats are territorial. They fight off intruders into their territory, so that the courtship ritual can proceed to copulation, uninterrupted.

Barnyard matings are, by human criteria, indiscriminate, promiscuous, transitory, and imposed by males. The same criteria may appear to apply to wild matings, though closer inspection reveals the complexity of male-female courtship. The American white-tailed deer is an example. The buck's mating territory is defined by his urinary odor, and by buck rubs, that is sapling trees on which he has rubbed off the velvet of his annually regrown antlers. He fights off rival males. Females in small herds seek out a male, and he serves all of them, after which the sexes separate until the next breeding season.

As in the case of sage grouse, the males and females of some antelope species meet for breeding on a lekking ground (Shuster, 1976). Males assemble annually at the same lekking ground, each one often on the same spot. There they await mate selection by visiting females. Even though some males are by-passed, there is no rivalrous fighting.

By contrast with multi-mated species, a small American rodent, the prairie vole, is monogamous, and has a family social organization (Getz and Carter, 1980; Getz, Carter and Gavish, 1981). Virgin females remain reproductively dormant so long as they continue to live with male relatives only. To become reproductively active, a virgin female must engage in nasogenital grooming of a male stranger. Direct contact with a pheromone present on the male's genitals brings the female into estrus within two days. The two copulate and become, lifelong, monogamously pair-bonded.

Troopbonding: Primates

Among species as varied as lions, elephants, gorillas, and chimpanzees, adult males and females live in a troop with their infants, juveniles, and adolescents until the latter reach adulthood and leave home. Each troop in many ways resembles the extended kinship family of many human societies.

Among the great apes (Nadler, 1984, and personal communication), gorillas and chimpanzees are troopbonding species. Orangutans in the wild are not. Pairs meet in the jungle. When the female is in heat, they mate, and then separate until their next encounter. Gibbons, like the siamang, are pairbonders. They do not form extended kinship troops, but families of two parents and children. Among nonhuman primates, they are said to most closely approximate the nuclear family of human beings.

In a chimpanzee troop, dominance is distributed hierarchically. The leading lady is the one with whom, during her times of estrus, the leading male copulates most frequently. The two may even go off into the jungle for a few days of "honeymoon." After she passes the peak of estrus, she may play around, copulating with junior males, and even juveniles of the troop. Under conditions of captivity, the sex lives of chimpanzees may become seriously disrupted. For example, one male raised in captivity and deprived of troop membership was unable to copulate, in adulthood, when released into a large enclosure with other chimpanzees. He would sit with his girlfriend, cuddling her and masturbating himself, but he was unable to respond coitally to her invitations (Kollar, Beckwith and Edgerton, 1968).

As compared with chimpanzees, and also with human beings, gorillas are very low-key and easy-going about their sex lives. A female usually initiates copulation, usually only with the dominant alpha silverback male, and only when she is in heat. Juveniles may intrude and make a nuisance of themselves. Adolescent and young adult males do not assert themselves or become competitive.

The great apes, being unable to talk, cannot tell us about their fantasies and the mental imagery of what turns them on, erotically. Under conditions in the wild, and by making an inference from their behavior, it would appear that males and females turn each other on, heterosexually, by something that first pertains to vision, smell, or sound, and then to touch and pressure sensation. In captivity, as an inducement to copulate and breed, a sexually lethargic pair of chimpanzees were shown movies of chimpanzee copulation (see Chapter 13). They responded to what they saw by becoming erotically aroused. Not enough is yet known to permit a good conjecture as to how or why one partner is more prepotent as a turn-on than is another.

Diversity: Linguistic and Sexuoerotic

Human beings, because they have speech, can talk about their sexuoerotic turn-on imagery in fantasy and in perception. Whether or not they are applied in practice, these fantasies document the wide-ranging diversity of what does get to be coopted in the service of erotic and sexual turn-on in our species.

No one has, as yet, formulated an indisputable hypothesis as to why the human organism is not developmentally programed to mature as inevitably and exclusively as heterosexual. The statistical evidence is indisputably clear that many kinky and paraphilic embellishments may enter the program, and so may deficits. Developmentally, the program of sexuoerotic turn-on has early origins, though it is manifested full-fledged only at puberty and thereafter.

This wide range of sexuoerotic diversity has its counterpart in the diversity of languages historically manifested in the human species, worldwide. In both instances, diversity may be an inevitable evolutionary trade-off—the price paid for the freeing of the primate brain to develop its uniquely human genesis of syntactical speech and creative intelligence.

Whatever the ultimate explanation, it is clear that the human species is phyletically programed in such a way as to permit many variations of the basic sexuoerotic imagery of mammalian mating. The basic imagery is heterosexual. It begins with proceptive attraction and courtship, proceeds to acceptive genital union, and concludes with conception, gestation, and delivery of the young.

Many species, such as the sheep, are hormonal robots in which the basics of the three phases, proception, acception, and conception are governed in toto by hormonal programing of the brain before birth (Clarke, 1977). Virtually nothing, it would appear, can be altered by what happens postnatally. By comparison, primates are sexuoerotically unfinished at birth, and are susceptible to postnatal inputs—human beings especially so.

Sexuoerotic differentiation and development in human beings has, as its counterpart, native language. In both instances, the brain must be born prepared. The completion of its programing, however, is dependent on postnatal input from the social environment through the special senses, particularly touch, vision, and hearing. It is during this phase of postnatal input that the human brain is susceptible to having its sexuoerotic programing augmented and embellished with what will, by puberty and later, be manifested as paraphilia.

---

1. Gerald Groemer, Ph.D.

3

Lovemaps: Their Development

Adam/Eve: The Sexual Brain

The three-dimensional map of the human sexual brain is like a satellite map of a planet in which the finite details have only begun to be resolved. Large portions are still permanently cloud-covered. To be complete, the map should be animated, showing the currents of air, the flow of liquid, the distribution of living things, and the spread of traffic over transit routes.

In the confusion of so much complexity, it is not surprising that today's scientific knowledge of how the sexual brain develops and maintains its governance of sexuality and eroticism is still very preliminary, and subject to continual revision. Present knowledge is pieced together from experimental studies of brain and sexual behavior in insects, birds, fish, reptiles, and mammals, and from clinical studies of brain, sexuality and eroticism in human beings.

The story begins early in prenatal life when the developing brain is susceptible to the influence of sex hormones. The primordial template of development is designed to create Eve, not Adam. Masculinization requires something to be added to the neurochemistries, typically a hormone. In experimental animals, it has been shown that the hormone, testosterone, will bring about masculinization of the brain. That seems to be logical, since testosterone is the chief hormonal secretion of the male testicles, and is secreted in prenatal life precisely at the time when the brain uses it. What seems not so logical is that, before the cells of the sexual brain use testosterone, they convert it into estradiol, an estrogen, which is chiefly a hormonal secretion of the female ovaries.

This apparent incongruity requires a revision of the concept of what is a male sex hormone, and what is a female sex hormone. Actually all of the sex hormones are human hormones. They are all made in the body from cholesterol. First progesterone is made. Enzymatically, it is converted into testosterone, and testosterone is converted into estradiol. It is the ratio of the three hormones that is different in males and females, not their presence or absence.

In addition to converting testosterone into estradiol, the masculinizing sexual brain cells probably convert some plain testosterone into dihydrotestosterone. The timing and region of these conversions is unquestionably important. There is some evidence that estradiol has a different effect on the right and the left sex-regulating regions of the brain's hypothalamus (Nordeen and Yahr, 1982). It is possible also that a hormonal effect differs according to whether the hormone is supplied continuously or in pulsatile episodes (Belchetz, Plant, Nakai et al., 1978; Wildt, Marshall and Knobil, 1980).

The very idea that sex hormones can program the unborn brain in such a way as to preordain the behavior of sex in later life is total anathema to people who believe that all human sexual behavior is under motivational control and voluntary choice. They separate animal nature from spiritual nature, and tolerate no compromise. Their position is, however, too extreme. There are similarities and differences between ourselves and other mammalian species. The differences are greater between human beings and the subprimate than the primate species. Sheep, as mentioned in Chapter 2, can be regarded sexually as hormonal robots. All of their mating behavior, from the first mating season onward, is preprogramed by a sex hormone of the steroidal type that gets into the sex cells of the brain before they are born.

The truth of this assertion can be observed on film (Short and Clarke, undated). This film shows experimental sheep that act like rams, and are reacted to as rams by other members of the flock, rams and ewes alike, at breeding time. Yet they are not rams, but masculinized ewes. Their brains were masculinized before they were born by precisely timed, large doses of testosterone injected into the pregnant mother. A brain so masculinized remains masculinized for the remainder of life, even though, in adulthood, the animal's own ovaries secrete female hormones. The animal is destined, therefore, to go through life acting like a ram, without male organs.

Monkeys: Sexuoerotic Rehearsal Play

It is not possible to produce so complete a hormonal robot effect in experiments with monkeys. Female monkeys with masculinized external genitals as a sequel to having been exposed to treatment with high-dosage testosterone, in utero, show more boy-type behavior in their juvenile play. When they reach adolescence, however, their sexual and erotic behavior does not exactly replicate that of normal males. Nor does it exactly replicate that of normal females (David Goldfoot, personal communication).

In monkeys, play itself has proved to be an essential precursor of male-female breeding in adulthood. The play of juveniles includes sexual rehearsal play with age mates. It begins at around three months of age as presenting and mounting, but in a jumble of confused positioning, front, side, and rear, irrespective of whether the playmates are boys or girls. In the ensuing three to six months, the positioning of the female presenting on all fours, and the male mounting from the rear, becomes perfected. Finally the male achieves the adult positioning of his feet, not on the floor, but grasping the legs of the female above the ankles.

Monkeys deprived of playmates by being isolation-reared grow up unable to present or mount, even when paired with a gentle and experienced mate. Therefore, they do not copulate. Thus, they do not reproduce their kind.

Even so short a playtime as half an hour a day proved sufficient to allow some monkeys to achieve the mating position. It was not sufficient for two-thirds of the group, however, and the remaining third were slow achievers. They were between eighteen and twenty-four months of age when they finally succeeded. Even so, in adulthood they were poor breeders and had a low birthrate (Goldfoot, 1977).

Monkeys allowed unrestricted play time, but only in all male or all female groups, engage in presenting and mounting play with one another when they become adolescent. Though normally reared partners of the opposite sex find them sexually attractive, they cower and are scared. A male does not mount the female, even though he inspects and touches her genitalia with curiosity. A female resists the approach of a male partner, who succeeds in copulating only if he is exceptionally gentle and skilled at not making her more scared. When back with their same-sexed friends with whom they played as juveniles, males continue to mount males, and females to mount females with a frequency unrecorded in males and females that grew up and engaged in sexual rehearsal play together as juveniles (Goldfoot and Wallen, 1978; Goldfoot and Neff, 1984; Goldfoot et al., 1984).

Sexuoerotic Development: Human

Sexual rehearsal play, so far as is known, occurs in all primates that live in social troops. Human primates are no exception. The earliest recorded manifestation of human sexual rehearsal is in the womb. By sonogram, it has been possible to take a picture of an unborn boy's penis in a state of erection. There is no technique, as yet, for recording the corresponding phenomenon of vulval vasocongestion of the unborn girl. Postnatally, the same applies to baby girls, whereas in baby boys erection of the penis is readily observed. It occurs during waking and sleeping. Episodes of nocturnal penile tumescence (NPT) average three per night and last for a total of between two and three hours. They are associated especially with REM (rapid eye movement) phases of sleep which are ascertained later in life to be associated with dreaming, including erotic dreaming. NPT continues throughout childhood, peaks at puberty (Karacan, Hursch, Williams and Littell, 1972), and does not disappear until advanced old age. Because of the difficulties of measurement, little is known about nocturnal vulval congestion in girls and women, other than that it does occur (Fisher, Cohen, Schiavi et al., 1983).

During the first year of life, human infants sooner or later discover the sensuousness of their genitals in response to rhythmic pressure, squeezing, rubbing, touching, and thrusting. By age three or four, at nap time or bed time, if children are in close proximity, side by side, rhythmic pelvic thrusting may be observed, perhaps in association with rhythmic thumb sucking. A boy who suckles naked at the mother's breast until this age may be seen to have an erection of the penis, and to pay it no heed.

Three or four is also the age at which children may be seen to engage in flirtatious rehearsal play. A parent or other older children of the opposite sex is often the recipient of their flirtatious attention, which is fairly obviously patterned after models in the social environment, including those seen on television.

By age five, or thereabouts, as the number of agemates increases at kindergarten or school, flirtatious play becomes boyfriend-girlfriend playmate romance. This also is the age when pelvic rocking or thrusting movements against the body of a partner while lying side by side gives way to the rehearsal play of coitus (Money, Cawte, Bianchi and Nurcombe, 1970).

The extent to which the positioning of coitus conforms to local traditions by being transmitted down the age ladder from older to younger children remains to be ascertained. It will be necessary to collect information from ethnic groups that do not veto sexual rehearsal play in their own children. In our own society some children assimilate erroneous information about what goes where, in sexual intercourse. Some children, indeed, equate coitus with kissing. For many children, sexual rehearsal play is equated with playing doctors and nurses, that being full extent of their knowledge and experience of genital contact.

At around the age of eight, two partners in sexual rehearsal play may become pairbonded in a love affair that might be defined as a pairbonding rehearsal. However, it is scarcely a rehearsal when, as happens in some cases, the couple remain intensely bonded through adolescence and into adulthood and beyond (Money, 1980, p. 148).

Lovemaps and their Vandalism

Lifelong lovebonding that begins at age eight and continues through marriage into adulthood demonstrates that the imagery of erotic attraction and genital arousal can, like native language, be well established at an early age. Since there is need for a name for this counterpart of native language, I have called it a native lovemap.

An eight year old's lovemap of the standard, heterosexual boy-meets-girl, girl-meets-boy design may be carelessly vandalized by adults. Though sincere in serving a tradition that decrees both neglect of children's sexuoerotic development, and disciplinary abuse of those who manifest successful heterosexual development too soon, these adults are vandals, nonetheless.

Widespread vandalism of children's sexuoerotic development by otherwise well-meaning adults is exceptional among the many aspects of child development. Nothing else in developmental pediatrics is so neglected and abused. Quite to the contrary! Doctors and scientists are unremitting in poking and prying into every other facet of child development. We poke with needles, pry under the microscope, measure with radioactive tracers or nuclear magnetic resonance, analyze chemistries in the laboratory, and subject children to long-term scrutiny and statistics. By contrast, sexuoerotic development is blanketed by an avoidance taboo.

On the basis of what can be ascertained ethnographically from societies that do not blanket their children's sexuoerotic development under such a taboo, it is reasonable to infer that the lovemaps of the majority, if not all of the children, turn out to be heterosexual (Money and Ehrhardt, 1972, Ch.7).

The taboo in our society condemns in childhood the very heterosexuality that it prescribes in adulthood. It condemns any genital manifestation of juvenile sexual rehearsal play as a sin that requires absolution or expiation. It defines some manifestations of eroticism, regardless of age, as perversions or, in lurid legalese, as abominable and unspeakable crimes against nature. They are so unspeakable that in some courtrooms the law specifies that a sexual charge need not even be stated in words.

Just as they absorb their society's native language, children absorb also its sexual precepts, negative as well as positive. Even as precepts of antisexualism are in the process of vandalizing a child's lovemap, they continue to be absorbed. Lovemap defacement may be extensive, but total obliteration is unlikely.

Catch-22 Dilemmas

Vandalism of the lovemap during its vulnerable developmental years may be synonymous with impairment of its positive growth secondary to deprivation and neglect. Conversely, impairment may be secondary to the invasive vandalism of prohibition, prevention, and abusive punishment and discipline. Impairment may also be secondary to being introduced precipitously, and without prior preparation, to one of the erotosexual practices that both exist in society, and are morally or criminally condemned by it. In consequence, the practice is experienced as traumatizing. For example, the children of a paraphilic sadist may be introduced to the sounds and sights of paraphilic sadism in the parental bedroom. In addition they may be abusively beaten and disciplined themselves, with or without sexual implications.

Vandalism of the developing lovemap under the aforesaid circumstances is effected because the experience constitutes entrapment in a catch-22. That is to say, the children are damned if they do, and damned if they don't disclose what has happened. The penalty of nondisclosure is continued entrapment with no escape possible.

One of the catch-22 dilemmas is being the younger partner in a pedophilic relationship with a wide age discrepancy between the two partners. Another is being the partner in an incest relationship. The greater the age discrepancy, the more difficult the dilemma, regardless of the sex of the partner. The lesser the age discrepancy, the less difficult the dilemma. In age-matched juveniles of the same household, sexuoerotic rehearsal play with relatives is equivalent to that with friends.

As in the case of any wound, a vandalized lovemap tries to heal itself. In the process it gets scarred, skewed, and misshapen. Some of its features get omitted, some get displaced, and some get replaced by substitutes that would not otherwise be included. Omissions transform an ordinary heterosexual lovemap into a hypophilic one. Displacements and inclusions transform it into a paraphilic one. The paraphilic transformation seems at the time to be a satisfactory compromise. It disassociates lust from its vandalized place in the heterosexual lovemap, and relocates it. In the long run, however, the relocation proves to be a compromise that is too costly. In a paraphilic lovemap, lust is attached to fantasies and practices that are socially forbidden, disapproved, ridiculed or penalized. The penalty may be very severe. It may be the death penalty.

The Vulnerable Years

Conjecturally, the most vulnerable years for lovemap vandalism are likely to be between ages five and eight. The systematic observations and studies of childhood erotosexual development needed to confirm this conjecture remain to be done. Undoubtedly, there can be adverse influences before age five, and the same may be true after age eight. The years between eight and the onset of puberty are not years of latency, as once they were deemed to be. Major erotosexual traumas during this period may disrupt the consolidation of the lovemap that would otherwise be taking place. Further disruption may take place during the peripubertal years; but after puberty, the lovemap, if it changes, does so chiefly by decoding what has already been encoded into it. Once a lovemap has been formed it is, like native language, extremely resistant to change.

Like native language, a person's lovemap also bears the mark of his own unique individuality, or accent. Even though it be a conventionally heterosexual one, it is usually quite specific as to details of the physiognomy, build, race and color of the ideal lover, not to mention temperament, manner, and so on.

In view of the present woeful lack of prospective studies of sexuo-erotic development in childhood, there is a corresponding lack of systematic knowledge regarding the genesis of one particular paraphilia instead of another in a person's lovemap. From the clinic there is some preliminary evidence from which to develop hypotheses for future investigation.

There are some cases in which there is sufficient confirmation of the retrospective sexuoerotic history to suggest that a paraphilic lovemap may be a sequel to an experience that is generally regarded as nonsexual, but which is experienced by a child as inducing genital arousal. Being given an enema is such an experience. It may generate a klismaphilic lovemap, especially if enemas are repeated with zealous regularity, and associated with a highly aroused sense of either genital titillation or of bodily harm.

As paradoxical as it appears, corporal punishment may affect the genitals and their sensations. In boys the evidence is visible, for they get a panic erection. The best explanation of this reaction is in terms of a spread of autonomic nervous-system activity governing the response to bodily injury into that which governs the sexuoerotic response. Such a spread or overflow is acknowledged in the vernacular of a former era in which sadomasochism was known as the English or the German perversion. This was in recognition of the harshness of repetitious corporal punishment of young boys in the elite schools of those two countries. The effect may have been supplemented by repetitious homosexual submission enforced by older boys.

The lovemap may develop paraphilically also as a sequel to a juvenile experience that is overtly genital and sexual. In the clinic, there are some cases in which the retrospective history can be sufficiently confirmed to support this position. There are various examples. In the juvenile history of exhibitionism, for instance, a young boy may overrespond to the excitement and the possible punishment generated by his display of his erected penis to girl playmates so that he becomes addicted to repeating the procedure. This is the reaction of defiant self-assertion, instead of defeat and submission to what might become a lifetime of impotence.

Even detailed peculiarities of the lovemap may be traced to early origins, as in the case of an exhibitionist who exposed his penis to elderly ladies in church, and then urinated on the floor. He had a history of being an abused foster child. One foster mother, a devoutly religious and church-going lady, punished him for being a bed wetter by requiring him to sleep on urine-stenched straw in the basement and to wear his urine soaked underclothing to school. In his next foster home, he had a positive relationship with younger parents. There he underwent the development of puberty. Proud of his first ejaculation, he showed his erected penis to his foster mother, for which he was expelled from the home by her husband. Thenceforth, he was permanently addicted to exhibiting in church, more frequently during periods of work or marital stress than at other times.

A lovemap may develop to replicate a juvenile sexual experience, but with the ages of the participants reversed. This phenomenon can be traced in the history of some pedophiles who, as boys, were themselves the younger partner in a mutual pedophilic relationship. In adolescence and adulthood, they remain sexuoerotically boyish, and are paraphilically attracted only to juveniles of the same age as their own when they became a pedophile's partner.

This phenomenon is not an inevitable sequel to being a juvenile partner in a pedophilic relationship (Money and Weinrich, 1983). It may require that the juvenile's pedophilic experience be supplemented by another, ongoing life experience the enormity of which renders the young person particularly vulnerable. Bereavement is such an experience. In one case, a boy's experience of pedophilic affection alone filled the personal void created by his mother's death. His loss was intensified by his separation from his father, and from everyone and everything familiar to him, when he was sent overseas to live as a stranger in a boarding school.

The sexuoerotic relationship of his parents together, when it is subject to disharmony and feuding, may have a paraphilic effect on a child's developing lovemap. The child is caught in the crossfire, so that his allegiance cannot be shared equally with both parents. In a case of somnophilia, or the sleeping princess syndrome, the juvenile history illustrates the subtlety of this dilemma. The boy would see his mother, in the aftermath of marital strife over the husband's infidelity, sleeping alone on the couch in the living room, clad only in a negligee. He was a favorite son, and he could imagine her pose being a solicitation. In recall, he cannot distinguish whether it was in actuality or in vivid fantasy that he performed cunnilingus on her. From adolescence onward, his paraphilia was to intrude illicitly on a sleeping woman and offer her the gift of cunnilingus. If asked to leave, he would. Eventually he was arrested, charged with rape, and imprisoned. It is quite possible that in actual paraphilic rape, as in this case of somnophilia, there is a high prevalence of incest, in fact and fantasy, in the history.

Pediatric Syndromes Inducing Paraphilia

There are some cases in which a paraphilic lovemap has its genesis in a lonely struggle in which other people are involved by default, not by direct participation. This type of struggle goes on in children who grow up stigmatized by a deformity that threatens their future eligibility as a romantic and sexuoerotic partner. Birth defects of the sexual organs exemplify this threat explicitly. One type of birth defect is micropenis (Money, Lehne and Pierre-Jerome, 1984). One youth with this defect discovered in himself at adolescence a paraphilic, gothic fantasy of bondage and death: after a wild sexual fling, he tied the woman to an ivy vine. By daybreak it had entwined her and so luxuriantly overgrown the wall of the house that her fate was never discovered. Nor was the secret of his small penis.

In another case, a woman with a mosaic chromosome pattern (45,X/46,XY) had a history of ambiguous genitalia at birth, and enforced sex reassignment from male to female at age 4½ years, which was thenceforth treated by the family as having never occurred. Parental feuding was extremely acrimonious, and was invariably blamed on this child. Her ultimate height was 4 ft. 4½ in. (133 cm). She required sex hormone replacement therapy, indefinitely. After a period of lonely isolation, she found a boyfriend, over six feet in height, whose sexuoerotic fantasies were of bondage, uniforms, and discipline. He was in the dominant role, and she in the submissive role, with great enthusiasm and mutual pleasure.

Another example is that of a boy whose stigma was the accelerated growth and premature puberty of the syndrome of congenital virilizing adrenal hyperplasia or CVAH (Migeon, 1979). He lived in the era before the treatment of the syndrome with cortisol had been discovered. By age six, he had the physique and general appearance of early teenage. His father, a chemistry professor, was too inhibited to be able to talk openly with him about his sexual learning and conceptions. At age six, he was discovered to be the unknown raider of the neighborhood who had taken a score of brassieres from clothes lines and hidden them at home. His second fetish was for women's purses, which he obtained by strategically moving around underneath the bleacher seating at college games.

At the other pubertal extreme, there is the stigma of pubertal delay and short stature. In this category, there is the case of a boy who at age 15½ years was only 5 ft. (152 cm) tall, and just beginning to enter puberty. He was a fan of competitive wrestling and weight lifting on television. He identified with the contestants, and fantasied their physique and strength as his own. Watching their demonstration of power became, as he developed pubertally, a stimulus to sexuoerotic arousal. His penis responded with an erection. Thus, his lovemap incorporated a modified form of scoptophilia, or watching.

Delay of the onset of puberty would have been permanent in another case, except for hormonal substitution treatment to compensate for the missing female hormones. This was a case of the androgen-insensitivity syndrome, formerly known as testicular-feminizing syndrome, in an XY female (Lewis and Money, 1983). In childhood the gonads appeared as lumps in the labia majora. At surgery, they were found to be not ovarian, but testicular in structure. They were removed, which was not necessary, as at the proper age they would have induced pubertal feminization. It was also not necessary to have identified the child as a male on the basis of the chromosomes and gonads, as on all other counts she was female. The family was very severely traumatized, and their trauma was trans-mitted to the child as she grew up. Her self-image grew to be that of a victim of birth defect, and a sexual freak. She repudiated feminization at puberty by not taking female hormone pills. In adolescence and young adulthood she was socially inept and romantically isolated. She found no partner to match her paraphilic lovemap. In this lovemap, she had been cheated out of a Christian heritage by reason of the secret conversion of her grandparents to Judaism. In paraphilic fantasy, she was the Jewish victim of a Nazi concentration camp. Her triumph over this adversity was to become the lover of the blond, blue-eyed stud who was the son of the camp commandant. Bound and tied, she was threatened and coerced into having sexual intercourse with him. At the time when she found enough resoluteness to disclose this masochistic fantasy, she would come to the clinic with a thick coat of pancake makeup on her nose, ostensibly to hide her ethnicity. Achieving exactly the antithesis, she kept one ap-pointment with a covering of peppermint-striped toothpaste on her nose, because her supply of makeup had run out.

Lovemap Age Synchrony

As in the preceding cases, a child who enters adolescence with an eccentrically developed lovemap will not readily find a partner whose lovemap reciprocally matches his/her own. In the absence of a sufficient degree of mutual lovemap matching, the first culmination of a sexuoerotic relationship in intromission is likely to be experienced as perfunctory, crass, exploitative, defiling, or traumatic. The dual buildup of sensual excitement that belongs to the limerent (Tennov, 1979) or love-smitten couple will be deficient or missing. The experience will have, rather, an aversive quality.

In a comparison of college men who sought sex therapy and those who did not, Sarrell and Sarrell (1983) reported that both groups could remember equally well the situation in which their first ejaculation, or semenarche, occurred. The sex-therapy group recalled the situation as predominantly negative, and the control group as positive. Situational components of women's first experience of intercourse (Weis, 1983) influenced also its negative or positive aftermath, according to their own affective ratings.

Not only at college age, but also during the developmental years of childhood, sexuoerotic rehearsal play, matching of the lovemaps for age synchrony and image reciprocity has a more healthy developmental outcome than does mismatching. One of the primary criteria of matching, insofar as one can judge from the available evidence of comparative ethnography and comparative primate ethology, is age synchrony. That is to say, early childhood sexuoerotic rehearsal play takes place predominantly between infants or juveniles whose lovemaps are developing in synchrony. The young may learn from the sexual activities of older children, or of adolesents and adults, but they do so from the periphery, with or without playful participation, rather than by reciprocating as an equal in status with the older partner. Synchrony of lovemap age in reciprocal sexuoerotic rehearsal play continues through the juvenile years, but may be less strictly adhered to with the approach of puberty.

Another criterion of lovemap matching in childhood sexuoerotic rehearsal play is male/female image reciprocity. In the earliest years, however, male and female positioning is sex shared, and not sex discriminant. That is to say, males and females may substitute for one another in cavorting around and playing at presenting and mounting. Homosexual and heterosexual practice serve the same function at the outset. Progressively, heterosexual pairing predominates.

When a society traditionally endorses age-synchronous male/female sexuoerotic rehearsal play in its children, then male/female, heterosexual differentiation of lovemaps predominates. In consequence, by the time the boys and girls reach adolescence, they are well synchronized in the genitoerotic roles of male and female, reciprocally. Postpubertally, they do not experience heterosexuality for the first time with alarm or negation. Moreover, the likelihood of mismatched lovemaps is rare, and perhaps even zero. Paraphilias may be nonexistent as, indeed, appeared to be the case in aboriginal Arnhem Land (Money, Cawte, Bianchi and Nurcombe, 1970). There the ancient freedom from a taboo against children's sexuo-erotic rehearsal play had been preserved, despite changes toward Westernization.

4

The Vulnerable Male

Male and Female Visual Arousal

From conception onwards, there is evidence of the greater vulnerability of the male as compared with the female. The ratio of 46,XY to 46,XX conceptions has been estimated at 140:100. At birth, the male:female ratio is 105 or 106:100. At all ages, male deaths exceed female. Around age 65, the male:female ratio is 70:100.

The risk of being male may well be a spin-off of the Adam principle, namely that the embryo will develop as Eve, unless something extra is added (Chapter 3). For the reproductive organs, the additive is chiefly testosterone, which is also the hormone important to the prenatal masculinization of the sexual brain.

Masculinization of the brain does not preordain any male/female difference as absolute, except insofar as males impregnate, and females menstruate, gestate, and lactate. Other male/female differences are threshold differences, not absolute ones (Money, 1980). Thus a given type of behavior will be shared by males and females but the threshold for its arousal and expression will be different. One of these threshold differences may well pertain to dependence on the sense of sight to initiate erotic arousal, prior to making an approach.

In a four-legged species like the dog, the nose is the organ that initiates and mediates the male's arousal, but it is of negligible significance for the arousal of the female. In primates, the nose loses its preeminence, and the eyes take over. In human beings it would not be too surprising should it eventually prove to be that the male's threshold for visual erotic arousal is set lower than the female's, prenatally. Conversely, the human female's threshold for tactile erotic arousal is set lower than the male's. At the present time there has been no study across cultures to investigate the degree to which these threshold differences may be culturally induced artifacts. That the differences do exist today in our culture is, however, not disputed, despite wide variability among individuals.

One source of evidence is that explicit erotic pictures, movies and videotapes appeal more to males than to females, whereas women turn more to tales of romance and soap operas of yielding and being taken.

Another source of evidence is that boys at puberty are greeted with very explicit visual images of eroticism in their wet dreams, for which there is no exact pubertal counterpart in girls.

The mental content of a boy's wet dreams, or his masturbation fantasies, does not appear out of the blue, but has its history in the development of his lovemap. In fact, it is a vivid presentation of his lovemap. His first wet dream may, in fact, be the first full unveiling of the design of the lovemap.

No one has yet made a systematic census of the content of the first wet dreams and first masturbation fantasies in the male. It is known, however, that the majority of men remember their first ejaculation; and that, among a group of college students, those who applied for sex therapy had experienced the first ejaculation as traumatic, whereas other male students had not (Sarrell and Sarrell, 1983).

Just as in the case of males, there has not yet been a census of the content of the first masturbation fantasies of girls, nor of their first orgasmic dreams. In general, girls are several years older than boys when they first have a dream with orgasm—or indeed, when they first have an orgasm (Kinsey, Pomeroy, Martin and Gebhard, 1953). Also, in general, girls begin masturbating at a later age than do boys.

To make up for the lack of census statistics on the prevalence of paraphilic dreams and fantasies, one turns to clinical and court statistics. They make it clear that from puberty through adulthood, males more than females are recognized as having erotic fantasies and dreams of a paraphilic type. If enacted in actual practice, some of them qualify legally as paraphilic sex offenses.

Even the most cursory glance at clinic and court statistics shows that not only are adolescent boys and men in the majority as paraphiles, but also that they present a far wider range of paraphilic imagery, or syndromes, than do women. According to my own observations, the paraphilic imagery of women relates to touchy-feelies and the skin senses;

to masochistic subjugation and the martyr role; and, more rarely, to sadistic torture and genital exploitation of men.

By contrast, the paraphilias of men, although they do not exclude the skin senses, are more explicitly visually represented in imagery and fantasy. Their content ranges over at least forty syndromes that can be distinguished from one another (see Chapter 26).

The amplitude of the male/female difference in paraphilic imagery and practice lends support to a hypothesis that the greater paraphilic vulnerability of the male is somehow based on his greater dependency on the visual image for the arousal of erotic initiative. His lovemap, like his native language, is not in place at birth. Its formation is dependent on input from the social environment, especially through the eyes. Just as boys are more vulnerable than girls to developmental speech and reading disabilities, so also are they more vulnerable to developmental lovemap disabilities. The imagery of their predominantly visual lovemaps is subject to a wider variety of paraphilic disruptions than is the predominantly tactual imagery of the lovemaps of girls.

Hypophilia and Paraphilia

It goes without saying that girls are developmentally exposed to vandalism of their lovemaps, just as are boys. Their response to such vandalism is in keeping with their lesser dependence on visual imagery than on tactual imagery and the skin senses for erotic arousal and initiative. Vandalism destroys or distorts their future potential to respond not to the romantic strategies and initial approach of the male, but to the follow-through in naked body contact, especially contact of the sex organs, and orgasm.

Vandalism of the lovemap in girls is more likely to issue in hypophilia than paraphilia. The canon of hypophilia includes erotic apathy or inertia, erotic revulsion, genital penetration phobia, lubrication failure, vaginal spasm (vaginismus), failure to climax (anorgasmia), and coital or postcoital pain (dyspareunia).

Hypophilia takes its toll of men, too. Some hypophilic complaints overlap those of women, whereas others are male specific, in particular impotence and premature ejaculation. Anorgasmia is rare in men as compared with women. It might well be that paraphilic imagery is a trade-off—the price of not being so readily affected by anorgasmia. Thus it may be that paraphilia is to men what anorgasmia and erotic apathy are to women.

Whereas paraphilias affect predominantly the proceptive phase of sexuoerotic initiative, the hypophilic disorders affect predominantly the acceptive phase—the acception of the two partners together, bodily, usually in genital union. Proception (Beach, 1976) comprises what happens in preparation for acception. In animals it is highly stereotyped on a species basis, and has been called the mating dance, and also courtship. Courtship in human beings sometimes means the preliminaries to a sexual invitation, prior to foreplay which is also proceptive. Human courtship can also apply to a much longer period preparatory to marriage, during which there may be many episodes of proceptive courtship.

Conception is the third sexuoerotic phase. It may or may not be a sequel to proception and acception on any particular occasion. It is important to the functioning of the acceptive phase insofar as the prospect of conception may be essential to acceptive fulfilment. Alternatively, aversion to conception may have the reverse effect. Paraphilia has no direct effect, either positive or negative, on gestation, except that it may interfere with completion of the acceptive phase, and so prevent impregnation and conception.

Sexuoerotic imagery and proception belong together. The distinguishing mark of a paraphilia is the imagery of its lovemap, which appears as dream or fantasy and gets translated into practice. Thus it is feasible to designate paraphilic disorders as disorders of proception, by contract with hypophilias, which are disorders of acception. The distinction is often fuzzy for, behind many a disorder of acception there lurks, covertly, a paraphilic proceptive fantasy. It may remain covert, even in the course of sex therapy, unless subject to explicit inquiry. Being disorders of proception, paraphilias are also disorders of pairbonding and, therefore, of falling in love. It is actually a misnomer to call them sexual disorders. They are disorders of love, not lust.

5

Saint and Sinner: Opponent Process

Love and Lust

In mythology and folklore, there are many versions of woman as the madonna and woman as the whore. Man is, correspondingly, the provider and the profligate. Female or male, one is the saint, and the other is the sinner. One typifies love. The other typifies lust.

The cleft between saintly love and sinful lust is omnipresent in the sexuoerotic heritage of our culture. Love is undefiled and saintly. Lust is defiling and sinful. Love exists above the belt, lust below. Love is lyrical. Lust is lewd. Love is heralded in public. Lust is hidden in private. Love displayed is championed, but championships for lust are condemned. Love is candid, and speaks its name. Lust is clandestine and euphemizes its name.

In some degree or other, the cleavage between love and lust gets programed into the design of the lovemaps of all developing boys and girls. In mild degree, it is accommodated in the lovemap by means of evasiveness or joking. In serious degree, it defaces the lovemap and leaves residual hypophilia, hyperphilia, or paraphilia in which the irreconcilability of love and lust is perpetuated.

In the hypophilic solution to the cleavage between love and lust, love and lovebonding may remain intact, but the organs of lust, the genitalia, become dysfunctional and infrequently used. In the hyperphilic solution, lust displaces love and lovebonding, and the genitalia function in the service of lust alone, typically with a plurality of partners, and with compulsive frequency.

The paraphilic solution is one in which love and lovebonding are compromised because the genitalia continue to function in the service of lust, but according to the specifications of a vandalized and redesigned lovemap, and often with compulsive frequency, also. The redesigned lovemap manifests itself in fantasy, and in the staging of that fantasy in an actual performance. A klismaphilic lovemap, for example, specifies both in fantasy and performance that the person's sexuoeroticism will be aroused, and orgasm achieved, only if the partner participates in a scenario of admininstering an enema.

As aforesaid, it is not fully correct to designate the paraphilias as sexual disorders. More accurately they are disorders of love and love-bonding. The idiosyncrasies of a paraphilic lovemap are personal and specific. There is a low actuarial probability, though not a total impos-sibility, of matching two paraphilic partners whose lovemaps reciprocate or mirror image one another.

For some paraphiles (or paraphiliacs, if you prefer an extra syllable), there is a two-step, or split solution. It lies in carrying out the paraphilic lust ritual on different occasions than when engaging in sexual activity with the regular partner. Then, while having sexual intercourse with the regular partner, the imagery of the paraphilic ritual is replayed in memory, in order to achieve genital response and orgasm. It is just such a dis-junction that astonishes the neighbors, the wife, and the family of the model husband and father when he is arrested as a Jack-the-Ripper lust murderer.

A transvestite, whose wife cannot tolerate his cross-dressing in bed, similarly may be able to perform genitally only by replaying, in fantasy, a cross-dressed scenario. The more it is replayed, the less effective the scenario becomes. It is then necessary to enact a new performance in actuality, so as to enlarge the repertory of replays in fantasy.

Disjunction between a paraphilic fantasy and the bodily performance of copulation includes the regular partner only as copulatory vessel. He/she is spared from the defilement of lust enacted in the paraphilia. Excluded from the dramatis personae in the replay of the paraphilia in fantasy, the partner has, albeit inchoately, a sense of being superflu-ous—an escort, maybe, wanted as a body, but not as a lover.

When there is no such disjunction between two people having a sexuoerotic encounter together, the conjunction of the erotic imagery of their matching lovemaps serves its arousal purpose during the proceptive phase. Then, as the proceptive phase assimilates into the acceptive one, lovemap imagery yields to the sensuousness and sensuality of bodily contact, especially the voluptuous feeling of approaching orgasm. The two partners become oblivious of all else as they correspond bodily with one another, and feel metaphorically merged as one.

As compared with such a complete matching of two lovemaps a partial match is like two chimeras, each pressurizing the other to fit its own image. There are three possible outcomes. One is to separate, either amicably or acrimoniously. Another is to stay together, feuding. The third is to stay together, one partner yielding to the other in what amounts to a collusion or complicity.

Stockholm Syndrome

Whereas any one of these three outcomes may apply to a relationship in which only one partner is paraphilic, it is the third that baffles most people, including doctors and judges. For the average person it is an enigma that a wife would stay married for 25 years to a husband whose paraphilic sadism was always injuriously abusive; or that an abducted ten year old boy would pass up many opportunities for escape from his pedophilic abductor and stay with him after witnessing the lust murder of another boy his own age; or even that the girlfriend of a paraphilic transvestite would advise him on fashions and cosmetics, help him cross-dress and then escort him in public, and eventually marry him, and get pregnant by him.

Had this paraphilic transvestite's wife not known of his paraphilia until after marriage, then it might appear that she had been duped. That, however, would not explain why, following the disclosure of the husband's transvestism, one wife divorces, whereas another adapts to a collusional type of marriage, despite the progressive diminution of sexual intercourse.

The collusional type of marriage may be maintained also when a husband, after revealing himself as a paraphilic masochist, becomes relegated to a role like that of a family dog, chained and locked in the house by his wife, totally dispossessed of all his savings and investments. After escaping with the help of friends, he then escapes from them and returns back to his domestic prison.

The postmarital collusion of a marital partner in paraphilia that was previously kept hidden suggests that there were some premonitory signs of temperament or personality by which the couple recognized themselves as mutually matched, before the details were spelled out. The premonition may be something as nonspecific as a recognition of who would be the domineering partner, and who the submissive one. The premonition may be reciprocal, or it may be one-sided. If one-sided, then the recruitment of the one partner into the other's paraphilia may be a by-product of falling in love.

It could be that the love affair marks the onset of a new phase of development in which partners assimilate each other's quirks and foibles, as well as the principles they live by. They may do it reciprocally, or it may be one-sided, with one partner being more dictatorial than the other.

To understand better the power that one person may have in shaping the destiny of another, it is necessary to think in terms of the phenomenon known as brainwashing. Among political prisoners, brainwashing is effected by means of torture, abuse, neglect, and privation of the senses. It brings about a predictable response known as identification with the aggressor—on the principle of "if you can't beat them, join them."

The bond that in some instances develops between captor and captive, or terrorist and hostage, is referred to as the Stockholm syndrome. This term originated in the case of a Swedish woman who became so attached to one of the bank robbers who held her hostage that she broke her engagement to her former lover and remained bonded, or in bondage, to her former captor while he served time in prison. The American case of Patty Hearst, kidnaped by the Symbionese Liberation Army on February 4, 1974, is another example. The same thing happens routinely with abused children. They become addicted to abuse. After rescue, they maneuver to return to their parents for more abuse (Money et al., 1985).

In the case of paraphilic sadism, the bond that develops between a lover or spouse and the paraphilic partner clearly resembles the bond between captor and captive. The Stockholm syndrome, more broadly defined, may be regarded as applying across the board to all of the paraphilias in which one partner exercises paraphilic power and the other becomes collusionally bonded to the paraphile as an accomplice.

Inclusion and Displacement Paraphilias

In the course of the genesis of paraphilia in childhood development, there are two principles according to which a regular, heterosexual love-map gets redesigned into becoming paraphilic. One is the principle of inclusion: something or someone not expected to be in a lovemap becomes incorporated into it. The other is the principle of displacement: one of the proceptive features of the lovemap becomes dislocated or displaced into the acceptive phase.

In both types of paraphilia, the feature included or displaced becomes prerequisite to the achievement of orgasm. An example of inclusion is the enema of a klismaphilic lovemap. Being given an enema by the partner is, for the klismaphile, superior to penovaginal conjunction and mutual thrusting for inducing the peak excitement of orgasm.

An example of displacement is the genital display of an exhibitionistic or peodeiktophilic lovemap. In primates, display of the genitals ordinarily is a solicitation or invitation that belongs to foreplay in the proceptive phase of a sexuoerotic encounter. In paraphilic exhibitionism, genital display to a startled stranger usurps the place of penovaginal conjunction and mutual thrusting with an established partner in inducing the peak excitement of orgasm.

The following excerpt, transcribed from an exhibitionist's account of what led up to yet another arrest for indecent exposure, illustrates the intensity of the excitement generated by his genital display: "When the urge does come, it comes so strong that you really want to do it. It just blocks off everything that makes sense, . . . everything else that could maybe stop you. . . . You want to do it so bad. . . . I was driving, and the urge just came out from nowhere to do it. . . . I must have passed up about ten or fifteen places where I could have done it, trying not to do it. . . . But it just kept tingling with me. Stop here! Stop there! Stop here! Go ahead! You can do it! And the feeling that I had inside was one like, if I didn't do it, I'd be missing out on something very, very great. It just kept on going. I ended up driving halfway to Annapolis, trying not to do it, just passing up places. And it got so strong I just had to do it. I just had to get out and do it."

Whether of the inclusion or dislocation type, paraphilic lovemaps generate fantasies and actions that range from harmless to noxious. Some paraphilias are ludic, or playful. Some are harmless, but an unwelcome nuisance to a partner with an unmatching lovemap. Some are dangerous and destructive, even to a consenting partner. Some are legally classified as criminal sex offenses. Sex offenses range from lust murder and assaultive rape to harmless offenses against public modesty, namely indecent exposure and peeping.

Tragedy into Triumph

A shared principle of all paraphilic lovemaps is that they represent tragedy turned into triumph. The tragedy is the defacement of an ordinarily developing heterosexual lovemap. The triumph is the rescue of lust from total wreckage and obliteration and its attachment to a redesigned lovemap. The new map gives lust a second chance, but at a price.

The price is that the new map dissociates the saint from lust, and the sinner from love. The madonna and whore are forever sundered, and likewise the provider and the profligate. Lust belongs only to the whore and the profligate, love to the madonna and the provider. The madonna and the provider are, like Dr. Jekyll, dissociated from the whore and the profligate, their equivalents, respectively, of Mr. Hyde.

A paraphilic lovemap is a ruse of sorts—a circuitous or behind-the-scenes way of getting a certificate of admission to the theater of lust. Paraphilia is almost always imbued with some degree of furtiveness, deviousness, and deceit. At the same time, it is histrionic, flamboyant, and self-incriminatory.

The paraphile whose lovemap is the means of his sexuoerotic survival is like the survivor of torture or catastrophe—or even surgery—who reiteratively dreams and tells, over and over, the story of how he/she turned the tragedy of suffering into the triumph of survival. This pride of survival is careless about self-incrimination. Paraphilia notoriously leaves incriminating evidence by which it may be traced.

Paraphilic Addiction: Opponent-Process Theory

The paraphilic triumph over tragedy has many affinities with addiction. In the language of common sense, an addiction always has a predicate: one is addicted to something, as in being addicted to alcohol, heroin, or other chemical substance. An alcoholic is addicted not to swallowing fluid or drinking in general. It is possible to become addicted to drinking water, and to take it in toxic amounts. Nonetheless, the alcoholic becomes intoxicated not on water, but specifically by drinking alcohol. It is not essential that he/she take it by mouth. The rectal route, as in a wine enema, is a satisfactory alternative.

Eating addiction has a parallel specificity. The obese binge eater is addicted not to eating in general, but to specific foods, such as chocolates or other sweets, carbohydrates, and fatty dishes. The same type of specificity applies also to sex. It is, however, currently fashionable to use the term, sexual addiction (Carnes, 1983), as though the addiction were to practicing anything and everything sexual, if not now, then progressively in a downhill slide. This doctrine of progression is a recrudescence of degeneracy theory—a leftover from antisexualism of last century (Chapter 20). It is just plain wrong.

Sexual addictions, like drinking and eating addictions, are extremely particular. The sexual addict is always addicted to something sexually specific. Thus a woman who sought therapeutic help because she despised herself as a nymphomaniac was, in fact, addicted to men whom she could pick up in a singles' bar. They were good for a one night stand, and then no more. She would resolve to quit her compulsive cruising, but the addiction proved stronger than her resolve, and she repeated it over and over.

In another case of compulsive cruising, this one in a male homosexual, the compulsion was to cruise gay bathhouses, peepshows, and other public places where he had already been arrested five times, and where he feared, and wisely so, the risk of contracting AIDS, the new and lethal epidemic viral infection. His addiction proved to be for large penises, the larger the better. He traced the origin of his addiction to the age of between four and five when, through an open door, he saw his father showing his big penis to his older sister, and he felt excluded and jealous. The insatiable quality of his addiction could be attributed to the fact that, as an adult with an adult-sized penis, he could never find one proportionately as great as his father's had been when his own had been that of a small boy.

In the first of the foregoing instances of compulsive cruising, the paraphilia belonged in the category of solicitation and allure (Chaper 11), and the second in the category of stigmata and eligibility (Chapter 10). Any paraphilia can be conceptualized as an addiction. The recipient person or thing of the paraphilia is what defines the addiction, and is its predicate.

Another illustration, from one of the fetishistic/talismanic paraphilias, is that of the male transvestite or transvestophile who can perform sexual intercourse with a partner, female usually, but in some cases male, only when he wears female garments, usually underclothes. He is addicted to women's clothing—the transvestophilic addiction does not, it would appear, occur in women.

The transvestophile's tragedy, in some cases on record in his early history, was his mortification at having been paraded in public in girl's clothes, in many instances as a punishment. The triumph is that the mortification is transposed into erotic and genital arousal. Thenceforth, dressing up is no longer a mortification, but a sexual and erotic thrill. At puberty, female garments are used as stage properties in the boy's masturbation fantasy and in the practice of masturbation. At a later stage, they become stage properties in his copulation fantasy and practice. Without them, he does not function in sexual intercourse.

Becoming positively addicted to what initially was negatively aversive is a manifestation of what the psychologist, Richard L. Solomon (1980), has formulated as the opponent-process theory of learning. Opponent-process is seen at work when daredevil stuntmen overcome their initial panic and terror and become addicted to their daredeviltry. Joggers and marathon runners transcend the bodily pain and exhaustion of their exertion and, becoming addicted, get euphoric and high from it. As aforesaid, even the victims of cruel child abuse become addicted to abuse so that, having been rescued, they maneuver to become abused again, as perpetual martyrs.

Opponent-process learning takes place quite rapidly. Like all addiction, it is remarkably resistant to change. As applied to the paraphilic addiction, opponent-process theory accounts for its resistance to change.

It is possible that the resistance of paraphilic addiction to change lies also in the fact that a paraphilic attraction is the equivalent of the normophilic attraction of falling in love. Love is blind, according to popular wisdom. Criticism of the beloved falls on deaf ears, no matter how rational and logical it may appear to the critics. Family interference meets with resistance and intensification of the bond with the beloved. So strong is the bond that the lover may, indeed, be said to be addicted to the beloved. Being love-smitten may even be the prototype of all addiction.

The opponent process can be discerned in all the paraphilias, insofar as they all predicate orgasm on an activity that only the paraphile appreciates as erotic. Others regard the erotization of that acitivty as completely inappropriate, and react with outrage, contempt, or ridicule. For them it would prevent orgasm, not build up to it.

The paraphilic opponent-process strategy for turning tragedy into triumph appears at first glance to generate a motley array of paraphilias, more or less at random. Upon closer inspection, however, it appears that the paraphilias are not generated at random, but that they subdivide into six classes or strategies. Each strategy is a means of triumphing over tragedy. The six are: sacrificial/expiatory; marauding/predatory; mercantile/venal; fetishistic/talismanic; stigmatic/eligibilic; and solicitational/ allurative.

In each of the six strategies, a paraphilia is a substitute for normophilia—heterosexual or homosexual, according to the sex of the partner. By definition, a paraphilia has a dual existence, one in fantasy, and one as fantasy carried out in practice. On the criterion of its mental imagery, a paraphilia is a mental template or lovemap (Money, 1983b) that, in response to the neglect, suppression, or traumatization of its normophilic formation, has developed with distortions, namely, omissions, displacements, and inclusions that would otherwise have no place in it. A paraphilia permits sexuoerotic arousal, genital performance, and orgasm to take place, but only under the aegis, in fantasy or live performance, of the special substitute imagery of the paraphilia.

Sacrifice and Expiation

Definition

The sacrificial and expiatory paraphilias are those in which sexuoerotic triumph is wrested from tragedy by means of a strategy that incorporates sinful lust into the lovemap, though only on the condition that it requires reparation or atonement, by way of penance or sacrifice, since it irrevocably defiles saintly love.

One or both of the partners may perform the atonement. The penalty ranges from humiliation and hurt to blood sacrifice and death. Self-imposed atonement is masochistic. Performed by the partner, it is sadistic. Either may be consenting or enforced.

Ecclesiastical Analogy

Martyrdom, as exemplified in the martyrdom of Saint Sebastian in Medieval and renaissance art, is a sexuoerotic turn-on for at least some paraphiles. They are among the masochists of the expiatory and sacrificial paraphiles who are religiously devout.

For sadomasochists, the ecclesiastical high period of history coincided with the persecutions of the Inquisition in the fourteenth through the sixteenth century. Victims of the Inquisition were accused of heresy and witchcraft. Under torture, they confessed their sexual sin: they had copulated at night with demonic incubi and succubi, or with Satan himself. They were declared witches, for which they were condemned and burned at the stake. The sexuality for which they died was supplanted by the sexuality of sadomasochism. The painting and sculpture of torture, sacrifice, and martyrdom glorified sadomasochistic imagery while apophasically denying that it did so.

The concept of atonement for sin has ancient origins in religion, and is a central principle of Christian theology. The principle of atonement by way of sacrifice or penance has diffused into the laws and penal systems of Christendom. The same principle has diffused also into the theory of aversive conditioning or punishment training in child rearing and education. In our society, it is virtually impossible for children to grow up without assimilating at least a rudimentary conception of penance or sacrifice as a reparation or atonement for sin.

It is also impossible for children to grow up without assimilating the concept that the genitals are a prime source of sin. Sexual sin, American children also learn, may be of such magnitude and abomination to their elders that it can be atoned for only in the electric chair, in the gas chamber, or on the lethal-injection gurney.

The price of sin and wrong-doing is usually measured in units of suffering. This metric fails, however, to take cognizance of the penitential metamorphosis of pain into ecstasy. The members of flagellant sects who scourge themselves may be not only paying penance, but also undergoing a transformation of pain into religious ecstasy. The same applies to other self-inflictions, like harnessing themselves to a heavy load by means of flesh hooks, and dragging it over a long distance.

When the same or similar transformation of pain into ecstasy has not a religious, but an erotic meaning, then it is defined as masochistic. It is an atonement for the past and present sin of sex. The sin of the masochist may be atoned for in private, autoerotically, without the collaboration of a successful partner.

Self-inflicted Atonement

The rituals of self-inflicted atonement for the sin of being sexual have their origin in the penances and retribution familiar in society. Binding, flogging, and hanging are old and familiar punishments. Of these three, only hanging is likely to end in death. Paraphilic strangulation and partial asphyxiation is commonly from a rope or noose tightened around the neck while masturbating to orgasm. Such a paraphilia has a history of having been successful on dozens or hundreds of occasions before being discovered. At the moment of orgasm, the paraphilic script calls for the rope to be released. The one occasion when the release procedure fails is the only failure, because it ends in paraphilic death. It is the failure that is discovered (Hazelwood, Dietz and Burgess, 1983). The death is usually construed as suicide. To the family of a teenaged boy who meets his death this way, there is an added mystery, in many cases: he is found dressed in articles of his mother's clothes. For him the sin of sex may have been not only the sin of masturbation, but also the paraphilic fantasy of son-mother incest.

Execution by lethal injection, today's tech-med chic of the death sentence, has not yet found its way into the self-atoning paraphilias. Atonement by electrocution, by contrast, has done so. Usually, the electrical shock is delivered through a home-made apparatus placed in or attached to the genitalia. The current is timed or stepped up to synchronize with orgasm. Death, when it occurs, is an unscheduled outcome. Some deaths have been precipitated by contact of the electrically charged, masturbatory apparatus with water, as in the bathtub.

Collusional Atonement

The masochistic drama of erotic death and atonement may be enacted not as an autoerotic monologue, but as a dialogue with a coopted partner in collusion. The partner is not necessarily a paraphilic sadist, but rather a daredevil hustler or mercenary given to trying almost anything for kicks, or for profit. This was the type of hustler whom a young man with a paraphilia of homosexual masochism would pick up, one or more at a time, on the waterfront. With his beguiling brand of macho, he would cue the hustlers into their roles in his masochistic drama. First he would supply them with squeeze bottles of mustard or catchup and a spray can of shaving cream to squirt on him as he lay naked, masturbating. Then he would direct them to bind him with rope, urinate on him, degrade and abuse him verbally, hit him, and kick him with their heavy boots, harder and harder, until he would ejaculate, not knowing whether a blow on the head would wound or kill him.

As a stratagem against dying prematurely, the star in this drama of self-planned assassination would record it on tape. At home he could replay his tapes and use them in masturbation fantasy, or while having a less dangerous, and by the same token less arousing relationship with a male partner. The lifetime of this ruse was six to eight weeks. Then the compulsion to cruise the waterfront and stage a new drama became imperious and irrefutable again.

There is a variant of the lethal drama of stage-managing one's own sexuoerotic assassination. The doomed players in the dramas have variable age and sex relationships with their killers. In the gay community, the younger partner is typically a hustler—certainly no saint. He does not define himself as gay, but as a heterosexual who, for a period of his youth, will have sex with an ephebophilic homosexual partner for money, or for gifts and favors, but definitely not for love.

Eventually the mercenary nature of the relationship is threatened by evidence of mutual attachment—evidence such as making more frequent visits without pay, being stigmatized by others because of the attachment, or being jealous over the intrusion of a rival, even though the rival is a personal friend. By history a rebel, the youth attacks this new obstacle of attachment to his patron by attacking the patron himself and killing him. Alternatively, he may kill a surrogate. Sometimes he murders with a friend as an accomplice. In some cases, the victim is known to have had a premonition of violence ahead, but his masochistic disposition to stage-manage his own assassination was too dominant in his paraphilic lovemap to permit him to heed the premonition.

Victim Sacrifice: Lust Murder

The obverse of self-sacrificial masochism is sadistic sacrifice of a victim. The sadist is the paraphile, but the partner is not. In sacrificial sadism, the paraphilic methods of sacrifice are as varied as those that inspire them and from which they derive, namely, the methods of humiliation, deprivation, abuse, violence, torture, maiming, piercing, and execution favored by tyrants, secret police squads, and correctional systems down the ages.

In the irrational syllogism of extreme paraphilic sadism, the transgression is postulated as the heinous and criminal pleasure of sexual orgasm. It requires atonement, and it is the partner who must be afflicted on behalf of the sadist. The most extreme penalty is death—erotic assassination or lust murder. Its technical name is erotophonophilia (Greek: Eros, the god of love; phonia, bloodshed or murder; philia, love), the erotic love of murder.

In the paraphilia of lust murder, the dying of the partner is the sacrifice that, in anticipation, arouses the paraphilic murderer, sexuoerotically. The culmination of the murder induces the culmination of orgasm. The very idea of lust murder is so gruesome to society that even professional investigators may fail to get details of the method of killing—often by strangulation—and of achieving orgasm with the corpse, which may be genital, oral, or in some more idiosyncratic way.

Lust murder shares a zone of overlap with necrophilia. The necrophiliac attachment, however, is to corpses, not to killing, the reverse being true in the case of lust murder.

There is a zone of overlap also between lust murder and paraphilic rape which is classified as a predatory paraphilia (see below). The paraphilic rapist, however, is addicted to lust violence rather than to lust murder, per se. When paraphilic rape terminates in murder, death is likely to be a by-product of violence and struggle, and not the paraphilic act itself, as it is in lust murder.

In paraphilic rape, the partner is characteristically an unsuspecting stranger rather than a social acquaintance. In lust murder, the paraphilic murderer is quite likely to have spent a period of time getting socially acquainted with an intended victim, and not to have stalked a stranger. A younger person may have been abducted and then given the status of companion. With an older person, the relationship initially may have appeared indistinguishable from ordinary affectionate dating. The bond of affection may have been consummated in sexual intercourse or other genitoerotic activity on several occasions prior to the fateful encounter that culminated in lust murder.

Lust as ordinary sexual intercourse seldom takes place only once in a person's lifetime. So also the enactment of a paraphilic ritual seldom takes place only once. The occasion when paraphilic murder is discovered is not necessarily the paraphile's first murder.

Self-incrimination is not atypical in the paraphilias. Thus, once traced, a paraphilic murderer may disclose the history and details of his killings—with a virtual vanity of achievement, on the one hand, and, on the other hand, relief that external intervention will, at last, do what internal forces failed to do, namely prevent further recurrences.

Collusional Killing

Paraphilic murder, like all the paraphilias of sadistic sacrifice, is not inevitably done in secret, without witnesses or accomplices. There are some cases in which the paraphile enlists the service of an assistant or assistants. It is possible that the assistant is another paraphile with the same paraphilic syndrome, and ready-made as a collaborator. Alternatively, the assistant, if devoid of paraphilia, may be entrapped in the role of apprentice. The compliancy of the apprentice seems mysterious and inexplicable, except by reference to the Stockholm syndrome (Chapter 5).

A well-publicized example from 1976 is that of the Baltimore pedophilic lust murderer, Arthur Goode (Waters, 1984). At the age of twenty, he abducted a newsboy from a professional family and coopted him as his boy lover. The child had opportunities to escape, even after he had been witness to the lust murder of another boy his age. Yet he was unable to take advantage of a single opportunity. His rescue was finally effected when, after the pair were recognized, the police were notified. Only then could he disengage himself from the mysterious bond with his abductor.

In some cases, there is not only one assistant, but a hierarchy of compliancy and collusion in which some members do not participate in the paraphilic rituals, but cover up for those who do. As bizarre and perplexing as such a hierarchy of obedience and conformity might appear, it is far from unique in human affairs. There are parallels. In 1978, for example, 911 Americans, all followers of the religious and sexual cult leader, Jim Jones, died in an orgy of mass suicide. As Jones exhorted them at the microphone, parents gave Kool-Aid flavored cyanide to their children, and then drank it themselves. In 1969, on the night of August 8–9th, members of "The Family," men and women, of another cult leader, Charles Manson, went on a murder spree at his bidding. The actress Sharon Tate and her guests were among the seven victims. A whole nation collaborated with Hitler in his mass genocide. Arbitrary killing, as exemplified by Jones, Manson, and Hitler, needs only to be enchained to sexuoeroticism to become paraphilic suicidal or homicidal assassination.

Sadomasochistic Repertory

Sadism, masochism, and sadomasochism (S/M) are generic terms. They encompass a repertory of expiatory and sacrificial paraphilic rituals that subdivide into five categories: corporal punishment, mutilation, bondage, servitude, and humiliation.

Punishment, mutilation, and bondage may be applied directly to the genitals only, and/or to other parts of the body. The methods employed include cutting, piercing, branding, burning, whipping, kicking, punching, pinching, squeezing, breaking, stretching, binding, and penetrating, in various standard or exotic permutations and combinations.

Servitude and humiliation both may pertain specifically to sexuoerotic practices, and/or to roles in general in a mutual, dominance/ submission relationship. The relationship may be stereotyped as master and slave, employer and servant, adult and child, male and female, or owner and pet. Humiliation is imposed both verbally and by enforced obedience to perform tasks that are menial, degrading, filthy, or disgusting to perform, according to ordinary criteria.

The premise of the sadomasochistic relationship is the unequal distribution of power and authority. In many sadomasochistic rituals, this inequality is exemplified by uniforms—different uniforms for the different disciplinary rituals in the S/M repertory. Military and police uniforms feature prominently. The uniform may, for some paraphiles, have a fetishistic quality as a sexuoerotic turn-on. There are standard S/M wardrobes for some roles: the tightly laced and corseted dominatrix with mask, spike heels, and a whip; the leather-studded jacket, pants, and jockstrap of the all-male motorcycle set, with chains and jackboots; and so on.

Coprophilia/Urophilia

Paraphilic fixation on excrement in sadomasochistic humiliation and servitude stems from the anatomical proximity of the perineal organs of excretion to those of reproduction and genitoeroticism. In childhood, those organs and their functions are equated with dirtiness and the forbidden. Prohibition of what is dirty in the perineum, therefore, does not differentiate playing with the sex organs from playing with the organs and products of excretion. According to the opponent process principle (Chapter 5), doing the dirty and forbidden is triumphal defiance over humiliating obedience. It is simultaneously a triumph over the equated dirtiness of the genitoerotic and the excremental functions. The equation signifies that the excremental and the genitoerotic are one.

The paraphilia of feces is coprophilia, and of urine is urophilia, also known as urolagnia and as Undinism (named for Undine, the water sprite). The two paraphilias involve ingesting, smearing, and spraying the excrement, and also urinating after intromission into either the anus or the vagina.

S/M Community

A partner who fakes a role in a sadomasochistic paraphilic ritual transmits no zest to the partner. It is more satisfactory if the two partners are genuine sadomasochistic paraphiles who can enter into a mutual collaboration or collusion.

Sadomasochists who lack a collusional player for their paraphilic dramas are nowadays able to take out membership in clubs and societies of like-minded heterosexual, bisexual, or homosexual people. They are able to establish contact with other members of the S/M community through personal advertisements in special-interest magazines and news-papers. In public meeting places, notably bars, strangers may use a color-coded signaling system in which different colored pieces of cloth showing in the hip pocket decode as different sexuoerotic predilections. Left/right wearing of keys or other accessories signals dominance/submission.

A signaling system, being also an advance warning system of sorts, enables sadomasochistic partners to match up more or less appropriately as sadist or masochist, master or slave, dominant or submissive, top or bottom, in rituals of bondage and discipline, humiliation, water sports (urophilia), scat (coprophilia), fisting (intromission of hand and arm into the vagina or rectum), piercing, and so on.

Signals of either/or do not identify those who engage both ways, as many do, on either the same or different occasions or with the same partner or different ones.

Either/or signals also do not identify those who have highly idio-syncratic paraphilic rituals, like the coprophilic "plumber," who would turn off the water in public toilets for males so that he could collect the feces left by particular strangers whom he had selected because they fulfilled the ideal specifications of his coprophilic love map. Back at home, alone, he used their feces in his coprophagic and smearing ritual.

A third deficiency of either/or signals is that they omit quantitative information regarding the degree of sadomasochistic playfulness versus harmfulness to be engaged in. Omission of quantitative signals may be attributed in part to the principle, widely accepted in the S/M community, that the S/M relationship is one of trust in which ultimate control resides with the masochist. The masochist is not portrayed as the hapless victim of a Dracula of horror, shock, brutality, and death. Dracula is said to be only a playful and harmless velvet dragon, obedient to the masochist's plea for humiliation, servitude, bondage, and domination.

The velvet dragon analogy does not necessarily hold up, however, if the velvet is replaced by the uniform and paraphernalia of the keeper of the dungeon. If at the beginning of a relationship a sadist omits to reveal the full range and culmination of sacrifice involved in his/her sadistic fantasy, then the partner may be destined to a role not of collaboration, but of abused sacrificial victim.

There is no hard-edged dividing line between the abusive and the playful sadomasochistic paraphilias. Nonetheless, many S/M people appear to be permanently anchored on the playful side. With a partner appropriately attuned, it may be possible for the fantasy to be staged as a piece of personal, sexuoerotic theater. Otherwise, it may remain forever coded in the lovemap as fantasy, exclusively. The expiatory and sacrificial paraphilias are not invariably malignant. For some they are benign. Statistically, those may rate as abnormal, but ideologically they are acceptable.

Marauding and Predation

Definition

The marauding and predatory paraphilias are those in which sexuoerotic triumph is wrested from tragedy by means of a strategy that incorporates sinful lust into the lovemap, though only on the condition that it be stolen, abducted, or imposed by force, since it irrevocably defiles saintly love.

The person with a predatory lovemap may be either the predator or the prey. Predator and prey may set themselves up as actors in a prearranged paraphilic drama or they may be strangers, the prey being completely unprepared for the imposed role of victim.

There are two classes of marauding and predatory paraphilia. One is characterized by attack, assault, and seizure; and the other by stealth, theft, and abduction. Together, they are characterized by taking something without consent.

Theft of Sexual Property

The social institutionalization of property ownership has, as its antithesis, the taking or usurping of ownership without consent. In a property-owning society like our own, therefore, the antithesis of being denied access to a consenting sexual partnership is to take or usurp it without consent. Even young children can deduce this antithesis when, at the age of sexuoerotic rehearsal play, they are punished and denied further contact with the partner. They do not need to make the deduction de novo, however. It is present in the mythological heritage and folklore of our culture, and is preserved in stories and films of the cave-man stereotype.

There is, for example, the theme of untamed savages who raid a neighboring tribe in order to carry off their women as wives or concubines. Some are enslaved sexually in the private harem of the chief, and some in the public harem, or brothel, of those with less wealth and power. There is also the theme that, in the ancient rites of warfare, the victorious plunder and rape the vanquished.

Whether the vanquished are raped or taken as sexual prisoners, they are taken away from someone else. Women are taken away from either their fathers or their husbands, if they belong to a patriarchal society in which women are legally the property of men. Under peacetime conditions in such a society, the crime of rape is the crime of despoiling someone else's property. Despite the woman's consent, having intercourse with her is still an offense against someone else's property. It is the offense of either fornication or adultery, for which the punishment might be the same as for nonconsenting rape.

Under the conditions of American slavery, for example, if a consenting white woman had a black lover, should the affair be discovered, he was automatically punished as a rapist. The woman's consent was irrelevant. He had despoiled someone else's wife or future wife. If she should have a child with a black father, the child could not be legitimate and raised by her in freedom. Being partly black, it could not be free. The child of a black mother and a white father, by contrast, could be declared a slave, born of a slave mother, and raised without a legitimate father. Thus, the white father had not legally committed rape.

An analogous situation exists at the present time with respect to statutory rape defined on the basis of age. If the female is defined by law to be below the age of consent, then no matter what the conditions of consent and agreement, if she has intercourse with a male who is older than she is, he is defined as a rapist. The female is her father's property, and his property has been despoiled.

Technically, the same should apply in reverse if a boy has intercourse with an older female partner, but in practice the eye of the law has no view of the male as sexual property, subject to sexual theft. The law sees the male only as the property owner and as the potential sexual thief.

Statutory rape excepted, the definition of rape as the taking of someone else's property is now a matter of history. Today, rape is defined as the taking of sexual intercourse from a partner without consent. The broader definition applies to both sexes, though in practice almost all rape charges are made against men. The offender need not be unauthorized to perform sexual intercourse by reason of being a marauding stranger. He may be a dating partner, a romantic acquaintance, or in some jurisdictions, a husband. The act of rape need no longer entail forced seizure, but only the clambering or coerciveness of a male insistent on a genital resolution to a state of sexuoerotic arousal already arrived at by mutual agreement.

Proposed or completed legalization of this expanded definition of rape is a spin-off of contemporary radical feminist militancy. In the first era of the women's movement somewhat more than a century ago, the price of antisexism was antisexualism. Emancipation from a career of childbearing did not mean a career of lust and prostitution, but a respectable career devoid of sexuality and eroticism. No longer were women accused of being witches obsessed with the sin of insatiable lust, as they had been throughout the preceding centuries of the Inquisition. Victorian women were, ideologically, able to experience love, but not lust. Reluctantly, they gave themselves up to the lust of their husbands, when they were obliged to, only to appease the man's animal instincts, and because coition was a regrettable prerequisite of motherhood.

The new radical feminism no longer idealizes feminine erotic apathy and inertia. It does not, however, endorse feminine lust and assertiveness as women's birthright. Instead, it portrays women as the victims of carnal knowledge without consent. Male lust is equated with rape, rape with violence, and violence with domination, raw power, and the degradation of women.

The feminist definition of rape as not a sexual but a violent act is itself a power play. As compared with the old ideology of witchcraft, it reverses the sex of the victim. The new heretics are men, not women, and the uncompromising evidence of their heresy is not only rape, but also pornography. Here lies the onset of a new Inquisition, this one directed chiefly at the lust not of wives and daughters, but of sons and husbands. It is already gaining momentum in the new bureaucracy of the bastard science of victimology which it has spawned. Victimologists are the Torquemadas of the new Inquisition. They judge sex as abuse of women and children.

The first Inquisition had the paradoxical outcome not of eradicating witchcraft, but of increasing the prevalence of witch trials. Analogously, the paradoxical outcome of the second Inquisition, if it remains unhalted, could be a progressive increase in the prevalence of accusations of marauding and predatory paraphilias. Then, as each new generation of boys matures into puberty, their manhood would, in progressively increasing numbers, be sexually traumatized and disabled. Girls also would not escape. Those of either sex who escaped a paraphilia might do so at the cost of being heterosexually apathetic and inert, or impaired in their genital functioning. Some would find themselves able to fall in love only with a partner of the same morphological sex as their own.

Paraphilic Seizure and Rape

As historically defined, rape means seizure by force or plunder. It also means carnal knowledge, without consent. In military history, raping women belonged in the same category as taking slaves. Paraphilic rape, by contrast, is a syndrome, in which the stark terror, screaming, yelling, and struggling of an unforewarned victim are integral to the assailant's lovemap. Victim compliancy instead of resistance incites the paraphilic rapist to an unremitting and compulsive crescendo of deadly threats, restraints, injuries, and violent assault, without which his erection may fail, or be lost. Rape of this paraphilic type needs its own name. In Latin it is raptophilia, and in Greek, biastophilia (*biastras*, rape, force).

The lovemap of a paraphilic rapist excludes the possibility that lust can be expressed by mutual consent. Typically, the partner is a stranger, ambushed and captured by force. Compliancy implies consent, and evokes an escalation of paraphilic intimidation and violence. The victim may, therefore, fare better by an escalation of panic and aversion.

Paraphilic rape or biastophilia may culminate in death. The death is not synonymous with lust murder or erotophonophilia, however, unless it is preprogramed in the lovemap to be the ultimate outcome. The paraphilic imperative of biastophilia is that the victim of assault be unforewarned, terrorized, tortured, and unable to escape. Erotophonophilic death, by contrast, is more likely to be a sudden act of annihilation. It concludes an encounter that appeared mutually amicable at its outset.

The predatory violence of biastophilia has a counterpart in symphorophilia (Greek, *symphoro*, disaster). This is the predatory paraphilia in which the symphorophile stage-manages a disaster or catastrophe which may claim victims. The symphorophile usually is a sexuoerotic spectator of the disaster at a distance. Mostly, the victims are chance bystanders, or those who are trapped in an arranged crash, explosion, or fire. The catastrophe may be arranged to annihilate aquaintances or relatives, and in some instances the self in a final act of sexuoerotic self-immolation. Symphorophilia then becomes as much an expiatory sacrifice as a marauding predation.

Paraphilic rape is not the same as the copulation of a domineeering and insisting partner with a reluctant lover or spouse whose resistance is disregarded. Nor is it the same as nuptial rape, in which a bridegroom imposes the right of defloration on a timid and sexually phobic bride. Nor, also, is it the same as statutory rape which is defined not in terms of force, but of legal age of consent.

Paraphilic Predation by Stealth

Paraphilic predation by stealth is exemplified in its most undiluted form in kleptophilia, the paraphilia in which stealing induces sexuoerotic arousal and excitement. Kleptophilia is the sexuoerotic counterpart of kleptomania, the nonsexuoerotic manifestation of apparently senseless, irrational, and compulsive stealing. In both types of stealing, the objects taken are of little or no evident value or pragmatic usefulness to the thief. They may be taken indiscriminately and at random, or they may be always typical of a specific fetish. One fetishistic kleptophile stole only left shoes from women walking on the street. He hoarded hundreds of them. Some kleptophiles do not hoard, but discard their loot.

Kleptophilia may be repetitiously associated with a ritualistic fixation on breaking and entering—through a window, for example, and never a door. The building may be either unoccupied or occupied. Typically it is a dwelling. If the dwelling is occupied, the pilfering may be the beginning of a ritual that progresses to the theft of sexual intimacy from an occupant. Or, the only theft may be that of sexual intimacy.

The stolen intimacies need not necessarily include penovaginal intercourse. The paraphilic fantasy may require that the occupant of the dwelling be asleep, so as to be awakened to the mystery of sex—the so-called sleeping princess syndrome, or somnophilia. When stealing oral or genital intimacy from a sleeping princess crosses the dividing line that separates stealth from seizure, then gentleness gives way to abuse which may be by abduction, coercion, or force.

From somnophilia there is a sort of stepwise logic to necrophilia. In this paraphilia, sexual intimacy is stolen only from a corpse. For a necrophile, a funerary career is a virtual imperative.

Hybristophilia: The Bonnie and Clyde Syndrome

The obverse of paraphilic marauding and predation is being sexu-oerotically turned on only by a partner who has a predatory history of outrages perpetrated on others. The name of this paraphilia, hybristophilia, derives from the Greek, *hybridzein*, to commit an outrage against someone. The criminal couple, Bonnie and Clyde (Neuman, 1967), have become eponymous for this paraphilic syndrome since their outrageous exploits were popularized by being commemorated in a movie. In their case, the man was the perpetrator and the woman the accomplice. The sexist stereotypes of our society dictate the popular assumption that it is always the woman who is led by the man into crimes of robbery, rape, and murder. However, the reverse may also occur. The partners in crime may also be same-sexed lovers, either two men or two women. There may be more than two in the partnership, witness Charles Manson's "family" of lovers and partners in killing (Bugliosi and Gentry, 1974).

The paraphilic appeal of the lover as criminal may entail that he/she be a convicted criminal who has been convicted and spent time in prison. The relationship between the hybristophile and the criminal may actually begin in the prison where the offender is serving time, and the partner is a visitor.

There is a variant of the syndrome in which the hybristophile taunts and provokes a lover or spouse to commit a criminal act, so as to fulfil the requirements of the paraphilia. The offender is then reported to the police and arrested, or a warrant is put out for his/her arrest. If the next step is imprisonment, then the hybristophilic role is to visit the prisoner, to incite sexual arousal, and then to thwart it, unfulfilled, when the visiting hour terminates. If the prisoner is finally released, and if reconciliation is consummated in sexual intercourse, then the experience of the reconciliation orgasm is one of extravagant intensity and ecstasy. It is the ultimate fulfillment of the imagery in the hybristophile's lovemap.

The hybristophilic lovemap excludes the possibility of oneself as the victim of an outrage successfully effected. So long as the two partners remain paraphilically bonded, then each victim, it is assumed, will always be someone else. If the bonding fails, however, then the hybristophilic partner may become the next on the list of victims.

8

Mercantile and Venal Strategies

Definition

The mercantile and venal paraphilias are those in which sexuoerotic triumph is wrested from tragedy by means of a strategy that incorporates sinful lust into the lovemap, though only on the condition that it be traded, bartered, or purchased and paid for, not freely exchanged, since lust irrevocably defiles saintly love.

Marriage, Payment and Property

In these paraphilias, the purchase price is a corruption of the bride price, or of the dowry, both of which belong historically to the institution of the arranged marriage. Today, as in history, families have a vested interest in the union of property, wealth, and power that can be effected by way of the marital union of eligible offspring. The counterpart of the arranged marriage is the elopement marrige in which the romantic love-bond defies all considerations of family expediency.

In the ecclesiastical tradition of arranged marriage, the more perfunctory the role of copulation as the prerequisite of procreation, the more highly spiritual it was deemed to be. The idealized conception was the immaculate conception. Romantic lovers united in carnal passion were sinners, not saints. Carnal passion belonged not to the madonna and the provider, but to the whore and the hustler.

The whore and the hustler, according to the tradition of carnal pas-

sion as sin, have a monopoly on sex as a wicked and sinful delight. They
are branded with the scarlet letter of the sinner—more because they
subvert the doctrine of the sinfulness of carnal passion than because they
are paid while doing so. Those who do the same without pay are subject
to the same social stricture.

Orgasm as Commodity

Harlots and hustlers, call-girls and call-boys, courtesans and gigolos,
all are merchants whose commodity is orgasm. In the private and direct
tradition, they deliver the orgasm in person-to-person participation. In
the public and indirect tradition, they deliver the orgasm or its simulation
live on stage for the sexuoerotic entertainment of spectators. Live on
camera, the same commodity is reproduced for mass circulation in print,
on film, or on videotape, as media entertainment.

The history of the orgasm trade is too ancient for its origins to be
retrieved. It may be presumed, however, to have roots in sexual slavery,
barter, or exchange, as well as in erotic temple obligations and sexual
worship.

Among the merchants and service workers of the orgasm trade today,
some are sold or self-placed as apprentices because no other source of
income is available to them or their families. Others are conscripted,
lured by the promise of big money and a higher standard of living than
would otherwise be available to them. Still others, however, enlist in
response to the dictates or pathology of their own lovemaps. Individual
differences notwithstanding, these lovemaps share the common denom-
inator of multiple partners whose only contract and commitment is to pay
for what they get, either in cash or possibly in kind.

Among the customers and clients of the orgasm trade, some are the
young getting initiated, or lacking the financial resources for marriage,
or the moral resources for premarital affairs. Some are transients, and
some are alienated from their regular partners. Some are revelers, seeking
erotic entertainment. Some are the partners of an erotically impaired or
constricted mate, buying erotic variety, as in oral sex, unobtainable at
home. Some are paraphiles, paying a professional to act the supporting
role in an otherwise thwarted paraphilic ritual.

For the somatically disabled and the genitally impaired, the relationship with a paid professional may be the equivalent of therapy. With

specialty training in sex therapy, the professional qualifies as a sex surrogate. The surrogate's clients are treated for erotic phobia, failure to erect or lubricate, premature orgasm, lack of orgasm, and related genital disablements. For the client, one of the surrogate's job specifications is ability to function genitoerotically with different partners, without becoming pairbonded in a love affair to any one of them. Conversely, the client's attachment in a love affair or other long-term bond is reserved for someone else other than the surrogate.

Buying and Selling: Business and Pathology

The high degree of respect in which the philosophy of the market place is held in our society perhaps explains why there are few specifically named paraphilias in the mercantile/venal category. Though widely condemned as a social and legal vice, the buying and selling of orgasm is customarily classified as business, not as pathology.

The difference between business and pathology can be examined in the context of the new telephone business of dial-a-fantasy. In this business, the customer pays in advance to have a professional respondent improvise a role in a sexuoerotic fantasy on the basis of cues provided as the phone call progresses.

The job specification requires only that the professional respondent be a good dramatic actor on the telephone, not a personally turned-on lover being spurred on to orgasm. The caller is the one for whom the telephone drama may be the equivalent of foreplay, culminating in orgasm. The paid call may be in the nature of sporadic recreation, engaged in casually and as a supplement to a more regular sex life. The paid call may also be a regularly repeated routine which constitutes the caller's sex life exclusively, or else is an imperative adjunct to a sex life with a partner.

Telephonicophilia, or getting-off on the telephone, to use the vernacular, need not be paid for. In the so-called obscene telephone call, the caller relies not on payment, but on guile as a confidence trickster to engage the listener's attention and keep the conversation going. Neither trickery nor money is needed if consenting friends talk each other off on the telephone. It is not making the telephone call, but paying for it that qualifies as a paraphilic pathology when, without the payment, sexuoerotic arousal culminating in orgasm, either on the phone or later, fails to take place.

Payment paraphilia extends beyond the telephone. In the business of burlesque shows, live shows, and peep shows, the regular customer has long been recognized in the stereotype of the man who masturbates in the front row, under the cover of his hat or raincoat. Prostitutes also have their regular customers whose paraphilic quirk is the fulfilment of their fantasy that the acme of sex can be achieved only if it is paid for.

Just as there are not only buyers, but also sellers in the sex trade, so also there are both buying and selling paraphilias. The Greek term, *chremistes*, for those who deal in money, applies to both buying and selling. Thus the term, chrematistophilia, applies to those whose sexuoerotic turn-on is dependent on either receiving or making payment, regardless of the type of service rendered.

Payment by Artifice

Paraphilic buying and selling may be engaged in not as an actual business contract, but as a form of play acting in a prearranged drama of an as-if contract. The symbolism of payment needed no interpretation in the case of a man of wealth who was unable to fulfill his role in a homosexual agreement, either alone or in a group, until the partner wrapped his genitalia in dollar bills. According to the terms of another idiosyncrasy, the arrangement is to have money taken from one's pocket or wallet, as if it is being stolen or, conversely, being paid indirectly through the ruse of being a thief.

The prearranged drama may be one of as-if prostitution, without exchange of actual money. Thus, a pair of lovers or spouses may play act a vernacular script of a prostitute and her trick, liberally using dirty words, so-called, that would at all other times be forbidden. A related version of this drama requires that a boyfriend or husband play the role of pimp who picks up a trick to have sex with his own partner. The invitation may be spoken, face to face; or it may be written—a message published in a personal advertisement column, or scrawled on a men's toilet wall, with phone number or meeting place, date and time. The responding stranger's role is to have intercourse with the as-if pimp's wife or girlfriend, as if with a prostitute, while her pimp-impersonating husband or boyfriend watches. By envisioning her as a saint degraded into a paid whore or adulteress, the husband or boyfriend is enabled to achieve an erection while watching her with the other man, and then to copulate with her, himself.

A threesome of this type is a paraphilic variant of troilism or *ménage à trois*, and of the larger polygroupings of four or more. Multiple simultaneous partnerships do not, per se, constitute a paraphilia, however.

There are some people whose sexuoerotic relationship is satisfactory when they live together before the official contract of marriage, whereas after they are legally wed it degenerates. The explanation rests on the familiar sinner/saint principle, for marrige legally transforms a disreputable and lusty sinner relationship into a respectably chaste and saintly one. In this circumstance, the survival of lust may be at the cost of adultery. The payment may be either direct or indirect. In a bygone era, the respectability of an arranged marriage was maintained by the expediency of maintaining a mistress or a gigolo as an extramarital partner in lust.

The venal/mercantile paraphilias merge with those of the solicitational/allurative type when carnal services are bought and sold not directly, *in vivo*, but indirectly as media representations in print or on film (see Chapter 11). The term for written and photographed carnal services is pornography, if moral and legal condemnation is implied. The more neutral term is explicit erotica, or erotography. Pornography in its Greek derivation means harlot writings. Erotography means erotic writings. It is a measure of our civilization that pornography, the most commonly used term to refer to explicitly depicted sexual and erotic activity, relates to what men do, not with their wives, but with harlots. Husbands and wives must be content with nonexplicit sexual and erotic activity euphemistically and evasively referred to as making love.

9

Fetishes and Talismans

Definition

The fetishistic and talismanic paraphilias are those in which sexuoerotic triumph is wrested from tragedy by means of a strategy that incorporates sinful lust into the lovemap, though only on the condition that a token, fetish, or talisman be substituted for the lover, since lust irrevocably defiles saintly love.

Miracles and Magic

Religion, mythology, and folklore in our society have, since ancient times, been replete with relics, talismans, amulets, fetishes, and charms that work miracles, protect from harm, have mystical powers of prophecy and magic. From an early age, children assimilate from their story books and television programs information about tokens and their powers. Children also associate tokens with sex, as they assimilate knowledge of diamond rings for engagement, gold wedding bands, and class rings or pins exchanged as a token of going steady in teenage. They also associate knowledge of a more specifically sexuoerotic nature with articles of clothing as tokens, namely, garments that cover parts of the body that, if exposed naked, are considered lewd. By way of the mental process of generalization, other tokens may become endowed with sexuoerotic significance. In particular cases, this is the basis on which a token may, in the ontogeny of development, attain the status of a paraphilic fetish.

Brassières, garter belts, hose, and high heels are standard para-phernalia in the visual turn-on of millions of American males, for whom they may be regarded as fetishes, but not to the degree of constituting a complete paraphilic pathology. They are not absolutely prerequisite to most men's erotic arousal to orgasm, but are rather an extra option. Their absence does not preclude ordinary sexual participation with a partner, nor are they a substitute for the partner. Wearing these garments is also not essential to the woman's sexuoerotic arousal and climax. They are worn as a concession to the man's sexuoerotic fixation on them. It is rare to hear of women with a fetishistic fixation on men's underwear. Homosexual males, however, may have a fixation on jockstraps and tight underwear that parallels the heterosexual male fixation on female un-derwear.

The tokens of the fetishistic/talismanic paraphilias are predomi-nantly, though not invariably, inanimate objects. A tactual fetish may also be a live creature, wriggling and/or furry. For example, in a female case of fetishism, the fetish was a small dog. It was placed by the woman in her crotch, as an adjunct to masturbation and orgasm. Instead of a dog, she could substitute a small infant in the same position—which made her childbearing years something of a nightmare for her (Chapter 25).

Feels and Smells

Fetishes can be classified as related either to haptic or olfactory imagery in perception or fantasy. Haptic pertains to the feeling of pres-sure, rubbing, or touch; olfactory, to smell or odor. Even if fetish objects, like undergarments, are visually an erotic turn-on when seen in pictures or at a distance, in fantasy their application is haptic or olfactory.

The haptic paraphilias belong together as the hyphephilias, and the olfactory as the olfactophilias. In the hyphephilic group, the feeling may be internally generated, as by an enema or inserted artifact. Externally, feelings are generated through the skin senses by the application of fab-rics, fur, hair, and such like, the feel of which has its early source in hugging, cuddling, and affectionate care (see Chapter 12).

Leather and rubber fetishes bridge the gap between touch and smell. Leather shoes and their smell, and rubber training pants and their smell are probably the respective early sources of leather and rubber fetishes.

Plastic is replacing rubber for training pants, and will surely change the paraphilic rubber fetish into a plastics one. The early juvenile onset of paraphilic fascination with rubber was shown in a British survey of the retrospective recall of a group of rubber fetishists (Gosselin and Wilson, 1980).

Klismaphilia, the enema paraphilia, is rare among the fetishistic/talismanic paraphilias in having its own Greek-derived nosological term. It is an appropriate distinction, for the touchy-feely element of klismaphilia is not from the enema syringe, per se, but from the fullness pressure of the enema water, internally. In some klismaphiliacs, water is replaced by wine, or by the urine of the partner discharged through the penis inserted into the rectum.

The talismans or fetishes of the olfactophilias characteristically carry the smell of some part of the human body. Shoes, for example, in shoe fetishism, carry the smell of sweaty feet. Fetishistic garments are those, like jock straps, underpants, and sweat shirts, that come in contact with exocrine or sweaty secretions of the crotch or the underarms. Crotch smells may include also fecal or urinary odor, and in women, menstrual odor. Brassières are a reminder of the smell of lactation, as well as of the shape of breasts. Some olfactophiles not only smell the fetishistic garment or article, but also suck or chew on it.

One man's meat is another's proverbial poison, and so it is that sweaty, excretory, and menstrual residues valued by an olfactory paraphile are labeled filth in the official terminology, namely mysophilia.

The talismans or fetishes of the touchy-feely paraphilias, the hyphephilias, characteristically relate to the hair and skin of the human body, or to the fabrics that cover the skin. The fuzziness of hair and fur has also a nonparaphilic importance in infancy: it is the texture of a security blanket, nuzzled sensuously to the nostrils and lips that suck a thumb or finger. The smoothness of fabric, including leather, is to fur as skin is to hair. The young boy or girl being cuddled feels both fabric and skin. Fetish fabrics are also those that cover the forbidden sexual parts of the body for which they become a paraphilic substitute.

For the transvestophilic male, the feel of women's clothing, especially the silky feel of undergarments, augments the visual significance of gender-transposed dressing as a female. The combined feel and appearance of the garments, in actuality or in fantasy, is prerequisite to the transvestophile's complete erotic arousal and attainment of orgasm. Transvestophilia is, therefore, also known as fetishistic transvestism to distinguish it from the act of cross-dressing or transvestism. The act of cross-dressing may be done occasionally for a drag queens' masquerade party for, say, Halloween or New Year's Eve. It is done consistently by a gynemimetic or a transexual in conformity with the lifestyle. The act of cross-dressing is not the same as the state of being a transvestophile. The act may be engaged in by either a male or female transvestite. The state of transvestophilia is either extremely rare or nonexistent in women.

Transvestophilia is only secondarily a fetishistic syndrome. Primarily it is one of the gender-transposition syndromes. In some instances it is an antecedent of transexualism, though transexualism may also exist without a prior history of transvestophilia.

The transvestophile's wardrobe may be age specific. Commonly it is that of an idealized teenaged girl. It may also, however, be that of a juvenile, in which case transvestophilia is a gender-transposed variant of juvenilism. Another and younger variant is infantilism, also known as diaperism and autonepiophilia. In both juvenilism and infantilism the garments have fetishistic significance. Both syndromes may also incorporate a masochistic element of spanking and verbal humiliation. In transvestophilic juvenilism, spanking is known in the argot of cross-dressers as petticoat punishment.

10

Stigmata and Eligibility

Definition

The stigmatic and eligibilic paraphilias are those in which sexuoerotic triumph is wrested from tragedy by means of a strategy that incorporates sinful lust into the lovemap, though only on the condition that the partner be, like a pagan infidel, ineligible to be a saint defiled.

Assortative Mating

To be ineligible as a saintly partner, in these paraphilias a person must be socially stigmatized or ostracized as an outsider not suitable for kinship by marriage. The criterion of exclusion may be age, race, nationality, language, religion, social class, occupation, wealth, health, physique, physiognomy, or some insignia of group membership such as the right to wear a uniform.

The criteria by which a person is judged as suitable for kinship by marriage vary according to family and community, time and place. Thus the criteria of the idealized lovemap are subject to historical as well as ethnographic changes of fashion. The advertising and entertainment media are, in the present era, powerful not only in spreading a new trend, but also in setting it. The Hollywood sex goddess and matinee idol bear witness to the power of the movies in setting standards for the idealized American lovemap, male and female, respectively.

By shaping an idealized lovemap, a social tradition serves also to ensure assortative mating within its own particular social, tribal, racial, or regional group. Assortative mating preserves group cohesiveness by preventing changes brought about by miscegenation and the hybridization of group values. Historically, the tradition of the arranged marriage has served the same purpose.

Individual lovemaps, though conforming overall to group tradition, may be extremely detailed in specifying divers characteristics of the partner. People vary widely as to which characteristics take precedence over others—thighs, buttocks, bosom, torso, face, teeth, eye color, hair, skin, weight, height, and so on, even down to such details as having a lopsided, crooked smile, or a multifurrowed brow.

These individual variations, despite their specificity, do not constitute a paraphilic syndrome if they are simply incidental to, but not absolute prerequisites of sexual arousal and orgasmic performance. Variations that are not incidental, but absolutely prerequisite to sexuoerotic pairing, and that do, therefore, constitute a paraphilia, may or may not be within the bounds of social and legal propriety.

There are two major groups of eligibilic paraphilias, namely those that specify the morphological status of the body of an eligible partner, the morphophilias; and those that specify the chronological age level of an eligible partner, the chronophilias.

Body Morphology

There are some morphophilias in which the eligible sexuoerotic partner must be a person who is handicapped, dependent, and in need of rescue and supportive care. Some morphophilias undoubtedly are misconstrued as altruistic self-sacrifice and do not have a name. Acrotomophilia is a morphological paraphilia that was not named in print until the late 1970s (Money, 1977).

Acrotomophilia is the paraphilia in which, to be eligible, a partner must be an adult amputee. Acrotomophiles call themselves amelotasists (Ampix, 1978), to signify their attraction to amputees, and to avoid a diagnostic status. In an acrotomophile's lovemap, the missing body part or parts may be specified in detail. Congenitally missing extremities, or phocomelia, as in thalidomide babies who have now reached adulthood, satisfy the specifications of some acrotomophilic lovemaps, but not others.

The obverse of acrotomophilia is apotemnophilia (Money, Jobaris and Furth, 1977), in which becoming an amputee with a stump instead of a limb is a prerequisite of one's own paraphilic lovemap. Apotemnophiles defy handicap and overachieve. In view of the near impossibility of obtaining surgical amputation of a limb upon request, an apotemnophiliac is obliged to engineer an accident so as to require a hospitalized amputation of the injured limb. Apotemnophilia is not restricted to limb amputation. It includes also self-castration and genital self-mutiliation. In some cases it is related to instability of gender status and carries implications of transexualism (Money and De Priest, 1976).

The morphological changes of the body specified in a morphophilic lovemap may be ornamental, rather than mutilatory, or a combination of both. Tattoo and scarification are examples, and so is piercing of the perineum, genitals, or nipples for insertion of ornamental gold bars or rings. Because they affect body morphology, these modes of adornment are stigmatic/eligibilic. However, because they are modes of adornment, they are also solicitational and allurative (see Chapter 11).

Age Matching and Disparity

The matching of partners by chronological age is more or less a social norm of sexuoerotic eligibility. In the chronophilias, this norm does not hold. Between the two partners, there is a discrepancy in chronological age. Chronological age is not the sole discrepancy, however.

Often, if not always, there is a discrepancy within the chronophile between chronological age and sexuoerotic age. In literature Peter Pan illustrates this point. Immortalized as the boy who never grew up, he was the sexuoerotic self of his creator, Sir James Barrie (1860-1937).

Barrie, alias Peter Pan, had intense attachments to boys who had not yet grown up. In particular, he had unabashed romantic love affairs successively with George Llewellyn Davies and his younger brother, Michael (Birkin, 1979). They were almost certainly sexuoerotic attachments until puberty. Then sexual maturity robbed them of their pedophilic attractiveness for Peter Pan. After they were orphaned, Barrie adopted them and their three brothers.

Barrie developed the drama of Peter Pan as an adventure for the three oldest Davies boys in the woods and on the shallow lake of his summer estate. Another famous pedophile, Rev. Charles L. Dodgson

(1832-1898), alias Lewis Carroll, recounted the stories of *Through the Looking Glass* and *Adventures of Alice in Wonderland* for one of the young girls to whom he became attached. Some of them, with their mothers' consent, he photographed nude. The image was on a glass plate, in that era. Carroll set them off, tinted, in landscapes or seascapes painted on or behind the glass (Cohen, 1978).

Barrie and Carroll both exemplify that the discrepancy between chronological and sexuoerotic age in the pedophile extends to social age. Various nonsexual social interests and activities are juvenilized and on a par with those of the pedophile's young friend. That gives the young person and the pedophile equality of status. In childhood, to be respected as an equal by an adult is rare, and greatly appreciated. Conversely, the pedophile greatly appreciates being given equal status as a juvenile by his young friend.

Sexuoerotic Age Discrepancy

In naming a chronophilia, the developmental stage of the sexuoerotic age is compared with that of the chronological age. The latter is loosely assumed to be the age of adulthood. The sexuoerotic age may be infantile, juvenile, or adolescent when it is younger than the chronological age of adulthood. There are no special names for the sexuoerotic age of progressive stages of adulthood.

There are some chronophilias in which the chronological ages of the two partners may be adult, but the sexuoerotic age of one, or less often both of them, is discrepantly younger or older than his/her chronological age. One of this group of paraphilias that has its own technical name is autonepiophilia (Greek, *nepon*, infant).

Autonepiophilia is a syndrome of paraphilic infantilism. It involves being the baby oneself, babified by one's partner. The ritual typically begins with being bathed, powdered, diapered and put to bed with a baby bottle.

For some autonepiophiles, the next phase is to be pampered, as by a parent, because the diapers are wet and need changing. For others it is to be scolded, smacked, or humiliated for wetting or soiling, in which case the erotic turn-on is masochistic. Either way, the erotic delight engendered supplants the usual sequence of interactions that lead up to orgasm, and may dispense with penovaginal copulation completely. One patient had his bedroom furnished entirely as a baby's nursery. Twice divorced, he said that he tried to have intercourse with his new girlfriend at least once a month, because he knew how much she enjoyed it. "But it is such hard work, doctor," he said, "because I have to keep on concentrating on diapers to keep going." Otherwise he lost his erection and could not climax.

The syndrome of paraphilic juvenilism, in which one of two chronologically adult partners is in the sexuoerotic stage of childhood may be more common than suspected. In women, for example, it may be manifest as a persistence of girlish inhibition and modesty in which the role of the partner is, in the paraphilia, equated with that of an intimidating parent. The woman's role is to maintain girlish virginity by resisting coitus as the equivalent of molestation or rape.

In men, a subvariety of paraphilic juvenilism is explicitly evident in association with transvestophilic cross-dressing. An affected individual cross-dresses as a little girl and engages in a ritual of being naughty, for which he gets a good spanking, provided he has been able to find an obliging partner. A partner who not only obliges, but is actually sexuoerotically aroused by spanking a juvenilized transvestite is rare. The paraphilia entails a discrepancy between the two in sexuoerotic age, though not in chronologic age.

In addition to paraphilic infantilism and juvenilism, there is also the unnamed paraphilia (paraphilic adolescentilism is a suitable term) that requires one partner to treat the other as a sexuoerotically inept adolescent still lacking the full complement of the skills and responsibilities, sexuoerotic and otherwise, of maturity. For the most part, this syndrome is recognized not for what it is as a whole, but only in terms of one of its salient sexuoerotic symptoms. Inability to make the developmental transition from autoerotic masturbation to two-person masturbation and foreplay is one such symptom. Without foreplay, the sex act may become a perfunctory act of intromission—the wham-bam and thank-you ma'am of popular parlance, in which only one partner achieves orgasmic climax.

At the other extreme, dependent on the actual personal history of adolescent sexuoerotic development, there may be a failure to make the transition from two-person foreplay to genital intromission—sometimes known as a penetration phobia. In the woman, there may be a failure of lubrication. In the man, there may be either a failure of erection prior to intromission or, after intromission, prior to ejaculation—two forms of what is commonly known as impotence. Alternatively, there may be a failure to hold an erection long enough before ejaculation occurs, commonly known as premature ejaculation.

Chronologic Age Discrepancy

The obverse of syndromes of the foregoing type are those in which
the discrepancy exists between not the sexuoerotic ages, but the chronologic ages of the two partners. If the older of two partners is chronologically adult in sexual maturity, and the younger one is not, then the
relationship is loosely, and often for legal purposes, defined as child
abuse, child molestation, or pedophilia. In the interests of scientific ac-
curacy, the developmental stage of the younger person should be recognized as infantile, juvenile, or adolescent, and the syndrome of
pedophilia subdivided correspondingly into *nepiophilia, pedophilia,* and
ephebophilia. Each syndrome is usually highly age specific.

There is no satisfactory terminology when the older of the two
partners is pubertal or early adolescent, and the younger one juvenile,
with only a narrow age discrepancy between them. There is also no
satisfactory legal differentiation of sexual play from sexual abuse or
molestation when both partners are young and close in age, but one is
more advanced into adolescence than the other.

The law has no precedent for dealing with a discrepancy such as is
presented when the younger partner has undergone precocious puberty
and is reproductively mature by age nine, whereas the older partner is
aged fifteen and is showing only the beginning signs of the onset of
puberty.

Among the young, irrespective of whether their ages are matching
or discrepant, the law does not recognize an age of consent to sexuoerotic
activity. After maturity, however, age discrepancy is of no legal concern.
Thus *gerontophilia* is not illegal, regardless of whether the older partner
is of grandparental or parental age, provided the younger, gerontophilic
partner, male or female, is no longer legally a minor.

Erroneous Stereotypes

There is no popular stereotype of the gerontophile, male or female,
as a sexual degenerate whose degeneracy will inexorably lead to sadistic
depravity and lust murder. A parallel stereotype does exist, however,
with respect to pedophilia. This stereotype lacks substantiation and empirical proof. It is erroneous. Its error is a conclusion, no doubt drawn
from observed facts, that is false and misconstrued. Thus, in some cases,

a lust murderer with the syndrome of erotophonophilia may have children exclusively as victims. However, affectionate pedophilia, which lacks violence or killing, is not the same paraphilia as lust murder directed toward children. Nor is it the same as rape (biastophilia) directed toward children. Typically, these paraphilias do not coexist in the same person, nor does one convert into the other. If such a conversion appears to have taken place, investigation of the history of the individual's paraphilic imagery commonly uncovers the presence of violence and murder in the sexuoerotic fantasy since early adolescence. At the outset, however, the fantasy did not translate into action. Only later did it burst out of bounds.

Another popular stereotype regarding pedophilia is that the syndrome is more prevalent in homosexuals than heterosexuals; and that the age of the partner lowers progressively from adult to adolescent to juvenile, as the paraphile becomes progressively jaded and degenerate with age. This stereotype also is not true. It is far more likely that heterosexual pedophilia is relatively more common than homosexual, especially if incest statistics are included. The paraphilic age range of the pedophile's partner of either sex is rather rigidly set as juvenile. Homosexual pedophilia has little overlap with homosexual ephebophilia, and both of these have little overlap with homosexual attraction for adults. The same applies heterosexually.

Incest, be it homosexual or heterosexual, does not qualify as a paraphilia simply by reason of its definition as sexual pairing within the kinship. First cousin marriage is forbidden as incest under some laws, and ethnically condoned or required under others. When there are no restrictions to be defied, then it is quite clear that the sexuoerotic relationship in a first-cousin marriage may be entirely unencumbered by paraphilia. It is the very fact of its being a sin that gives incest the potential status of a paraphilia on the basis of the saint/sinner principle. According to this principle, lust and incest are reconciled as both are sins, whereas lust contaminates the saintliness of a legally permitted, consenting partner, even a spouse. Without this principle, there is no rational explanation of why a parent of either sex disengages from the husband-wife sexuoerotic relationship and, very often if not always, with the silent collusion of the spouse, engages in a parent-child relationship. To qualify as paraphilic, this switch is not a sporadic lapse, but a consistent one. Further, in some cases, it applies not only to one junior partner, but to two or more of them, over a period of time, and possibly over two generations.

In some cases of age-discrepant incest, the fact of kinship may be less important than the fact of age. That is to say, incest may mask in the older partner a primary syndrome of either pedophilia or ephebophilia, or possibly and more rarely, infantophilia. In such a case, there may be other eligible junior partners who are not kin, as well as those who are.

In evaluating the paraphilic quality of incest, or its absence, the relationship may be that of the household, not the genealogy. That is to say, the participants may be related by marriage, adoption, or fostering. The boundaries of permissibility are blurred in such households. Take, for example, a test case. Two age-concordant partners grew up unrelated until they married at, say, age fifteen. They then shared a household with the mother of one and the father of the other. These two adults then got married. Presumably their already married children would suddenly become partners in incest, since they would share the same parents. Or should the prior marriage of their children be considered to have made them related to one another, so that their own marriage would be incest?

Although sibling and step-sibling sexuoerotic contacts qualify technically as incest, they should more properly qualify simply as sexuoerotic rehearsal play, especially if the two partners are age-concordant juveniles. This kind of play in childhood, or early in adolescence, is not a precursor of paraphilia, insofar as it does not exclude a subsequent sexuoerotic relationship with a partner who is not kin. The same may be said of other, age-concordant, nonsibling relationships in which kinship is either genealogical or by marriage, adoption, or fostering.

The adverse effects of kinship on a sexuoerotic relationship is, in the ultimate analysis, that of the catch-22 outcome (Chapter 3) of being damned if you do, and damned if you don't make a disclosure. In other words, it is their very forbiddenness that ensures the possibility of a pathological effect—and all the more so if incest belongs in the lovemap of only one of the two partners, making the relationship asymmetrical. The probability of asymmetry is greatly increased when there is a wide discrepancy in the age of the two partners. Usually it is the lovemap of the older of the two which takes priority over that of the younger. Regardless of age or kinship, mismatching of lovemaps makes for an encounter or relationship that has negative sequelae expressed as, for example, disgust, guilt, elective mutism, phobia, panic, or rage. For this reason, reciprocal mutuality and matching of lovemaps in the first love affair, or the first affair that includes genitoeroticism and coitus, is an important precursor of a successful sex life subsequently. Sarrell and Sarrell (1983), already referred to in Chapter 3, found that college youth reporting for sex therapy recalled their first ejaculation at puberty as having been negatively imbued, whereas their controls recalled it as positively imbued. In a study of first coitus in women, Weis (1983) found a parallel phenomenon, namely that the situational context correlated with the affective sequelae.

Developmental Dissynchrony: Sexuoerotic and Chronologic Aging

In the pedophilic lovemap, the idealized image of the lover does not advance in age in synchrony with the advancing chronological age of the pedophile. Instead it remains forever juvenile. Thus, the pedophile's love affair with a young partner does not survive the young person's chronological advance into adolescence. The void that ensues can be filled only with another juvenile lover.

This developmental sequence is not unique to pedophilia. It has its counterpart in ephebophilia and, though not widely known, in gerontophilia, also. No name has yet been given to the paraphilia in which the idealized lovemap-image of the partner remains forever in young adulthood.

Failure of the idealized image of the lover in a person's lovemap to advance in age goes hand in hand with failure of the sexuoerotic age of the person to advance in synchrony with his/her chronological age. This dissynchrony may apply to one or both of two partners or spouses. In either case, it may by middle life deplete the partnership of its bonding power, and allow it to fall apart in separation or divorce. Neither partner may be able to formulate an explanation of what has happened. It is not necessary for a rivalrous attachment to another partner to have preceded the breakup.

Cross-species Attachments

In classical erotic art, the mythical satyr, half-man, half-goat, copulates with a human partner. There are erotic paintings of the middle east, three and four centuries old, in which a man is depicted copulating with a camel or a sheep. According to the Hindu tradition of erotic painting and sculpture which is still extant, as in Nepal, a human being copulating with an animal is, in fact copulating with a deity. The god is incarnate in the form of an animal, like Ganesa, the god with an elephant's head.

Not only in art, but also in life, the mores of human-animal sexual contact vary ethnographically. There is an ancient pre-Columbian custom among Indians of the Caribbean coast of Colombia, for example, that associates the attainment of manhood with the exercise of copulating with donkeys. It is considered that adolescent youth will not achieve competence in marriage unless they practice coitus with animals. The custom happens also to be an expediency that allows girls not to get pregnant until married.

In our own culture, pet animals are for petting, though not for copulating with. Lovers copulate, but they also engage in petting. Those who have no lover, being too young, lonely, sick, or old, may have a pet as a substitute companion to kiss, hug, cuddle, and curl up asleep with. The pairbond between owner and pet is notable for its strength and durability. No one has statistics on the prevalence of sensuous crotch contact with pets, nor on more explicit contact of the genitals.

There is a farmboy folklore of copulation with sheep, or occasionally with other animals in heat, and of being licked by a calf or puppy. Boys joke about such experiences. They are transient adventures on the way to maturity. Semantically, they constitute zoophilic acts, but not a zoophilic status or syndrome. To be a genuine paraphilic syndrome, zoophilia would exclude contact with a human partner as a source of sexuoerotic arousal and orgasm—or, at least the animal contact would surpass a human one. In this sense, zoophilia would seem to be fairly rare. A highly specific form of zoophilia is formicophilia in which arousal and orgasm are dependent on the sensations produced by small creatures like snails, frogs, ants or other insects creeping, crawling, or nibbling the genitalia and perianal area, and the nipples.

11

Solicitation and Allure

Definition

The solicitational and allurative paraphilias are those in which triumph is wrested from tragedy by means of a strategy that incorporates sinful lust into the lovemap, though only on the condition that a solicitational/allurative act belonging to the prelimary or proceptive phase be substituted for the copulatory act of the central or acceptive phase, thus ensuring that saintly love be not defiled by sinful lust.

Proceptive Signals

Paraphilic tactics of solicitation include displaying and watching, touching and rubbing, talking or listening, and writing or reading, in such a way as to convey sexuoerotic arousal. These same tactics have a place in the preliminaries of foreplay between consenting partners. As foreplay, these tactics do not occupy center stage, as they do in the allurative paraphilias. Paraphilically, they usurp the place of the coital genital relationship as the high point of erotic excitement and orgasm. This usurpation takes place even when coitus takes place, for the prior performance of the paraphilic act facilitates subsequent arousal and orgasm. Or else, its replay in imagination takes on the facilitatory function.

A sexuoerotic solicitation or invitation may be visually signaled either explicitly by presenting the genitalia, or implicitly in eye-talk, finger-talk, or overall body-language and appearance. A vocal invitation likewise may be either direct and explicit, or indirect and allusive, the signal being less the words than the modulations of the pitch, speed, and volume of the voice. Tactual invitation also is direct and explicit, if it is candidly applied to a person's genital or other erogenous region. It is indirect and implicit when feigned as a casual or inadvertent reaching, rubbing, or pressing against some part of another's anatomy.

As is the case with the paraphilias in general, the solicitational/allurative paraphilias tend to be manifested phenomenologically in antipodean pairs. Exhibitionism and voyeurism, for example, are antipodes of one another, on the polarity of signal output and input, transmission and reception, respectively. To exhibit is to transmit a solicitation, whereas to peep as a voyeur is to receive an alluring image.

Uninvited Overtures

Exhibitionism as a paraphilia comes to the attention of the court or the clinic as a phenomenon of public exhibition, exposure, or flashing of the male genitalia. For this reason, and to distinguish it from overall histrionic display or a theatrical type of attention-getting, it needs its own term, peodeiktophilia (Greek *peos* penis; *deiknunain*, display).

A peodeiktophilic lovemap in a male prescribes that the recipient of the paraphilic tactic should be a stranger. She should be startled into a reaction of either surprised pleasure and amazement or, conversely, of fear and panic. A neutral or indifferent response spells peodeiktophilic failure.

Answering a question before a group of medical students, a peodeiktophilic exhibitionist on one occasion gave an example of indecent exposure before a group of three young women at a bus stop. One of them asked if he didn't know that he was supposed to keep his penis in his pants in public, and told him to put it away. Thereupon, his paraphilic compulsion broke. He did as he was told and spent the remaining waiting time in social conversation.

In classical times, the women of a besieged Greek city would, by standing on the walls and displaying their genitals, turn away the enemy (Greek *apotropaia*, turning away)—a genital, but not an erotic act. As an act of paraphilic exhibitionism, a woman may display her genitals in public if she wears no panties and, with a short skirt, sits so as to expose the pudenda. Another possibility is to arrange to copulate in a park or other public place to attract onlookers, and to assume a position that allows display of the genitalia.

Men to whom a female exhibits usually do not take offense and do not call the police, whereas the reverse is far more likely to be true in the case of the male exhibitionist. The particular act of exposure that leads to arrest is not necessarily the first or only one of that particular occasion. Others may have preceded it. The flasher's penis may stay erect during a prolonged phase of excitement without reaching the phase of ejaculatory orgasm. Whereas one flasher may masturbate, another may not. The ritual of exposure, and whose attention to attract, where, and how, is highly individual and idiosyncratic. What the great majority of flashers share in common is that their paraphilia is limited to showing the penis to a stranger, without proceeding further into a genital relationship with her. Exhibiting the penis is not a prelude to rape, contrary to popular supposition. Peodeiktophilia is not the same as biastophilia. Convergence of the two syndromes in one individual is atypical and rarely reported.

A flasher who has a regular beat returns to a particular location, rather than to a particular person or persons to whom to expose himself. The voyeur or Peeping Tom who prowls a regular beat has his own directory of particular unshaded windows through which to glimpse a particular woman undressing, or having intercourse with her partner. If he stands there masturbating, he is, indeed, exposing himself. However, his paraphilia is to look, more than to show. If his paraphilic love map permits him to peep without attracting attention, then he may remain anonymously paraphilic indefinitely. All paraphilias being overt rather than covert syndromes, however, the night prowler usually does contrive to attract attention. One tactic, already mentioned, is that of somnophilia, the syndrome of awakening the sleeping princess, or prince—which leads to an accusation of unlawful entry and rape (Chapter 7). Paraphilic rape (biastophilia) rarely coexists with paraphilic voyeurism.

Exposing and peeping are visile paraphilias. Vision being an exteroceptive sense for processing stimuli at a distance, the visile paraphilias are also distancing paraphilias that keep the paraphile and the other partner spatially separated. The analogous audile paraphilia is not just one of talking and evesdropping, incognito, but of doing so on the telephone. This is the paraphilia of the obscene telephone call (Chapter 8), or telephone scatologia, or telephonicophilia.

The paraphilic telephone caller may be gay, though most is known about those who are heterosexual and who call a woman. In at least one known instance, a gay caller was able to talk himself into an orgasm without any responsive dialogue whatsoever. Usually, however, in order to avoid termination of the call, a telephone paraphile must pose as a pollster, bureaucratic official, blackmailer, victim in need, or someone else in an "I know you, but you don't know me" role, in order not to have the phone call precipitously terminated. Part of his trickery is to have researched some biographical details of the listener, and to play on that person's curiosity, pity, or fear, in order to maintain contact while the conversation becomes explicitly erotic. For the listener, the caller poses a threat because he knows the name and address of the person he has dialed, while retaining his own anonymity. There are some cases in which personal threats are verbalized, but evidence of their having been carried out is negligible.

The proportion of paraphilic telephonists who happen to contact someone who reciprocates in an explicitly erotic conversation is unascertainable. In the 1960s, Dan Basen, an art student now deceased, designed a program for a Happening. He dialed from his home at night the numbers of payphones on downtown streets in the entertainment district. His anonymous responders were men. They engaged in uninhibited and explicitly erotic conversation.

Instead of through the eyes or the ears, an uninvited sexuoerotic signal or aproach to a stranger may be initiated through the sense of touch. The paraphilia, frotteurism, of rubbing or pressing the genital zone or other part of one's own body against that of a stranger, usually in a crowd, is known from the French term, *frottage*. Toucherism involves touching with the fingers. It may be done prankishly, and not, as in frotteurism, under the pretext of being jostled in a crowd, or by the swaying of a moving bus or train.

One of the defining characteristics that differentiates rubbing/touching as a paraphilia from an egregious flirting tactic is the phenomenon of paraphilic distancing: there are no other friendly overtures—no smiles, no conversation, no encouraging response. Encouragement would signify consent, which is not written into the paraphilic lovemap of the frotteur/toucheur. In its place is either indifference, disgust, or alarm. If the recipient does become alarmed, it is usually because the rubbing or touching is misconstrued as a prologue to rape. This is another example of the confusion, in the popular mind, of the paraphilias of solicitation and allure with those of marauding and predation. As in other solicitation/allure paraphilias, there may be a time lapse between the excitement of the rubbing or touching ritual and the attainment of orgasm—which may then be either autoerotic, or with a partner.

The fable of the princess who turned a slimy frog into a handsome prince by not rejecting his overtures is, in fable form, the antipodean form of the paraphilia of rubbing and touching a stranger. The princess waits to feel a stranger's touch or rub. Like the paraphilic fantasy of waiting to be taken or possessed, it may never be fulfilled in the absence of a lure designed to attract the frog's attention.

To Lure an Audience

It is a basic tenet of our culture that women are supposed to lure men. Therefore, insofar as luring itself is a paraphilia of women, it is usually not recognized as such. Instead, it is misconstrued either as normal, or as so-called frigidity, namely, inability to progress from proceptive luring to acceptive, penovaginal intromission. It may also be misconstrued as hypersexuality, or nymphomania. As mentioned in Chapter 5, nymphomania manifests itself as a paraphilic compulsion to lure a succession of casual partners, this being the only strategy that permits sufficient arousal to achieve orgasm. The build-up of arousal may culminate in orgasm with each new partner, and/or it may be expended with the long-term partner, who may be a man or a woman. In men, this form of hypersexuality goes under the name of satyriasis or Don Juanism. In the gay vernacular, the synonym, compulsive cruising, alone is used. Pejoratively, it is also promiscuity, whether gay or straight.

The converse of compulsive cruising is unilateral limerence (Tennov, 1979) and compulsive fixation on an unattainable lover, despite desolate failure to lure a reciprocal response. This autistic form of lovesickness goes by the little known name of Clérambault-Kandinsky syndrome (Chapter 16), and may lead to suicide or homicide.

In our society, men are formally stereotyped not as lures for women, but as those who make overtures to women whose allure entices them. Formal stereotype notwithstanding, men do use macho lures. They follow fashions in hirsutism and barbering, in civilian and official uniforms, and in some instances in decoration of the body with tattoo, pierced jewelry, or other decorative accessories, accouterments, and apparel.

Tattooing, scarring, and piercing the body may become incorporated into a paraphilia of allure. It is named stigmatophilia, after the Greek, in the special sense of having markings branded, pricked, cut, or pierced into the body, especially into its erotic regions. Thus, tattoos may be applied to the genitalia as well as other parts of the body. Piercing of the perineum, genitals, or nipples enables gold bars, rings, or chastity locks to be worn and used for erotic allure, analogously with gold earrings.

Stigmatophilia belongs, as the name indicates, partly with the stigmatic/eligibilic paraphilias. It has affinities also with sadomasochism, since those who get marked are likely to engage in erotic mutilation and other expiatory/sacrificial paraphilic ceremonies in either a masochistic or sadistic role. Receiving the stigmata of stigmatophilia may be a masochistic procedure, but thereafter they serve to announce the bearer's eligibility as a particular type of partner, and to lure new admirers.

The macho lure of tattoos and pierced gold genital jewelry is often favored by those whose erotic uniform (Chapter 6) comprises high boots with chains and spurs, studded leather jackets, pants and wristbands, leather cockstraps, and other macho paraphernalia. A uniform has power to lure an audience of admirers.

Another erotic lure, at least among people not yet satiated, is a live sexual performance. The commercial live-show trade is exploitative and mercenary, but not exclusively so. Some live-show performers are in the business that allows them to put their paraphilia to work to earn a living. Their paraphilia is autagonistophilia. The word is derived from the Greek terms for self (*auto*) and contestant (*agonistes*). People who get turned-on by having an audience watch them copulate do not necessarily have to get paid. One such man would lure an audience by putting on a live show on the roof of his office building. The audience watched from the windows of higher neighboring buildings. He had also launched a scheme to act in explicit erotic movies. He was typical in his paraphilic defiance of the predicted risk to his professional career and his income. The outcome was conviction and imprisonment.

It is quite common not only for autagonistophiles, but paraphiles in general to keep a photographic record of themselves in an erotic performance, despite the risk of self-incrimination later. Being the audience at their own performance on film is a narcissistic version of the antipode of autagonistophilia, which is subdivided into scoptophilia and pictophilia. Both terms pertain to being turned-on by being an invited guest at someone else's erotic performance. Scoptophilia (also spelled scopophilia) is limited to opportunities of live groupings and the observer. Explicit erotica in print or on film provide virtually unlimited opportunities for pictophilia.

Being a guest at someone else's erotic performance, either in pictures, on film, or live, is far more likely to be an occasional pastime than a paraphilia. Observing qualifies as scoptophilia or pictophilia only if it is an imperative on which one's own arousal and orgasm depend. Unlike voyeurism, scoptophilia is with the consent of the participants.

Narratophilia is to pictophilia as words are to pictures. Telling erotic stories, listening to them, or reading them is, like looking at erotic movies or videotapes, far more likely to be an occasional pastime than a paraphilia. Erotic stories, like their visual counterpart, may occupy a casual place, either in private or shared with company, in a person's or a couple's sex life. For the narratophile, however, they are not casual, but genito-erotically essential. To illustrate: a man who lost his job and his family after being arrested and publicly exposed for engaging in homosexual activities in a men's toilet, had kept the secret of his homosexual proclivity from his wife for fifteen years of marriage. He had functioned as a bisexual, having intercourse with his wife every Saturday night. To become aroused, he would narrate stories from his days of military service about the masturbatory exploits of soldiers, keeping their homosexual interaction silent and private in his own fantasy only. He told his stories explicitly and in the vernacular. His wife indulged him only until he reached his orgasm. Then her ultraprudishness resumed, and any mention of sex was prohibited until the next Saturday night.

Pornography

The narrative/pictorial paraphilias qualify as partly of the venal/mercantile type insofar as a customer purchases media productions of carnal services to serve as lures or artifices of arousal in the proceptive phase. Whether used alone and autoerotically, or shared together with a partner, they are defined pejoratively as pornography, and meet with the same condemnation by madonnas and providers as do the harlots (Greek, *pornos*) for whom they are named.

The appeal of commercial pornography far exceeds the audience of paraphiles who are turned on by it more than by sexuoerotic interaction with a partner. The existence of the larger audience serves to demonstrate the point that paraphilic imagery is not an all or none phenomenon, but a matter of degree. The person with a pornography paraphilia is an addict for his/her particular type of pornography, whereas the ordinary citizen who uses pornographic publications exercises an option, not a compulsion. Commercial pornography is experienced not as a substitute for a relationship with a partner, but adjunctively, as a pastime or as an entertainment in the preliminary phase of foreplay.

The ordinary citizen cannot, however, turn on to any and all kinds of erotic material, but only to that which has a place somewhere in his/her own lovemap. You cannot learn someone else's lovemap, or borrow someone else's fantasy. It won't work!

Ordinary people who are consumers of commercial erotica do not become addicted to it. On the contrary, they become rather rapidly satiated. Thereafter, it occupies a peripheral place in their sex lives, to be called upon when the occasion and the circumstances are fitting.

Visual pornography is typically two-dimensional, but it may be sculptured in three dimensions. Attraction to naked statues with the genitalia depicted has been called agalmatophilia. This term refers to erotic aesthetics, however, rather than to a syndrome of paraphilia.

Phylisms: I

Definition

Despite the extent of their variety, the range of the paraphilias is not infinite. The limiting factor would appear to be phylogenetic as well as ontogenetic. That is to say, the phylogenetic development of the species sets a limit to the repertory of paraphilic sexuoerotic practice and/or imagery that is distributed ontogenetically among individual members of the species.

A repertory is a collection or inventory of items to be performed. There is need for a name by which to identify the items or units in the repertory of behavioral practices and/or images and ideas that are found in individuals and which are characteristic of the species. There is no adequate name for these units of behavior, action, or conduct, and/or the imagery and ideation in which they are, it may be presumed, represented in the brain/mind. The name I have coined is phylisms (Money, 1983a), for which a synonym is phylon.

The term, phylism, is derived from the Greek *phylon* (Latin *phylum*), tribe or race. A phylism is a unit or building block of our existence that belongs to us, as individuals, through our heritage as members of our race or species. A phylism is observed as a behavioral manifestation. It may or may not be self-observed in thought or imagery, and reported in words. Its governance is complex and, in almost all instances, resides ultimately in the brain.

Some phylisms have everyday names like breathing, coughing, spitting, sneezing, blowing, hiccuping, drinking, swallowing, licking, biting, chewing, pissing, shitting, fucking, laughing, crying, walking, grasping, holding, hitting, kicking, pressing, touching, itching, sweating, shivering, hurting, tasting, smelling, hearing, seeing—the complete list has not been arbitrated. Others have Latinate names like masturbation, fellatio, cunnilingus, lubrication, erection, orgasm, ejaculation, and so on. Still others remain unnamed, or have been named only recently, for example, pairbonding and troopbonding.

In the genesis of a paraphilia, a phylism that is not ordinarily programed into sexuoerotic functioning becomes disengaged from its regular context to become enlisted in the service of sexuoeroticism, and enchained to it. Whether or not any phylism, picked at random, could be so enchained is a moot question for which the answer is not presently known. What is known, on the basis of the paraphilic record to date, is that the number of phylisms enchained in the service of the paraphilias is limited to the six strategies described in the preceding chapters.

Judging from these six strategies, it would appear that the phylisms that may become attached to sexuoeroticism so as to form a paraphilia are those which, in the course of early development, are brought into some degree of propinquity with genital arousal and sexuoeroticism. Phylisms of internal pressure and perineal touch associated with receiving multiple enemas, for example, may become enchained to sexuoerotic arousal and so generate klismaphilia, the enema paraphilia. It is possible that a plethora of enemas in infancy and early childhood alone may generate the klismaphilia; but other variables such as their frequency or volume, or the degree of traumatization or genital titillation experienced, may also be significant supplementary determinants. There may also be a critical age effect.

Expiatory/Sacrificial Phylisms: Masochistic

In the expiatory and sacrificial paraphilias, the phylisms that become attached to sexuoeroticism are those that are elicited initially in response to warnings, threats, and punishments associated with the genitals and sexuoerotic rehearsal play. The paraphilias thus generated prescribe that sexuoerotic indulgence requires a sacrificial expiation or atonement.

Self-imposed sacrifical atonement variously involves insult, humiliation, pain, injury, and even stage-management of one's own death. These are the masochistic strategies. They are elaborations of self-mutilation, a phenomenon found in non-human, as well as human primates, particularly as a sequel to prolonged and frustrating deprivation and iso-lation. In lesser form, self-mutilation appears in those who bite their fingernails to the quick, and thereby keep the hands occupied and tem-porarily less likely to strike out.

On the basis of subjective report, self-mutilation has a paradoxical effect of reducing tenseness and agitation. The calmness that ensues may expand into euphoria and even reach a peak of mystical ecstasy. Such a transformation is probably a correlate of the release by the brain of one of its own morphine-like neurochemicals, endorphin. The masochistic paraphilias should provide an ideal source of data for future investigation of this proposition. In infancy, self-mutilation has a prototypic form, namely head-banging and, associated with it, rocking. One young adult head-banger's self-report was quite explicit with respect to the trance-like euphoria that he had experienced from head-banging since childhood. The initial pain from bruising his forehead quickly metamorphosed into euphoria.

In asphyxiophilia, asphyxiation by self-strangulation or hanging in-duces oxygen deprivation which, in turn, may enhance orgasm. It may have its origin in the phylism of prolonged apnea, the breath-holding seen in young children during a crying tantrum.

In the squirrel monkey there is a urinary phylism related to chal-lenging a stranger. Even to the image of its own face in a mirror, a male squirrel monkey's penis will unfurl from its retracted position and direct a stream of urine at the mirror. It is possible that this phylism could become sexuoerotically entrained, and manifested as urophilia, but its restricted occurrence among primates makes it unlikely to have human significance. It is more likely that inspecting the genitals by licking them, a widespread primate phylism, becomes related to urophilia and maybe coprophilia, also. This phylism may also be related to paraphilic ingestion of ejaculate, as a sequel to fellatio. Some male monkeys lick semen from the penis after copulating, or swallow it after either manual masturbation or self-fellatio.

Among primates, there is also a phylism for playing with one's own excrement, smearing or ingesting it. Such behavior may emerge in early infancy, and reemerge again, later, under conditions of extreme sensory and cognitional stimulus-starvation, monotony, and boredom.

Another phylism that is a candidate for sexuoerotic enchainment in urophilia and coprophilia is the general mammalian phylism of cleaning the perineum of an infant by licking it, and ingesting the products of urination and defecation. This phylism is observed in higher primates.

In the human species its occurrence has been reported in Eskimo infant care when, under severe climatic conditions, no washing water is available.

Still another coprophagic phylism, recently identified in experiments with rats (Moltz and Lee, 1983; Moltz, 1984), relates to the immunological incompetence of the newborn to resist acute infection of the gut, and death from necrotizing enterocolitis. Fourteen days after the onset of lactation, the mother begins to release a fecal pheromone, a prolactin-induced derivative of cholic acid in bile. The pheromone attracts the young to eat their mother's fecal pellets. The pheromone-containing pellets are rich in deoxycholic acid, also a derivative of cholic acid in bile. It protects against bacterial endotoxin, for example, of *E. coli*. The young need protection beginning at day fourteen, which is when they first ingest bacteria-containing solid food. By day twenty-eight, the young produce their own deoxycholic acid, and cease eating the mother's fecal pellets which no longer contain the pheromonal attractant.

In the human species, necrotizing enterocolitis is more prevalent among premature than full-term babies (Moltz, 1984). The premature are less efficient in bile-acid production. There is no known human counterpart of neonatal coprophagia in rats, so the possible relation of this phylism to maternal coprophagia, and subsequently to human adult coprophilia is speculative.

Similarly speculative is a hypothesis put forward by Hopp (1980) regarding coprophagia, incidental to ingestion of feces from the gut of the prey eaten by carnivorous predators. Bacteria ingested in this way eventually are shed in the feces of the predator. The proximity of the anal and genital openings allows for the transfer of microorganisms from the gut into the female genital tract at the time of copulation. In this way, Hopp conjectured, genetic information from another species may splice itself into the DNA of a chromosome belonging to an embryo about to be formed, and become a permanent feature of its genetic code. Complex transformation of genetic information is thus achieved at a rate far more rapidly than is possible by random mutation alone, as postulated in classical Darwinian evolutionary theory.

In human coprophilia, carnivorous human beings eat only the feces, not the flesh of the partner. The phyletic mechanism proposed in Hopp's hypothesis may be presumed to be the same, however, if it applies at all.

Expiatory/Sacrificial Phylisms: Sadistic

The antipodes of the masochistic strategies are the sadistic ones, in which atonement or expiation is imposed on the partner who is insulted, humiliated, smeared, pained, injured and, at the sadistic extreme, ritualistically murdered in a brutal form of love-death.

When two sadomasochistic partners get together, then sadomasochistic phylisms, one sadistic and the other masochistic, may be distributed reciprocally, one to each partner, respectively. Or, they may be reciprocally reversible, each partner taking turns. When the partners have no initial acquaintanceship and consenting sadomasochistic agreement, then a sadistic paraphilia merges into a predatory one.

Sadism and masochism are two of the earliest named of the expiatory group of paraphilias. For this reason they tend to be generic in the sense of encompassing a broad variety of specific phenomena, each of which may in time need its own name. Whipping, for example, is different from cutting and piercing; and fisting, with the hand or arm in the anus or vagina, is different from stretching and binding the genitals, and from licking boots or being led, like a dog, on a leash. Coprophilia and urophilia, aforementioned, are two of the subvarieties of sadomasochistic humiliation that do have their own name.

The two expiatory paraphilias that carry the self-imposed death penalty do so, true to opponent-process theory, as in the deadly game of Russian roulette. It is a gambler's game in which only one bullet is loaded into a revolver. Chance decides whether it will be the loaded chamber or an empty one in place when the player pulls the trigger against his own head. The two paraphilic games of death are asphyxiophilia, or self-strangulation; and autassassinophilia, or staging one's own masochistic assassination or murder. In erotophonophilia or lust murder, the staging of another's erotic bloodshed or homicide, there may also be an element of chance as to when the final act will actually be performed, if the victim is not a stranger.

In lust murder, the translocated phylism could conceivably be killing for food. Paraphilic cannibalism is, however, virtually unknown. Moreover, food intake rarely seems to get hitched onto sex and eroticism in paraphilia formation. One exception might be that the renunciation of food, as in the syndrome of anorexia nervosa, is actually a negation of paraphilia, its affirmation being bulimia, or autoerotic binge eating, climaxed by induced vomiting.

Instead of cannibalistic killing, the phylism that subserves paraphilic killing is more likely the primate phylism of attack and killing to protect the troop and its boundaries against invading predators. Lust murder and other rituals of uninvited violence thus overlap with predatory paraphilias. By stealth the predator stalks and captures the prey.

Marauding/Predatory Phylisms

In the marauding and predatory paraphilias, the phylisms that become attached to sexuoeroticism have to do with taking something by
either stealth or seizure. Simply taking something, like a breath of fresh
air, a swallow of water, or a bite of food is, self-evidently, very basic
to living things. In carnivorous species, to take food is to seize it, and
to kill. In diecious or two-sexed species, because procreation requires a
contribution from male and female, taking or giving that contribution
may be an act of reciprocation. It may also be an act of stealth and
seizure.

The praying mantis, like some spiders, sometimes seizes her copulating mate and eats him. This cannibalistic phylism of insects appears
to be inapplicable to mammals. Despite the mammalism phylism for
cannibalizing the placenta and, when parturition is disrupted, maybe the
young also, paraphilic cannibalism is, as aforesaid, virtually nonexistant.
The connection between sexuoeroticism and seizure has other phyletic
sources.

The most likely source lies in the phylism of troopbonding. A great
many primate species are troopbonders, including the three closely related
species, human beings, chimpanzees, and gorillas. Troopbonders are
territorial, and they mark out the boundaries of their territory. Territorial
marking in four-legged mammals is accomplished principally by odors,
or pheromones, secreted from specialized marker glands, or in the urine,
under the control of sex hormones. In primates, territorial marking is
principally visual. The troop defends itself against the intrusion of ma-
rauders and predators. More precisely, the young adult males are the
ones that do the defending, possibly at the cost of being killed and eaten
by a predator. As compared with juveniles and breeding females, young
adult males are expendable, for the birth rate can be maintained with an
unequal sex ratio in favor of females.

With an unbalanced sex ratio in which females predominate, maintenance of the birthrate will require a formula for sharing male copulatory
service. The sharing may be random; or it may be on the basis of a special
attachment, or pairbondedness, of two or more females to one male. The
male provides not only breeding service, but also some guarantee of
protection.

Pairbondedness and partner sharing need not necessarily be mutually
exclusive. Either the female may share her partner with others, or the
male or both may share partners. The less the potential for sharing, the

greater the potential for rivalry; and if females outnumber males, the greater a male's jealous possessiveness of the females that share him. Mating rivalry generates attack and fighting between competitors of the same sex. Jealousy generates attack and fighting also between male and female.

One of the phylisms indicative of surrender and appeasement is the presenting position which is also the phylism to invite copulation. Males and females both present as a sign of appeasement, the evidence being particularly clear in juvenile play, according to studies of rhesus monkeys. The victorious animal, whether male or female, responds by mounting the one that presents. Mounting is a phylism of hierarchical dominance as well as of copulation.

The appeasing animal is in a position not only to be taken in an actual or a simulated sexual act, but also to be abducted. After abduction or kidnaping, another phylism may come into play, the phylism of becoming addicted to abuse, or enslaved to it, and to enter into collusion with the abuser (Chapter 5). Such collusion is common in the battered child syndrome. It also occurs in political and other prisoners subjected to torture and brainwashing. The fact that such a phenomenon exists is not widely appreciated. It seems to fly in the teeth of common sense, so that evidence of its phyletic existence is discounted, especially by the judiciary in its assumptions about responsibility and guilt.

A kidnaped sexual partner who foregoes opportunities for escape remains in a strong bond of attachment to the kidnaper. Until the bond is broken by outside intervention, it persists with all the defiant resistance of the phylism of infatuation and the limerent love affair.

Abduction or kidnaping may take place while two rivals are fighting or competing over a mate. Behind the rivals' backs, so to speak, the disputed mate may be abducted by a third competitor. Or, by stealth, the two may take advantage of the opportunity and elope.

Abduction may involve another phylism, namely the departure of a newly mature young adult from the family or home troop. It may either break away, or be taken away to establish a new breeding troop, or to join one already formed.

Fighting over a mate, possessive jealousy, raiding a neighboring tribe to kidnap a mate, and mutual elopement are all ancient themes in human history, mythology, and folklore. They show how close is the connection between the phylisms of fighting, abducting, and mating. It is from this closeness that the predatory paraphilias are generated, developmentally.

The stealth and stealing paraphilias that have their own names as syndromes are kleptophilia, somnophilia, and necrophilia. The seizure and assault paraphilias are biastophilia (raptophilia) and symphorophilia, the paraphilia of catastrophes.

The phylism to which biastophilia and symphorophilia become attached is probably the ungovernable rage of an infantile temper tantrum. The victims of the catastrophe are, like hostages, stand-ins for the original enemy.

The syndrome in which it is the partner who is more exciting and paraphilically desirable if he/she has a criminal history of marauding and predation, or can be incited to embark on such a history, is hybristophilia.

13

Phylisms: II

Mercantile/Venal Phylisms

In the mercantile and venal paraphilias, the phylisms that become attached to sexuoeroticism are those of operant training and token economy. Operant training, using reward tokens, measures behavior progressively and more efficaciously against a criterion standard. The tokens may be utilized one by one, or they may be accumulated and exchanged, like trading stamps, for something else. Coins have been tokens of trade since time immemorial.

Children are trained with punishment training and incentive or reward training. The attachment of punishment to sexuoeroticism is what generates the sacrificial/expiatory and the marauding/predatory paraphilias. Conversely, the attachment of incentive, and particularly a cash incentive, is by definition what generates the mercantile/venal paraphilias and gives them their characteristic quality.

It is improbable that children, or at least most children, get direct training in attaching a cash value to genital services, as either buyer or seller. However, they certainly do get direct training in earning coins as tokens, and in trading. They are exposed also to the possibility of over-hearing household feuds and accusations linking sex and money. Sooner, rather than later, they are likely to learn something about prostitution, indirectly. Some may even apply the learning in childhood sexuoerotic rehearsal play, bargaining for a peek, or a feel.

The idea of buying and selling genital relations is a venerable part of our social heritage. It is hypocritically condemned and condoned at the same time. It is more or less attributed to the phylism of greed or getting more, and to the ostensible depravity of males and their exploitation of destitute and abused women. Whatever the merits of this attribution, it fails to take into account the male prostitute, hustler, or gigolo. It does not apply universally. It masks the existence of bona fide mercantile/venal paraphilias among those who buy and sell sex.

Consequently, these paraphilias remain mostly unnamed, unless one uses combination terms like paraphilic harlotry. and paraphilic hustlerism. Just as there is no paraphilic name for those who are erotosexually turned-on by selling themselves for sexual intercourse, so also is there a lack of terminology for those whose turn-on is paraphilically dependent exclusively on purchasing sexual intercourse.

A similar terminological deficiency applies also to those whose paraphilia is as if commercial—like the wealthy man who could not obtain an erection unless he pretended his wife was a whore. There is one named paraphilia in this category, namely, troilism.

Nymphomania and satyrism, or satyriasis, are names for obsessional multiple partnering that, if paraphilic, are predominantly solicitational and allurative (see below) and only marginally commercial. They do not necessarily involve a transaction on a fee for service basis. Gifts and entertainment are more likely.

Fetishistic and Talismanic Phylisms

In the fetishistic and talismanic paraphilias, the phylisms that become attached to sexuoeroticism belong in the general category of smells and skin feelings that initiate and are essential to pairbonding. Developmentally, the first pairbonding in mammals is that of mother and baby. The program for establishing a pairbond is sequential. If the sequence is broken, the baby is neglected, not suckled, and does not survive.

Mother-baby pairbonding is developmentally a precursor of what subsequently is the male-female pairbonding of mating. Animals in which mother-infant pairbonding is phyletically programed to be robot-like, are equally robot-like in the pair-bonding of mating, regardless of how long the mating bond lasts.

In subprimate mammals, parental and mating pairbonding both are under the influence of specific odors or pheromones, as they are technically named, with some input from touching and body contact. In species like the sheep or goat, for example, nuzzling of the baby against the mother's teat, in suckling, is a pairbonding stimulus for both. In the few hours before this happens, however, the mother must engage in licking and smelling the newborn baby. Her own odor contributes to the smell-bonding of the two.

When the young one reaches maturity, smell again plays a major role in pairbonding. A pheromone released in the vagina of a female in heat reaches the nose of the male and alerts him to the female's readiness to cooperate in the ritual of courtship and mating which is highly stereotyped, species specific, and phyletically programed into the individual, as if into a robot.

In rodents, not only mating, but also the timing of the onset of sexual maturation, is under the influence of pheromones released by other members of the colony. After a female copulates with a male, the onset of pregnancy may be prevented by the interference of odor from another male's urine (Parkes and Bruce, 1961).

In primates as compared with subprimate mammals, the role of the sense of smell in the process of pairbonding is to a large extent supplanted by vision. But the eyes do not completely take over from the nose. Touch and the skin senses remain important.

The ritual of courtship and pairbonding in higher primates is phyletically programed only in part. It is subject to additional programing from cognitional input in the course of individual development. Female chimpanzees and gorillas in captivity, for example, parent-bond with, and care for their firstborn better, if they have a social history of living in a social group that includes mothers and the offspring they have delivered and cared for.

With respect to human courtship and mate-bonding, the extent of phyletic programing has not yet been investigated. It almost certainly applies to presenting, mounting, and mutual thrusting, and perhaps also to body clasping and hugging. Genital inspection, smelling, and licking may also be included, at least in some human beings. Other stimuli and incitements to mating are superimposed, and are subject to cognitional exposure in the course of development.

One way in which the great versatility of cognition, an attribute of the cerebral cortex, expresses itself in human sexuoeroticism is in the variety of smelly things and textured, feely things that can become attached to sexuoerotic arousal. These things, when they become imperative to arousal, and replace in importance the person from whom they are derived, are the talismans of the two classes of the fetishistic/talismanic paraphilias, the olfactophilias and the hyphephilias.

Olfactophilia and hyphephilia, like fetishism, are generic rather than specific terms. The specific paraphilias under them do not have Greek-derived technical terms, except for mysophilia for filth, and klismaphilia, for enemas. It would be possible, using Greek roots, to coin a name for each of the festishisms on the basis of each different fetish object. Eventually it may be useful to have such names. In present usage, it suffices to use two-word terms, like shoe fetish.

There are two more paraphilias that need special nosological consideration among the fetishisms. One is transvestophilia—paraphilic transvestism or cross-dressing. The other is infantilism (autonepiophilia) or paraphilic wearing of diapers. The terms stand for two phenomena. One is a fetishistic paraphilia for a particular type of attire. The other is a nonfetishistic transposition of status on the criterion of age or sex, respectively, or both. In some people, the two phenomena, paraphilic and transpositional coincide. In other people they do not. For this reason, nonparaphilic transvestism is herein classified as a gender transposition phenomenon. Paraphilic transvestism or transvestophilia qualifies as a paraphilic clothing fetish in which a degree of gender transposition occurs episodically, and concordantly with cross-dressing.

Stigmatic and Eligibilic Phylisms

In the stigmatic and eligibilic paraphilias, the phylisms that become attached to sexuoeroticism have to do with assortative matching and mating. The animals saved from extinction, in the fable of Noah and the flood, matched themselves according to their own kind and went into the ark, two by two, as breeding pairs. In diecious species, chromosomal matching is genetically preordained as an imperative of reproductive survival. In species and subspecies that are able to hybridize, assortive matching and mating is achieved on the basis of a variety of phylogenetic formulas.

Immature songbirds, for example, listen to and memorize the song pattern, normally that of their own species, that they hear in infancy. They practice it only months later, when the first mating season approaches (Marler and Peters, 1981). Then, under the influence of androgen that stimulates the song brain, males begin to sing. Females do not sing unless their brains have been experimentally masculinized by androgen treatment at the time of hatching (Gurney and Konishi, 1980).

Untreated females listen and respond to the song as the mating call of their own species, and exclude males of other species.

In birds that are not songsters, the phylisms responsible for assortative mating that prevents hybridization are visual as well as auditory, as when the peacock displays its tail and struts around, screeching, and the peahen responds. In both males and females, the configuration and color of the plumage, and its use in a courtship display or dance, are each important as signals that invite pairbonding. In the majority of avian species, pairbonds are lifelong.

In the sight-bonding of birds, the actual appearance of the plumage is phyletically preordained, and is under the governance of sex hormones. Whether or not the courtship dance-ritual is similarly preordained, or is a product of individual or ontogenetic programing added onto species or phylogenetic programing, is not yet known.

The two-stage programing of song-bonding as a determinant of assortative mating in birds has no known counterpart in the pheromonal-bonding of subprimate mammals, which is phylogenetically programed exclusively. However, there is a counterpart in the visual-bonding of higher primates, and particularly of human beings and their assortative mating. We follow the birds!

There are some phyletically imposed constraints on our assortative mating, but they leave ample opportunity for ontogenetic variation to be added on the basis of individual biographical development. These variations are the product of social input through the special senses, especially the eyes, into the lovemap of the brain. They may be a product either of specific training; or of a more diffuse type of assimilative learning; or possibly of that rapid and addictive type of opponent-process learning that is analogous to imprinting. Each individual product is a template within the lovemap that gives the specifications that must be met before a person qualifies as an eligible candidate for assortative mating.

Human assortative mating may be simply the following of an encrusted tradition by which a people or tribal group keeps itself segregated from hybridization. Alternatively, it may be an explicitly articulated religious, legal, racial, linguistic, or social-class policy to prevent hybridization or miscegenation with outsiders.

Assortative mating is not, in and of itself, paraphilic. It qualifies as paraphilic when it so tyrannously restricts the range of eligible partners that it effectively precludes a reciprocal relationship. In nepiophilia and pedophilia, for example, the younger partner relates to the older one on the basis of the phylism of parent-child bonding, whereas in the older partner parental bonding fails to keep itself distinguished from the phylism of lover-lover bonding. The discordance between the two phylisms of bonding is possibly subject to compromise, but not to resolution. Even the compromise fails when the younger person gets older and too mature to be sexuoerotically eligible as the partner of respectively, a nepiophile or a pedophile. However, a friendship with no sexuoerotic component may remain.

Except for the difference in age between a juvenile and an adolescent, the phylisms of ephebophilia more or less parallel those of pedophilia. They apply conversely to gerontophilia. When a gerontophile and an ephebophile match their respective phylisms of hero and hero-worship, a long-term, pairbonded love affair is possible. Otherwise, one of the partners in an unreciprocated paraphilia sooner or later feels trapped and leaves; or else exploits the other in retaliation, perhaps even with the use of blackmail. The disillusionment then resembles that of a nasty and vindictive divorce.

Age discordant paraphilias involving relationships between family or household members involve not only a translocation between the phylisms for parent-child and lover-lover affectional bonding, but also a failure of the phylism that prevents sexuoerotic bonding between kin reared together.

This phylism has been demonstrated to be olfactory in the monogamous American prairie vole (see Chapter 3). Female offspring simply do not ovulate and come into heat provided they stay within the family group and encounter no males other than the father and brothers. Only if they lick and smell the perineum of a strange male will their reproductive physiology and mating behavior be activated, whereupon the pair becomes monogamously bonded for life.

Among troop-living primates, there is a phylism, known only by its behavioral effect, whereby adolescent males, and in some instances, adolescent females depart from their mother's troop, eventually to take up residence with another troop, or to form a new one of their own.

This phylism of departure from the troop has a counterpart in human beings, according to the research of Shepher (1971) on the marriages and love affairs of a kibbutz generation of Israelis. He found a total absence of marriages between boys and girls who had been reared together from earliest infancy in the same children's house, as if they were siblings. They were, in fact, genealogically unrelated. In infancy and early childhood, their sexual rehearsal play had not been forbidden or punished. When they reached adolescence, however, their early playmates evoked no romantic or erotic inclination in them. Love affairs, pairbonding, and marriage took place exclusively between partners who, in the first six years of life, grew up in separate children's houses or in a nonkibbutz household. The effectiveness of the phylism of departure in preventing as-if incest among kibbutz youth remains to be explained, as does also the failure of the phylism in other instances to prevent incest between siblings or other members of the same household.

Zoophilia, also known as bestiality, contravenes the phylism of assortative mating, for it is a manifestation of sexuoerotic interaction between two species that do not hybridize. The phylism that underlies it is the pairbonding imprint that becomes established, in certain instances, between an infant of one species and a foster parent of another. The young one may then grow up to respond to other members of the foster parent's species as if they belonged to its own species. A similar cross-species relationship may develop when two juveniles of different species are reared together, as pets sometimes are. There is no special name for this equivalent of zoophilia between two nonhuman species. It has been documented by Maple (1977).

Zoophilia as a genuine paraphilia is probably rare. Most instances of sexual contact with another species do not exclude, or take the place of person-to-person pairbonding.

Solicitational and Allurative Phylisms

In the solicitational and allurative paraphilias, the phylisms that become attached to sexuoeroticism are actually reattached, but out of sequence. They belong originally in the preparatory or proceptive phase of the sexuoerotic sequence. Their reattachment is to the acceptive phase, the phase that leads to the climax of orgasm.

There are three subgroups of solicitational and allurative paraphilias. They relate, respectively, to showing, touching, and narrating, and conversely, to looking, being touched, and listening to or reading.

Showing the genitalia as a maneuver of solicitation is a fairly typical phylism among subhuman primates, both male and female. In some species brightly colored genital swelling signals estrus in the female. Visual solicitation changes to touching, rubbing, and maybe smelling, as two animals approach one another more closely. Each partner then may inspect, lick, or touch the genitals of the other. If the solicitation is mutually acceptable and leads to copulation, then, among troop-living primates, other members of the troop, including juveniles, may take an active interest, and may become sexuoerotically aroused themselves. This effect of watching others mating was used experimentally at the Chessington zoo in England in 1973. To encourage the zoo's chimpanzees to breed (Chapter 2), their keepers showed them movies of other chimpanzees mating. They did then become responsive to their cagemate partners (Chicago Tribune, 5/30/73).

Narrating explicitly erotic stories orally or in print is, it goes without saying, an exclusively human maneuver of solicitation, as is listening to them or reading them.

The showing and looking allurative paraphilias are exhibitionism (peodeiktophilia, or displaying the penis) and voyeurism (peeping); autagonistophilia (being on view in a live performance) and scoptophilia (being a spectator). There is no special term for the female's exhibition of her genitals. Stigmatophilia (being tattooed, scarified, or pierced for genital ornamentation) is partly allurative.

The touching and rubbing allurative paraphilias are toucherism and frotteurism, respectively.

The narrative or graphic story-telling, allurative paraphilias are narratophilia, pictophilia, and telephonicophilia. The latter is also known as obscene telephone calling or telephone scatologia.

There is a strong element of paraphilic solicitation and allure in the hyperphilias of so-called nymphomania and satyriasis already referred to in Chapter 13. These hyperphilias are associated with compulsive and promiscuous cruising and picking up of casual partners who, after a one-night stand, are rejected. Continuity of the relationship lacks intrinsic interest for the hyperphiliac. The role of the pickup is to prove that the hyperphiliac's power to solicit and allure strangers is limitless. Long-term relationships may actually be experienced as confining and dangerous.

Solicitation and allure enter also into the amputee paraphilias, acrotomophilia and apotemnophilia, which are primarily stigmatic/eligibilic, though also related to expiation and sacrifice.

14

Paraphilia and Gender Transposition

Concordant Variables

In the common sense of everyday life, the status of being male or female is attributed to a person on the basis of the anatomy of the external sex organs. If this part of the anatomy is concealed from view, then male or female is inferred on the basis of the visible anatomy and voice, in conjunction with clues from clothing style, haircut, cosmetic adornment, body movements, and ways of behaving. It is taken for granted that all these different signs or clues will be concordant with the anatomy of the sex organs, male or female, respectively.

Most of the time it is safe to take perfect concordance for granted, but there are exceptions. Some exceptions are found in cases of birth defect of the sex organs. In other exceptions, the sex organs appear normal to everyone except their owner, for whom they are a mistake of nature, and should be replaced by the sex organs of the other sex. Until then, a subjective state of gender dysphoria is said to apply.

Gender Dysphoria/Transposition

Gender dysphoria is a state of mind or being. The evidence from which it is adduced is gender-transposed conduct and utterances. Gender transposition is empirically ascertained as a gross discrepancy between, on the one hand, the manifest sexual dimorphism of the body, and on the other hand, the manifest signs and expressions of that part of gender status which, in the ultimate analysis, is encoded in the brain and mind, irrespective of its origins. The components of gender status subject to transposition cover a wide range from trivial, arbitrary, and transient, to major, obligatory, and persistent.

The extreme of gender transposition is transexualism or cross-sexualism. Complete transexualism involves becoming sex reassigned cosmetically, socially, legally, hormonally, and surgically. Hormonal changeover from female to male is, in general, physiologically more effective than from male to female. The converse is true surgically. Male-to-female surgery of the external genitalia is technically more effective than female-to-male surgery. Vaginoplasty, the making of a vaginal cavity, is surgically feasible, whereas phalloplasty, the making of a penis capable of erection, is not.

The gender transposition that justifies hormonal and surgical intervention is deeply ingrained, persistent, and not reversible by known methods of intervention. In many cases, this complete degree of gender transposition spans the life history. There are some cases, however, in which the gender transposition during the earlier part of the biography is episodic, and takes the form of two names, two wardrobes, and two personalities—even two occupations (Money, 1974). The duration of each episode is variable.

Episodic gender transposition is generally referred to as transvestism. Transvestism is not a very satisfactory term, for it means simply cross-dressing, not episodic gender transposition, nor even episodic cross-dressing. Some people cross-dress sporadically for a masquerade party. Others, like transexuals, do it routinely. Thus it is necessary to differentiate the act of cross-dressing from the syndrome of transvestism or transvestophilia which is also the syndrome of episodic gender transposition with two names and two personalities, one of each to fit with the two wardrobes, respectively.

The syndrome of transvestism has been recorded predominantly, if not exclusively, in men. In this respect, it resembles the majority of the paraphilias. More precisely, it not only resembles a paraphilia, but it is, in fact, one of the fetishistic or talismanic paraphilias (transvestophilia) as well as gender transposition. In the paraphilia of transvestism, an adolescent boy or adult male is dependent on wearing female garments, especially underclothes, in order to achieve sexuoerotic arousal and orgasmic climax—either alone, masturbating, or with a partner who may be male, though more likely female. In fantasy, the transvestite's female partner may be transformed into a male, and the transvestite paraphile himself in the same fantasy, into a copulating female.

Paraphilic transvestism is not the only bridge between paraphilia and gender transposition. Transexualism may also constitute a bridge between paraphilia of the eligibilic type and gender transposition. According to the transexual's own conviction, sexuoerotic eligibility demands that the body be not that of the sex of birth, but of the other sex. Eligibility here requires changing the morphological sex of the self, so that it will not be the same as that of the partner. The matching of the postsurgical transexual with the partner usually is conventionally heterosexual, but depending on individual idiosyncracy, it may also be lesbian or gay. In transexualism, changing the body by ridding it of its original genitalia and other sexually dimorphic features has priority over coital competence which, no matter how important, is secondary to genital appearance.

Gynemimesis

Hormonal sex reassignment without surgery constitutes another form of gender transposition. It also is the antipode of an eligibility paraphilia. On the criterion of the genitalia, the person would be known in theatrical parlance as an impersonator. In biomedically new terminology, such a person is a gynemimetic (Money, 1980; Money and Lamacz, 1984), if impersonating a female; and an andromimetic, if impersonating a male (see Chapter 22).

A gynemimetic may have a history of gender transposition dating so far back into childhood that the gender identity and its expression as gender role may belong not as second nature, but as if they were first nature. Under that circumstance, ordinary people have no clues by which to judge the gynemimetic as other than an ordinary woman. There are, however, some men for whom the term, gynemimetophile, has been coined (Money and Lamacz, 1984). Gynemimetophilia is an eligibilic paraphilia in which the ideal of eligibility is a partner who is a gynemimetic lady with a penis. Sexuoerotically, the gynemimetophile is specifically attracted to a lady with a penis, more than to a lady without one. It may be a transient infatuation, but it may also be a durable attachment, more passionate than a prior attachment between the gynemimetophile and a conventional female lover or wife.

A gynemimetophile who becomes a member of a network of friends in the gynemimetic community of a large city is likely to meet members of the network with a postsurgical, male-to-female transexual history. Then, a potential sexuoerotic attraction between the gynemimetophile and a transexual may have no follow-through, once he discovers that the lady who formerly had a penis has undergone surgery and become a lady with a vulva. On the same basis, an attachment that is successful pre-operatively may dissolve following sex-reassignment surgery.

It would seem logical if the attachments of andromimesis were the counterpart of gynemimesis. In fact, there seems to be a difference. There is an absence, or at least a very great scarcity, of evidence that there are andromimetophilic women whose specific attraction to an andromimetic partner is that the latter is a man without a penis. Rather the attraction of a woman toward an andromimetic is that of a woman toward a man despite the missing penis. In nature's scheme of things, there is perhaps a connection here with the fact that andromimesis itself does not have an exact correspondence with gynemimesis, for there is no andromimetic syndrome of episodic transvestism in women that is the counterpart of the gynemimetic syndrome of episodic transvestism (transvestophilia) in men.

Homosexual/Bisexual/Heterosexual

Homosexual and heterosexual, like many other sexological terms, have two meanings, one as an act, and the other as a status. Anyone may engage in a homosexual or a heterosexual act. All that is required is that two people with, respectively, the same (homosexual) or different (heterosexual) genital morphology engage, directly or indirectly, in an act that in some way involves or implicates the genital organs and/or their sexuoerotic sensibility. Imagine standing on the parapet of a skyscraper viewing the panorama. You are accosted by a sex terrorist who demands that you suck his penis (or vulva), or vice versa. Otherwise you go over the edge. Would you or wouldn't you?

If you saved your life, and if the terrorist were of the same genital sex as yourself, you would have committed a homosexual act; but you would not have taken on a homosexual status. The criterion of a homo-sexual status, and of a heterosexual status as well, is the morphology of the sex organs of the partner with whom you fall in love. Falling in love is not subject to voluntary control, as anyone who has been lovesick can readily attest to.

Completely symmetrical bisexuality would meet the test of falling in love with either a male or female partner, on a 50:50 basis. Asymmetrical bisexuality, like 60:40, means that the lovebond with a partner of one sex would be stronger and more durable than with a partner of the other sex. Extreme asymmetry, like 90:10, in favor of heterosexual attachment would require an exceptional circumstance, like being sex-segregated in prison on a long sentence before the very weak degree of homosexual attachment could find expression (Money and Bohmer, 1980).

Both homosexual attachments and heterosexual attachments, whether alone or bisexually related, may or may not incorporate any of the various types of paraphilic imagery and practice. That is why, in the interest of scientific simplicity and parsimony, neither homosexuality nor heterosexuality, per se, are classified as paraphilias. Nor is masturbation (autosexuality) or abstinence.

As a gender transposition, homosexuality may apply only to the sexuoerotic component of gender status, and not at all to the occupational and recreational components, nor the sartorial or other social components. That is why it surprises or astonishes many people when one partner in a homosexual love affair is a football star, or a police officer, or heavy machinery operator, whose work role typifies the idealized stereotype of rugged masculinity. Correspondingly, a woman in the idealized role of fashion model, wife, or mother may have a lesbian lover.

For the sake of precision, the terminology in such cases is that the person has a homosexual gender status that is restricted exclusively to sexuoerotic attachments. The gender transposition is partial and is defined exclusively on the criterion of the same sexual morphology of the two lovers or partners as compared with the heterosexual criterion, namely that the sexual morphology of the couple differs. It is not correct to make a statement such as, "Joe College, a star athlete, has a male gender identity but a homosexual object choice or partner preference," because, by definition, a total male gender identity includes heterosexual partnering.

Moreover, homosexuality, like heterosexuality, is not a matter of preference, choice, or voluntary decision. It is a status, like being tall, dwarfed, or left-handed, and it is not changed by desire, incentive, will power, prayer, punishment, or other motivation to change.

Homosexual transposition of gender status which is not restricted to homosexuoeroticism, exclusively, may extend to the other components of gender status in variable degree. Transpositions that affect body language and mannerisms create the popular stereotype of the effeminate, or faggot homosexual male, and the mannish, or butch-dyke lesbian. In both instances, homosexual status is distinguished from transexual status and from gynemimetic (or andromimetic) status, because there is no fixation on altering the morphology of the body. It is distinguished also from the syndrome of transvestism, transvestophilia, because there is no paraphilic clothing fetishism.

Cross-Cultural Comparisons

Gender transposition is not a local phenomenon, but a worldwide one, with regionally different traditions of how it is integrated into the larger society. People who cross-dress and impersonate the other sex are condoned in our society provided they work in the entertainment industry. There they avoid accusations of impostering or conspiring against morality. They do not need to be unmasked, because their impersonation is advertised in advance.

In India, gender-transposition in males is socially institutionalized nationwide in what is partly a caste, and partly a religious cult with its own mother goddess, Bahuchara Mata, who is conventionally symbolized as a yantra, or vulva. Members of this nationwide gynemimetic organization are hijras. They come from families of Hindu, Muslim, Christian or other faith. They contributed to the recent comprehensive, ethnographic study by Nanda (1983). In their traditional practices, hijras had no sex hormones for feminization, but they did have the ancient transexual practice of emasculation, performed without anesthetic, by one of their older and experienced gurus. The complete hijra is a complete eunuch. The penis is amputated, as well as the scrotum and testes.

A hijra typically has a history of gynemimesis in childhood and early adolescence. While still living with his family, he will recognize the affinity that exists between him and the local or visiting hijras who sing and dance at various public festivals. When he leaves home to join the hijras, it may be to escape defamation and abuse, or to relieve his parents of the embarrassment of his presence, and his brothers of the duty to postpone their own marriages while he remains single.

A new member of a hijra household is on probation before he is initiated into having a female name and clothing. A hijra is required to earn a living. The least desireable option is begging for alms. Hijras are also, by tradition, the keepers of public bathhouses, used by those who lack domestic hot water for bathing. By tradition, they are also singers and dancers who have the right to demand money from the wealthy for performing at their marriages, when a son is born, or on the occasion of other celebrations. Some hijras are also renowned for their careers as prostitutes, which may be either full time, or part time, and as kept concubines. They engage in anal, oral, and interfemoral intercourse. Some hijras have no sexual interests at all, and others are sexual enthusiasts who enjoy being in the role of women servicing men.

The members of a hijra household are not cut off from contacts with their families of origin, nor from helping them financially. Those are matters of individual option.

Another recent ethnographic study of gender-transposition was done in Oman (Wikan, 1977). In Oman, a gender-transposed male is known as a xanith (pronounced hanith). This term is also more widely used in Arabic as the translation of the English, homosexual. Xanith is applied in Oman only to the gynemimetic partner in a homosexual coupling, that is, to the one who consistently performs as if in the sexual role of a woman with a man. It does not apply to the partner who, when having sex with a xanith, consistently performs as if in the role of a man with a woman.

In Oman, the xanith may gain public status as a man instead of a xanith, provided he enters into a marriage arranged by his family and produces the public evidence, namely a blood stained cloth, of successful vaginal penetration of the virgin bride. He gains this status despite the persistence of his feminine demeanor in facial expressions, voice, laughter, and movements. He may relinquish his male status and revert to that of xanith.

The xanith always retains his male given name. "He is not allowed to wear the face mask of purdah, nor other female clothing. His clothes are intermediate between male and female: he wears the ankle-length tunic of the male, but with tight waist of the female dress. Male clothing is white. Females wear patterned cloth in bright colours, and xanith wear unpatterned coloured clothes. Men cut their hair short, women wear theirs long, the xanith medium length. Men comb their hair backward away from the central parting, xanith comb theirs forward from a side-parting, and they oil it heavily in the style of women. Both men and women cover their head, xanith go bareheaded. Perfume is used by both sexes, especially at festive occasions and during intercourse. The xanith is generally heavily perfumed, and uses much make-up to draw attention to himself. This is also achieved by his affected swaying gait, emphasized by the close-fitting garments. His sweet falsetto voice and facial expressions and movements also closely mimic those of women. If he wore female clothes, it would in many instances not be possible to see him to be, anatomically speaking, male and not female'' (Wikan, p. 307). Nonetheless he has no tradition of feminizing the body either by becoming a eunuch, or by the contemporary method of taking sex hormones.

The xanith is publicly recognizable in Oman as having the status of neither male nor female, but of xanith. Like his clothing, his role in society resembles that of women, but does not replicate it. Unlike men, he is permitted to move freely among women behind purdah, and to share their social life, intimate gossip, domesticity, and activities. At a wedding, whereas musical instruments are played by men, the xanith joins the women singers. Unlike women, the xanith is not ruled under the power and dominion of a man. Like men, he has the right to go about in public unaccompanied. He also has the right, exclusive to the role of xanith, to live alone, to be hired as a house servant, and to be hired by men as a prostitute. Female prostitution is outlawed and, like adultery, is subject to severe punishment. Wikan estimated the prevalence of xanith in the small town of her study to be 2% of the 3,000 adult males.

Childhood Antecedents

In childhood, the developmental antecedents of the mimetic, transvestic and transexual transpositions are not clearly differentiated from one another, nor from the antecedents of the more limited transpositions of homosexuality and bisexuality (Money and Russo, 1979; 1981). In some instances, the juvenile antecedents of adult gender transposition may be sufficiently unobtrusive that they pass unnoticed by adults. Agemates, however, are often more astute in recognizing the gender nonconformist. They confer the sobriquet of sissy on a boy primarily because he backs away, instead of fighting the competition for a higher rank in the dominance hierarchy of childhood. It is far more stigmatizing for a boy to be called a sissy than for a girl to be known as a tomboy. She earns that sobriquet not because she fights, but because she is competitive against boys in energy expenditure, especially in playing their sports, and joining their teams.

A juvenile history of having been called a sissy boy or a tomboy girl is not equivalent to a prophecy of a gender-transposition affecting sexuoerotic function, postpubertally. Insofar as there is a carry-over, however, the outcome is far more likely to be the bisexual or homosexual transposition, rather than the mimetic, transvestic, or transexual one (Chapter 15).

15

Strategy and Phylism in Gender Transposition

Definition

Gender transposition, like paraphilia, is a strategy for resolving the saint/sinner sexuoerotic antithesis. This strategy dispossesses the lovemap of a potential partner of its franchise to be defiled by sinful lust, and thus elevates the potential partner to the status of lust-free saint. Dispossession is effected by transferring the franchise to a deputy who becomes the one to be defiled by sinful lust. The deputy may be oneself. In the case of a disparity of sex between the saintly one and the deputy, then a gender transposition may take place, in which the deputy assimilates gender characteristics of the other sex. For example, if the sex of the deputy is male, and if he has disfranchised potential female partners of their lust and enshrined them in saintly, lust-free purity, then the deputy may himself become womanly, at least to the extent of lusting after other men. If the transposition is more extensive, he becomes more effeminized. The corresponding phenomenon, when the sex of the deputy is female, is lesbianism.

Gender transposition is not an invariable concomitant of the deputizing strategy. In deputized incest, for example, the deputy may be a pubertal daughter who rescues her mother from defiling lust by becoming a little wife and housekeeper in her place. Nonincestuous adultery also, in some instances, features the strategy of paraphilic deputizing for another.

At the lesser extreme of gender-transposition, the partnership in lust is one of simple homosexual pairing in which penovaginal intromission is variously simulated or circumvented. At the greater extreme, the deputy in lust undergoes complete transexual reassignment and is metamorphosed so as to assume the sexuoerotic status of the disenfranchized saint.

Role Inconstancy

In attributing cognitive order and system to their existence in a social environment of selectively withheld sexual learning, some children are more, and some less versatile than others at dramatic play-acting and theatrical make-believe in gender-inconstant roles and strategies (Green and Money, 1966). Those who are more versatile constitute a population at risk for gender inconstancy and possible gender transposition, if they are born of parents whose reciprocal compatibilities and incompatibilities, in their careers as mother and father, and in their sex lives as husband and wife, remain perpetually unreconcilable. In this formulation, the key concept is that of versatility. If one defines gender transposition as pathology, then the concept is not versatility, but vulnerability to gender inconstancy and transposition.

The development of gender inconstancy and transposition can be observed, and has been documented in children as young as three to four years of age. It is either more exaggerated and frequent in boys than in girls, or else it generates more alarm in those adults who take action toward changing it. In our society today, sissy boys are severely stigmatized. Tomboyish girls are not (Chapter 14).

In boys, gender transposition expresses itself in playing with girls' toys and associating with girls instead of boys, in wearing clothing and accessories of feminine style as often as possible, in expressly wanting to be a girl, and in avoiding aggressive combat. In the early stages of gender transposition, a child is able to walk, talk, and gesture like either a boy or a girl.

Less is known about gender transposition in girls than boys, in part because clinical referrals are far less common. In general, gender transposition is less conspicuously expressed in girls than boys. It is more a matter of repudiating the historical stereotype of the idealized little girl than of impersonating a macho boy, though there are exceptions. In extreme cases, the girl with a gender transposition has a macho alliance with the father, and with the mother a contemptuous, dominating, and abusive relationship.

Father-Son Allegiance

Contrary to established beliefs, the fathers of sissy boys are typically blandly indifferent to the signs of their son's nonconformity to the standard of masculinity in boyhood development. They write it off as something the boy will grow out of.

For years, I did not know what to make of this indifference. I had no hypothesis until a few years ago when a psychiatrist consulted me about his own son, aged five, the younger of two children, both boys. He and his wife excluded the boy from a family appointment, ostensibly to spare him from stigmatizing himself as abnormal. They distanced themselves from one another, spatially and verbally. Their matrimonial relationship was that of wedded adversaries practicing insidiously clever strategies of mutual sabotage. For example, even, though he was a professed agnostic, the husband criticized his wife for being religiously too laissez faire. She reacted by becoming a conservative fundamentalist. Family religious observances became a source of unending dispute.

The rift thus created was additionally widened in disputation regarding acoustic sensitivity. For her, loud music was noxious, so that he was obliged to pursue his interest in live rock performances without her. In fantasy, he anticipated that his younger son would become his companion in music. The older son, by contrast, already at age eight had coerced his reluctant father into sharing his all-boy interest in fishing and the outdoors.

Professionally trained to be self-analytic, this father was also self-revealing. After soliciting my prognosis of his son's cross-dressing and girlish inclinations, and hearing that it was not obligatory to be pessimistic about gender-transposition at so young an age as five, he asked why he was feeling so angry with me—and angry because of what I had said. My reply was to the effect that perhaps he didn't wholly want his son's transposed gender manifestations to desist, and did not want to be robbed of the one member of the family whom he might consider his special escort.

Subsequently I dictated a note "to put on record a new hypothesis or formula regarding the role of the father in the genesis of feminism in a son's G-I/R (gender-identity/role)." This is the formula: "the father covertly courts his son's allegiance in place of what he finds missing in his wife, and casts him in the role of a wife substitute, if not for the present, then for the future." The son, for his part, may solicit his father's allegiance as a formula for keeping him in the household, and for preventing a parental separation. If the father has already gone, or even if he had died, the son's gender transposition may serve to solicit his miraculous return.

Within a family, the allocation or reallocation of roles is not necessarily covert. It is more or less inherent in the idea of naming or nicknaming a baby after an ancestor, parent, or other relative; and also in the wisdom of the kin regarding whom a particular child takes after. Parents have favorite children—mommy's boy, and daddy's girl—just as children may favor one parent over the other, or one relative over another.

The young son who becomes self-allocated to the role of daughter, and thereby becomes a bonding agent who keeps the family intact, is likely to keep the role of bonding agent in perpetuity. The evidence of one longitudinal, outcome study (Money and Russo, 1979; 1981) is that such a son reaches adulthood with not a transexual or transvestite gender status, but a nonparaphilic homosexual one.

Parental Compatibility/Incompatibility

There is now new preliminary evidence, unpublished, that the transpositional course of events may be changed if the child can be relieved of the self-imposed responsibility of keeping his parents together. In one case, that of a three-year-old, the gravity of the boy's responsibility for keeping the parents together could be measured against the intensity of the father's response when confronted with the possibility of losing a custody battle, in the event of divorce. That was absolutely out of the question, he said, so far as he was concerned, and he hinted darkly at homicide rather than permitting it to happen.

The boy's change away from girl-imitative behavior ensued with unexpected rapidity in the immediate aftermath of the family's first visit—a marathon five hours of individual evaluations and joint discussions. The change in the boy was concomitant with a change in the parents, as they achieved more focus on their compatibility, and less on their incompatibility.

They were strongly compatible in their professional and domestic lives, and equally incompatible in their sexual and erotic lives. In four years of followup, their sexual and erotic incompatibility has remained stubbornly intractable to change. Nonetheless, there was only one brief occasion when it threatened to bring an end to their compatibilities. It was then that a resurgence of effeminacy threatened in the boy. It was transient. It did not, as had been the case in the original diagnostic toy-play sessions, generate dramas of desperation in which members of a toy family became victims of catastrophe, abusive violence, and murder.

This boy's play enactments did not include any dramas of explicit erotic or sexual content. Nor was there a history of overtly initiated erotic or sexual conduct other than age-typical masturbation in private, which the parents did not condemn. If the boy experienced erotosexual imagery in dreams and fantasies, then their content remained private and undisclosed. Explicit erotosexual fantasies with the father as partner have been retrospectively dated to boyhood by some young adult homosexual men, however (Silverstein, 1981).

In a young child's development, gender transposition is a rudimentary and inchoate response to diffusely mixed covert and overt signals that seem to indicate that, by being a girl with a penis, or a boy with a vulva, a child will somehow be more satisfactory to each parent. Thus the two parents can be retained in, or restored to an intact family unit, and their continued allegiance to one another mutually ensured. This formulation sounds outrageous and absurd only if it is elevated to the status of being sufficient, instead of only a necessary condition in the genesis of developmental gender transposition.

Adam/Eve Principle of Prenatal Hormonalization

In gender transposition, the phylism responsible for the transposition and its attachment to sex and eroticism is epitomized in the Adam/Eve principle (Chapter 3), namely, nature's rudimentary principle of sexual differentiation, which is to differentiate a female and to have to add something to differentiate a male. In gender transposition, the successive phases of differentiation, beginning prenatally and continuing postnatally, do not proceed concordantly in the usual orderly fashion. Discordance may begin prenatally under hormonal influence so that, at birth, a baby is at risk postnataly for a transposed gender status, provided convergent social influences and experiences increase the risk.

Historically, gender transposition of the complete type was explained as hereditary. However, the hereditary attribution has proved too simple and is now anachronistic. The contemporary explanation is hormonal. Like its hereditary predecessor, the hormonal explanation applies to development that takes place before birth. This development is governed not by the genetic code, directly, but by sex hormones that program the sexual differentiation of the brain (Money, 1981b).

According to the Adam/Eve principle, simply stated, if the fetal brain is not hormonalized, it will develop from its early, sexually bipotential stage to be, like Eve, feminine. To be like Adam, it must be hormonalized. The hormone is testosterone or one of its derivative metabolites.

Masculinization/Defeminization

Brain hormonalization is not inevitably an all-or-none affair. It may be a matter of degree. It is possible to be masculinized without being also completely defeminized or, conversely, to be feminized without also remaining completely demasculinized (Baum, 1979; Baum et al., 1982; Nordeen and Yahr, 1982; Ward, 1972; Ward and Weisz, 1980). Thus it is possible for a boy to be born with a brain that is both masculinized and feminized (that is, not defeminized) to some degree—and correspondingly for a girl. At birth, and immediately after (see below), the masculine/defeminine ratio in boys, and the feminine/demasculine ratio in girls is potentially widely variable.

The source of variability could be spontaneous. It might be secondary to stress that changes the pregnant mother's own hormone levels, which then affect the fetus (Ward, 1984). It might also be induced within the intrauterine environment or through the placenta by substances breathed, swallowed, or otherwise absorbed by the mother. For example, it is known that barbiturates may have a demasculinizing effect on a fetus; and that in the last half century literally millions of pregnant women have taken sleeping pills and other medications containing barbiturates (see review by Reinisch and Sanders, 1982).

In most instances of gender transposition, regardless of degree, it is impossible to reconstruct the prenatal sex-hormonal history in retrospect. Ethically, it is not possible to conduct experiments on pregnant women in order to find out everything that needs to be known about the causes and the timing of prenatal masculinization and defeminization of the sexual brain in boys, and of its prenatal feminization and demasculinization in girls. Therefore, it is necessary to garner whatever evidence one can from spontaneously occurring clinical syndromes or so-called experiments of nature.

Clinical Syndromes

The relevant syndromes are those in which the prenatal sex-hormonal history is known to have been atypical because the baby is born with a sex-hormonally generated hermaphroditic (or intersexual) ambiguity of the reproductive organs. There are also syndromes in which the postnatal hormonal history is atypical, for example in adolescent gynecomastia, but in which the prenatal hormonal history has not yet been spelled out, though it too may be presumed to have been atypical.

In order to make an inference regarding the prenatal influence of sex hormones on the sexual differentiation of the brain, it is necessary to follow a patient clinically into teenage and young adulthood when masculine and feminine sexuoerotic behavior and imagery may be expected to be fully expressed (Lewis and Money, 1983; Money and Daléry, 1976; Money and Lewis; 1982; Money and Mathews, 1982; Money, Schwartz and Lewis, 1984).

The evidence from clinical studies suports the hypothesis that there is in human prenatal development a sex-hormonal effect on sexual brain differentiation, but that it does not have a hormonal-robot effect of the type described for sheep and other subprimate mammals (Chapter 3). Rather, the effect is one of laying down a threshold so that behavior that is generally defined as masculine or feminine, respectively, is expressed either rapidly and unhindered, or only after surmounting a barrier. The only irreducible sex difference is that men impregnate, and women menstruate, gestate, and lactate. Other behavior that is commonly regarded as sex different, including aggression, is actually sex shared. It is the threshold for its elicitation and expression that distinguishes most men from most women.

Postnatal Gender Differentiation: Identification/Complementation

Whereas sex hormones are responsible, prenatally, for programing individual variation in the sex-divergent thresholds of sex-shared behav-

ior, postnatally the sex-hormonal influence goes into a period of dormancy. In girls, sex-hormonal dormancy begins at birth. In boys, by
contrast, there is a great surge of testosterone beginning at about two
weeks of age. It becomes spent by age three months and remains so until
the onset of puberty (Migeon and Forest, 1983). The effect of this testosterone surge remains to be ascertained. It could be the grand finale
of sexual brain differentiation, according to David Abramovich in Ab-
erdeen (personal communication).

When the sex hormones flow again at puberty, they activate
male/female erotosexual programs or schemas already differentiated in
the brain. Contrary to popular assumption, they do not cause behavior
to be masculine instead of feminine, or vice versa (Parks et al., 1974;
Sanders et al., 1985). That is why among other things, it is not possible
to change heterosexuality into homosexuality, or the other way round,
by giving injections of sex hormones.

During the period between birth and puberty, when male/female
erotosexual programing of the brain is no longer affected by sex hormones, the special senses take over. The eyes, the ears, and the skin
senses, more than the senses of smell and taste, are the brain's gateways
to information about the gender status and erotosexual programing of the
people among whom the child grows up. Gender related information,
like information about native language, is assimilated through usage and
experience, and not simply as a product of training and indoctrination.

Listening and being heard together are imperative for the brain to
be successful in allowing a native language to take up residence within
it. Likewise, copying and practicing gender-divergent behavior together
are imperative to the establishment of one's gender status within the
brain. Gender copying is conventionally referred to as identification with
persons assigned the same gender status as oneself. The converse, gender
practicing, only recently has been referred to as complementation or
reciprocation (Money, 1972). That which is assimilated and learned by
way of identification is put into practice with persons not assigned the
same gender as oneself. To illustrate, the little girl learns to dance by
identifying with her mother or sister and copying them, but she dances
with her father or brother, complementing them. The same two principles
apply across the entire spectrum of gender divergent status, sexuoerotic
rehearsal play included (Chapter 3).

Brain Schemas

Identification and complementation each have their representation
or schema implanted in the brain. One is the schema of one's own gender

status. The other is the schema of the other gender status to which one must complement one's own. On the basis of actuarial statistics, one expects that the identification schema will differentiate to be concordant with the morphology of the genitalia of the self, whereas the complementation schema will be concordant with the morphology of the genitalia of the other sex. It is when this expectation is not realized that one has a gender transposition.

The degree of transposition is variable, from total or obligative to trivial or adventitious. Table 1 shows a 2 × 3 classification of gender transposition on the criteria of duration and degree of pervasiveness. By itself alone, a transposition is neither an asset nor a debit. It becomes one or the other on the basis of the value judgments, both informal and official, of other people.

Table 1
GENDER TRANSPOSITIONS

	TOTAL	PARTIAL*	ADVENTITIOUS
CHRONIC	Transexualism	Gynemimesis andromimesis, male androphilia, female gynophilia	Androgeny of gender-coded education, work, legal status
EPISODIC	Transvestism	Androgynophilia (bisexualism)	Androgeny of gender-coded play, body-language, grooming, ornament.

* Gynemimesis and andromimesis mean impersonating a female and a male, respectively, on a full-time basis. Male androphilia means erotosexual attraction between men, and female gynophilia between women. Androgynophilia means erotosexual attraction, to some degree, to men and women.

Dissociation

The Self Divided: Jekyll and Hyde

What shocked the American conscience most about the stabbing death of 28-year-old Kitty Genovese was not that Winston Moseley, her killer, was a lust murderer, but that at least thirty-eight neighbors in her apartment building in Queens, N.Y., turned on their lights when they heard her screams for help at 3 a.m., on March 13th, 1964, and then did nothing—except for one man who opened his window and yelled to the street below, "Let that girl alone" (Time, June 26, 1964). Moseley went back to his car. No one came to the woman's rescue, so he stalked her into the lobby of her building, continued stabbing her until she was unresponsive, tore off her clothing and attempted to have sex. As is quite typical in paraphilia, after having been arrested, Moseley himself narrated all the self-incriminating details of his crime, and of others that had preceded it. He told a psychiatrist he got no thrill sexually unless the woman he had accosted would no longer live.

Moseley was 29 years old, the father of three children, and a well-paid accounting machine operator. He belonged to a fundamentalist religion, owned his own home and car, and raised pedigreed dogs. Confronted with a battery of cameramen in the police station, he said: "I have a father out there. I also have a wife, and this is a pretty shameful thing. Would it be all right with you people, if I cover up my face?" He had no explanation for his crime, nor of himself as the perpetrator. He had no alibi, and no repudiation of guilt except by reason of legal insanity. Anyone accused of such a crime, he said, if he had really done it, deserved the death penalty.

Moseley, the family man and wage earner by day, could not adequately account for the predatory werewolf, alien to his daytime self, that he turned into on murder nights. Not being fully able to attribute one's paraphilic behavior to oneself, as well as recognizing oneself subsequently to be subjectively remote from it, is in varying degrees, pathognomonic of the paraphilias. The self is divided.

For a great many people, this phenomenon of the self divided is morally incomprehensible. It is also legally incomprehensible in a judicial system the very existence of which depends on the doctrine of personal responsibility, free will, and the voluntary control of all of one's own behavior in conformity with the precepts of the law. Judge J. Irwin Shapiro, who tried the Moseley case, spoke for all those who do not comprehend the pathology of paraphilia when he said from the bench: "I don't believe in capital punishment, but I must say this may be improper when I see this monster. I wouldn't hesitate to pull the switch myself." Less than three hundred years ago, similar utterances were being made by those who did not comprehend the phenomenon of the self divided in the witches of Salem.

Introspectively, this sense of the self divided is stated rather clearly in a letter from a prisoner serving time for attempted rape: "I've gone over and over in my mind on what led up [both times] to the final act. Somewhere along the way a child was involved, not necessarily personally involved, just a main factor. Whatever activated my sexual behavior, I couldn't control it afterwards [after it was activated]. It's like something else took control of my body entirely. Most people don't accept that as plausible. I really don't want to either, because it scares the hell out of me. And yet I know it's the truth, which makes it even worse sometimes. It scares me so much I used to lie to whoever I talked with, just to conceal it. What worries me now is, where does it all end? My behavior and fantasies haven't ceased, only intensified. I go on now only because there's a possible treatment available. My question to myself, is, will it be made available soon enough? I sent a copy of the [Depo-Provera] treatment program to the governor of the state . . ."

The phenomenon which this prisoner found so scary, and which is evident in Moseley's case, is referred to in Chapter 5 as the two personalities of Dr. Jekyll and Mr. Hyde, named for the novel by Robert Louis Stevenson. The law-abiding Dr. Jekyll cannot explain his metamorphosis into the paraphilic Frankenstein monster, Mr. Hyde, regardless of what it may seem to be attributable to. Though he seldom experiences a complete amnesia, or memory blackout, for what he did as Mr. Hyde, he has no guarantee that what he does remember is a faithful replication of what actually happened. To an unknown extent, his recall is blurred, or deranged.

Ordinary people can try to make sense of the Jekyll/Hyde experience by comparing it with nightmares. The nightmares of a survivor of catastrophe incorporate both the imagery and the panic of the original experience into the nightmare. When the dreamer wakens, he knows that he had a nightmare, even though the details may be confused. He also knows that, now he is awake, he is not the same as he was while having the nightmare. The panic no longer holds him in its terrifying grip, regardless of how shaken it has left him.

Fugue States, Seizures, and Brain Surgery

A nightmare, by definition, takes place in the sleeping brain. The corresponding experience in the waking brain, if it is extremely vivid, may be recognized as hallucinatory. However, there are lesser degrees of altered states of consciousness which are recognized as trances or trance-like states. The medical term is fugue (Latin *fuga,* a flight) or fugue-like state.

An epileptic fugue is one that occurs in asociation with an epileptic seizure. Though it may precede or follow a major, convulsive seizure, more typically it occurs alone, and is itself a type of seizure. It is variously known as a psychomotor or temporal-lobe seizure, or as a psychic seizure or psychic equivalent of a major epileptic seizure.

Some paraphiles have, concurrently with their diagnosis of paraphilia, also a diagnosis of epilepsy, documented clinically and on the EEG (electroencephalographic) tracing. The seizures may be of the grand mal (convulsive) type; or the petit mal type, also known as absences; or the temporal lobe type. The relationship between the two syndromes, paraphilia and epilepsy, has not yet been worked out; nor has the relationship between the ictal attacks, the interictal period, and the paraphilic enactments.

There are a very few noteworthy cases, published in the neurosurgical literature, of paraphilia associated with temporal lobe epilepsy of the type in which the focal brain lesion was surgically removed. For example, there is a case reported by Mitchell, Falconer and Hill (1954) of a man in whom a seizure would be induced if the man carried out a recurrent urge to gaze at a safety pin. Immediately after the seizure, while still in a confusional state, he would then sometimes dress in his wife's clothing. All the symptoms were relieved after the epileptogenic lesion was surgically removed in a left temporal lobectomy.

Davies and Morgenstern (1960) reported a case of a man in whom the onset of both transvestism and temporal lobe seizures occurred in middle life. In a similar case (Hunter, Logue and McMenemy, 1963), brain surgery, namely a left anterior temporal lobectomy, relieved the patient of both transvestism and temporal lobe seizures.

The proportion of paraphiles who are also epileptics, and vice versa, has not yet been ascertained. Nor has the proportion of paraphiles with EEG abnormalities in the absence of clinical epilepsy. Standard EEG tracings may not be an adequate method for measuring paraphilic fugues. It is possible that an EEG abnormality would be registered not by surface electrodes, but only by depth electrodes implanted in the limbic system. It is also possible that a tracing would indicate brain dysfunction only during periods when the paraphilic fugue-like state is in progress, and not at other times. The same holds true for PET (positron emission tomography) scanning, a new technique for mapping brain function and dysfunction which has not yet been applied to the investigation of paraphilia or paraphilic fugues.

The PET scan provides a visual picture in color of how much glucose or other neurochemical substance is being used in different regions of the brain at different times, and under different conditions, such as during a paraphilic fugue state.

The lack of prevalence statistics with respect to clinical epilepsy and EEG anomalies in paraphilic fugue states applies also to statistics on the coexistence of paraphilia with either neurological and brain diseases, like multiple sclerosis; or soft-neurological signs, so-called, that are documented behaviorally but not physiologically. Exactly the same can be said of chromosomal anomalies, as in the 47,XYY syndrome (Money et al. 1975), and in the 47,XXY (Klinefelter's) syndrome, which is known to engender an excess of all types of psychopathology (Hambert, 1966; Nielsen, 1969; Nielsen et al., 1969). In clinical referrals, however, there appears to be an excess of both neurological and chromosomal anomalies associated with paraphilia.

No matter how rare the conjunction of the epileptic and the paraphilic fugue states, the very fact that the conjunction sometimes occurs is of theoretical significance to future advances in understanding where and how the paraphilic fugue state exists in the brain. Whereas paraphilic fugue may well prove to be too distantly related to epileptic fugue for today's instrumentation to register the changes in brain functioning that take place while a paraphilic fugue is in progress, tomorrow's technical advances may permit subtle changes to be detected.

Paraphilic Fugue: Stimulus/Response

One tactical difficulty, no matter what the test, is to be able to synchronize testing with the actual occurrence of a fugue state. The timing of the onset of a paraphilic fugue in some cases cannot be predicted. In other cases, however, the onset is precipitated by a particular stimulus. In the case of an acrotomophile, for example, it was sufficient for him to see a female amputee.

He described what happened to him thus: "I get a feeling in my stomach . . . a warm feeling. I feel flushed. I feel as though this is the only thing there is for me to look at. There could be a multialarm fire going on, and this would be the only thing I would look at, this amputee. I get nervous. I get edgy—the feeling in my stomach. It's all encompassing . . . If I see her, this individual, without any warning, it seems just for a minute that there's nothing else around me. That's the only thing there is . . . What I'm concerned about is I work outside, on highrise construction. I'm a foreman. I don't want to be where I would have to make a decision and then see an amputee, where I would lose, for a second, my train of thought, job-related . . ."

Queried about what happened to his penis in the course of the foregoing type of experience, he said: ". . . sometimes I get a full erection, but there is always at least a partial erection . . . on the job, of course, I can't masturbate; nor if I'm out with my wife; but normally that's the only type of relief that I'll get. It's just a built up feeling like I'm almost ready to explode. My wife has said that I get extremely quiet. Like either intercourse or masturbation is a relief . . . maybe intercourse more so than masturbation . . . After I see one of these people, I guess she is in a fantasy while I have intercourse, but later on, a week or so later, sometimes yes, and sometimes no . . ."

Unable to formulate a cause for his amputee reaction, he said: "I'm so confused about it. I don't want to see an amputee, and I do want to see them. If we do go out, my wife and I, I'm always looking ahead, trying to prepare myself, if I do see one. I don't like the control they

have over me. I have no control for those few minutes or so. That's what
I don't like.''

His own account of losing control was independently corroborated
by his wife. From his reactions, she would know that he must have seen
a woman amputee, and upon looking around would confirm it.

Two Names, Two Wardrobes, Two Personalities

The fugue state has been recorded on film or videotape in a few
instances of paraphilic transvestism of the type characterized by two
names, two wardrobes, two personalities, and two occupations (Chapter
14; Money, 1974). The change is manifested in body language, as well
as spoken language and vocal pitch. It becomes quite evident during the
change of clothing, and makeup. In the case of a male transvestite, for
example, James became transformed into a very chic, attractive Jennie.
For details of Jennie's history and personality, she was a far better in-
formant than James; but to be herself and tell her own story, she had to
be wearing her own clothes, not James's—and vise versa for him. It is
easy to miss important segments of a paraphilic history by omitting to
inteview the two personalities.

If each of the two personalities does not dress differently, and if
each does not have its own name or nickname, which is often enough
the case in some of the paraphilias, then it is easy enough to overlook
the existence of one of the two. Such an oversight is all the more likely
if the one personality withholds information about the other. The listener
then assumes the existence of a single, unified personality, which is
readily misconstrued as being paraphilically sneaky, devious, and dis-
sembling.

Clérambault-Kandinsky Syndrome

It is customary to denote the fugue-like transition from one personality to another in dual or multiple personality as hysterical or dissociative,
and as being psychogenic. It may even be glossed over as voluntarily
theatrical and inconsequential; or joked about and ridiculed, like the
transition from being unattached to being madly in love.

In proverbial wisdom, it is said that love is blind, or that the person newly love-stricken, or limerent, has stars in his/her eyes. At the very prospect of encountering the beloved, the lover undergoes changes of physiology, behavior, and cognition which, added together, signify an altered state of consciousness. It would be stretching the meaning of language too far to equate this alteration with a fugue-like state, despite some similarities. However, when love is unrequited, or threatens to be so, the changes inflate into the full-blown syndrome of lovesickness. The victim of intense lovesickness does experience fugue-like states that, at their most morbid, include a fixation on suicide or homicide.

In the case of John Hinckley, the fugue-like dissociation of his onesided attraction to his movie actress idol, Jodie Foster, was epitomized in the note he wrote to her, dated 3/6/81, 1:00 a.m., on the morning of his attempt to assassinate President Reagan. One side of the page reads: "Goodbye! I love you six trillion times. Don't you like me just a little bit? (You must admit I am different). It would make all of this worthwhile, of course. John Hinckley." On the reverse side is only the name of the hapless Jodie Foster.

The Hinckley pathology of love goes by the name of the Clérambault-Kandinsky syndrome (Jordan and Howe, 1980). In this syndrome, the more ordinary vicissitudes of love unrequited or unfulfilled are greatly magnified. Similarly, the extremes of paraphilic fugue state are also magnifications of less extremely altered states of consciousness. There are many instances in which the transition from the nonaroused to the aroused, fugue-like paraphilic state escapes attention, or is more or less equated with what ordinarily happens in the transition from being sexuoerotically quiescent to aroused, in response to a present or potential partner.

There are also cases, however, in which the evidence of the fugue-like state is not recognized because neither the patient nor the observer has a name or a concept by which to identify it. In trying to find words with which to report his subjective experiences, a paraphile has no ready made terminology for a fugue-like state. He must use his own vocabulary and idiom, the true meaning of which may be overlooked in the clinical history-taking, except by someone specially trained to recognize it. The following case of a young man illustrated this point.

Imagery Disentranced

At the age of nineteen, he was remanded by the court for psychiatric evaluation. He had been charged with repeated misuse of the telephone to advise his neighbor that "I want to kidnap your kid [Calvin, aged six] and I want to kill." After some weeks in the hospital, he was observed by one of the staff to go into a dazed state of fixed staring while watching television.

Eventually it became established that this reaction was synchronized with television programs or commercials featuring young boys, and it was interpreted as evidence of pedophilia. The patient's own account was not solicited until some time later, when he saw a sexological consultant. He then explained that the image of the boy on the television screen would become Joey, who proved to be his alter ego. When he was not Joey, he was Frank. Joey would project his own fantasy drama onto the television screen. Joey's fantasy was triggered by the television image, but was otherwise unrelated to it.

Synoptically, the fantasy had a secularized religious theme of death and resurrection or reincarnation. In the patient's own words: "My desire," he said, "was to kill myself and kill Calvin, and somehow be born as Calvin. I don't know how that would have worked out. I wanted not only to be Calvin; but [his parents] Jeff and Kay seemed like such good parents toward Calvin that I would have loved to fall into their hands. I wanted them as my parents. I was suicidal at the time; and, because it seemed so close to actually happen, I thought: "Let's go all the way with it." So [it seemed as if] I accelerated the desires, and the feelings intensified more, and I didn't—I wanted to be Calvin, but deep down inside, I didn't really want to hurt the boy. So I started sending letters, threatening letters, and I started making phone calls . . . I said I was going to kidnap Calvin, and I was going to kill him."

Prior to the onset of this religion-derived fantasy of death and resurrection, the patient had gone through a prolonged teenaged period of intense religious obsessionalism. "I felt that you not only had to pray seventy times a week, but if you remembered something that God did for you, or something good, you had to drop everything and pray, and thank Him, or say you are sorry, that very second. I had a document that I had drawn up, about the size of this desk top. I had nothing but rules on it, and prayers that I had to follow . . . like you couldn't use old English handwriting, except for religion. You can't use a green pen, but only for religion . . . I was up to 500 prayers a week . . . I was so overwhelmed by all of this . . . I prayed to God to help me, and slow it down."

By around age eighteen, it had slowed down, but the time consumed by praying was taken over by Joey and his fantasies of being kidnaped and killed, kidnaper and killer. These fantasies had by now become explicitly eroticized, and were masturbation fantasies. Earlier in teenage, Joey's fantasies had borne no relationship to masturbation. There had sometimes been an erection induced by actual or pictorial images of young boys, and thoughts of touching them. "It was sexual," the patient said, "but I didn't know it was sexual. I didn't know what it was."

The patient's prior sexual history had been one of total deprivation of sexual learning at home and among peers who had teased and stigmatized him because his behavior did not conform to their standards. There had been, at age six, a traumatic incident, confused in the recall, but confirmed by the parents, of their spying on him in the bathroom, and three times beating him for not desisting from masturbating on one occasion while taking a bath.

Frank was an early adolescent when Joey came into being as a second personality. Joey's age was six, and he never grew older. Joey, the six year old, was the one whose destiny was to be kidnaped, murdered, and reincarnated as a better person.

At first Joey's death was scheduled to be effected by suicide, but that failed on three or more different attempts. Then it was effected pictorially. The technique was to tear out magazine fashion pictures or take actual photographs of young boys in shorts or T-shirts, and to superimpose over them an acetate sheet on which he painted wounds and blood, strategically placed to represent inflicted injuries and, ultimately, lust murder. The composite pictures served as a stimulus for sadomasochistic and lust-murdering masturbation fantasies. The stimulus figure could represent either Joey or the boy who had posed for the picture or photograph. Disassembled, neither the acetate sheet nor the picure betrayed their conjoined sadomasochistic and murderous secrets. Calvin, the boy next door, was one of those whose photograph had been used under an acetate sheet.

Eventually the pictures became an insufficient substitute for sexuoerotic contact. That was when Calvin and his parents began receiving phone calls and letters. The caller was Joey, but his voice was recognized as Frank's, the quiet, religious neighbor who attended the same church as Calvin and his parents.

The upshot was that the patient was summoned to the police station. "I thought to myself," he said, "this is the perfect opportunity to grab a gun . . . and just blast your brains out. But I didn't want to do it until after I made my confession, because I don't want to be pictured as a child killer, or a child murderer. I wanted people to understand where I was coming from . . . I just poured out my guts . . . We tape recorded the conversation . . . what I wanted all along was to get to jail. I said I wanted to be arrested and to go to jail . . . and I wanted to kill myself.''

Fortuitous Cues

In the foregoing account, it was more or less fortuitous, first, that the youth's dazed staring state was recognized and put on record; and second, that he was referred to a specialist who understood that the dazed state was premonitory of the paraphilic fantasy, too unspeakable to have been hitherto disclosed. It is quite likely that the signs of an altered state of consciousness will be recognized more often, once professionals become alerted to their existence.

In another case, signs of a fugue-like state would have escaped observation had not the patient found his clinical supervisor still at work, after hours, when he arrived at the clinic forty-five minutes late for his evening appointment. Customarily, he arrived thirty minutes early for each appointment, so as to have time in the cafeteria to compose himself over a cup of coffee, after a long drive. It was never his intention to take an indirect route or to be behind schedule, no matter what his destination. On this particular evening, however, he had detoured for what seemed to him like five minutes when he saw his gas tank was low. He asked the gas station attendant for the time, and discovered that he had been driving round with a whole hour unaccounted for.

Too distressed to report for the final fifteen minutes of his scheduled appointment, he took the elevator to my office, instead. Standing in the doorway, he could not give an adequate account of why he was there, or of what he wanted. He looked visibly shaken and distraught. His speech sounded panicky and out of breath. After he became more calm, he said his pulse had been racing, his hands sweaty, and his mouth dry.

The story that unfolded had its beginning on the highway, as he was driving to the clinic. Two school buses ahead of him took an exit ramp. That was the signal that triggered in him an episode of dromomania on wheels, forcing him to leave the highway at the next exit. Had he been accompanied by a driving companion, it would not have happened. "If somebody was with me," he said, "they would want to know why, and I would have to explain what I'm doing—and I can't explain it. And, also, it's easier to just carry on a conversation and keep going, so that it doesn't happen, anyway."

He did not expect to pick up the trail of the two buses. He did not, in fact, know specifically what he was going to do, except to drive around with a premonition of finding a church. "A church is like a signal," he said. "I drive past it . . . I'm on one side of the church, and I have to drive to the other side." According to the premonition, he would there find a youth at the age of puberty with whom he would strike up a friendly conversation, and then, utterly without warning, punch and kick him, and drive away. It was to prevent the materialization of this premonition that the patient had, eighteen months earlier, referred himself to, and then been accepted in the program of combined hormonal (Depo-Provera) and counseling therapy (Chapter 17).

The patient's premonition had been only partly fulfilled on this particular occasion for, on the far side of the church, there was only a little boy playing. "I didn't stop," the patient said. "I went on past, but I had to come back again. And after I came back the third time, I just, I just like, uh, relaxed; and I was able to pull myself together, and come on into the city. I don't know what happened. There was a change. Just all of a sudden I quit driving around."

Though he could not account for what precipitated the sudden change he here spoke of, the patient was aware that episodes of driving in search of a church had been virtually eliminated during the previous eighteen months on Depo-Provera—which accounted for his dismay at having had this one relapse.

Thinking biographically, the patient could not come up with a hypothesis of how the church got into his driving ritual. There is a possible connection, however, with the schizophrenic psychopathology of his mother's personal history. He was a boy of eleven when she had her first major breakdown. "God and Jesus—she thought they were talking to her. The Devil, too . . . Everybody was trying to humor her—her delusions. So, when everybody told her they believed that God was talking to her, and I heard them say that, I thought they believed it too, you know."

Even though the patient released more information about the paraphilic content of his altered state of consciousness on this occasion, so soon after an actual episode, than on other occasions, it was not easy for him. He repudiated cruelty. His paraphilic imagery of kicking or punching boys in the crotch and injuring them genitally was inconsistent with his idealized self-image as a pedophile. From the vantage point of his almost autistic introversion, he could become attached only to a boy around age eleven to fourteen, and his attachment was exclusive, affectionate, generous, and faithful.

Orthodox/Unorthodox

The paraphilic fugue or fugue-like state constitutes a dissociation or splitting of the personality so that the sexuoerotic component that constitutes the paraphilia is on one side of the divide, and not the other. The extent to which other components are also split varies. Thus, the personality on the paraphilic side of the split may not only have its own name, but may also dress differently, speak differently, and have different body language than the personality on the non-paraphilic side of the split. It may also have a different social age, and even a different social sexual status. It may have a different balance of traits of temperament—violence versus martyrdom, for instance, in association with the expiatory paraphilias. It may be more dependent on medications and/or street drugs, and more subject to injuries and paroxysmal aches, spasms, and related acute physiological symptoms.

Overall, the paraphilic personality may be more antisocial on the criteria of lying, stealing, gambling, breaking contracts and appointments, failing to carry through on promises, duties, and obligations. All told, the personality on the paraphilic side of the split is more likely to be unorthodox than orthodox with respect to conventional criteria of morality. It could hardly be otherwise. Sexuoerotic dissociation or splitting has its childhood genesis in personal inability, for whatever reason, to conform to the interventions imposed on sexuoerotic development in the name of obedience to someone else's moral authoritarianism which is unjustly imposed. The devious ruse of the paraphilia is the childhood solution to this otherwise unnegotiable imposition.

The dissonance between the unorthodox, paraphilic side of the personality split, and the orthodox, morally-conforming side, generates in some paraphiles a degree of sneaky deviousness which is virtually pathognomonic, and without which the paraphilia cannot be kept masked from public view. One formula of deviousness, the formula of "having your cake and eating it too," is to become a secret agent who legally entraps paraphiles as a vocation, and illegally fraternizes with them as an avocation.

Exposés of some of the most morally self-righteous crusaders, preachers, and legislators of antisexualism have revealed that their secret personality practiced in private what their public personality crusaded against in the media and elsewhere. In the aftermath of exposure, it is quite possible for the tables to be turned, so that a person crusades in favor of that which he formerly crusaded against. This turning of the tables may also occur in the aftermath of treatment, as when a former paraphilic rapist becomes an advocate of women's sexual rights; or when a former pedophile becomes an advocate of sexual age-matching. Such a turnabout may, or may not be accompanied by religious conversion, extreme self-righteousness, and not only an altered, but an exalted state of consciousness resembling that of the paraphilic fugue state itself.

The turnabout phenomenon precludes the emergence of a substitute paraphilia. Paraphilias are, indeed remarkably specific. Even a paraphilia that appears to be incremental over time, on closer inspection proves to have been, in fantasy, the same complex paraphilia all along, like a play with different scenes that, though enacted separately, are part of the whole.

Hyperorgasmia

Hyperorgasmia is a frequent, though not invariant, phenomena of the paraphilic fugue state for which an adequate scientific explanation does not yet exist. As based on the reports of many male paraphiles, hyperorgasmia means regularly and compulsively having an orgasm at the rate of four to ten per twenty-four hours, either alone or with a partner. The more frequent, the less the amount of the ejaculate. Neurophysiologically, hyperorgasmia is not a simple correlate of sex hormonal level in the bloodstream. It almost certainly will prove to be a function of neurotransmitters and neuromodulators, as yet unknown, in the brain and/or the peripheral nervous system.

17

Treatment

Steroid Hormones: Naming and Sex Stereotyping

The hormones secreted by the testicles and the ovaries were isolated, and their chemical structure identified in the 1920s, little more than half a century ago. By the end of the 1930s, the technique for their synthesis had been worked out, and they were on sale commercially.

The names of the three major sex hormones were given on what was initially recognized as their dominant *in vivo* effect. Androgen (Gk. *andros,* man) was named for its masculinizing effect. The chief androgen was named testosterone, because it is produced in the testes or testicles. Estrogen, from the ovaries, was named for its effect in inducing estrus, or heat, in female animals that have periodic or seasonal estrous cycles, at which times they ovulate and accept the male. Progesterone was named not for its ovarian origin and postovulatory peak, but for its placental origin and role in maintaining gestation or pregnancy.

The early methods of measuring hormone levels in blood or urine were crude and imprecise. Therefore, it was easily assumed that androgen belongs only to males and estrogen and progesterone only to females. It was also easily assumed that androgen controls every aspect of masculinity, behavior included; and correspondingly that estrogen and progesterone do the same for femininity.

This assumption would eventually prove to be too broad, and in error. It was in error, for example, with respect to male homosexuals. Treated with testosterone, they did not become heterosexual. What the body does in response to an excess level of exogenous testosterone is to suppress the secretion of testosterone from its own testes. If the blood level of testosterone remains still too high, because of a high treatment dosage, then the excess amount of the hormone is secreted in the urine.

The assumption that male hormone causes masculinity, led to yet another assumption, namely that estrogen given to a male would make him more feminine and, according to the stereotype of femininity, less sexually aggressive and intrusive. Thus, estrogen was tried as a treatment for aggressive and intrusive sex offenders.

Estrogen treatment of a male does have a feminizing effect, insofar as it induces the growth of breasts. It does not make a man want to be a woman, nor want to have a male as a sexual partner. The effect of estrogen on the testicles is the same as treatment with testosterone: it suppresses their own secretion of testosterone. Thus the body's circulating supply of testosterone may be reduced by estrogen to the same low level as that of a prepubertal boy. In consequence, the subjective experience of sexual drive may become more quiescent, and less urgent and demanding. However, the subjective effect is variable. Male-to-female transsexuals treated with estrogen do not typically become dropouts so far as their sexual life in partnership with a male is concerned.

Because of the effect of estrogen in suppressing the secretion of testosterone by the testicles, it is classified as an antiandrogen. It has a history of having formerly been used for its antiandrogenic effect in the treatment of prostatic cancer. Its disadvantage is that it makes the breasts grow, which is mortifying to most men.

Estrogen given to a male is able to have an antiandrogenic, suppressive effect on the secretion of testosterone by the testes because, like testosterone, it is a steroid hormone. So also is progesterone. All three hormones are, metaphorically speaking, first cousins of one another. The precursor substance of all three of them is cholesterol. Using a complex system of enzymes, both the ovaries and the testes are able to convert cholesterol into progesterone, then to convert progesterone into testosterone, and testosterone into estrogen. Since this sequence takes place in both men and women, there are, to be absolutely precise, neither male nor female sex hormones, but only gonadal sex hormones. The same hormones are found also in other animals. Men and women differ in the ratio of the three hormones they have, not in their absolute presence or absence. If women had no androgen, they would lack axillary and pubic hair, and they would, in all probability, be deficient in the subjective experience of sexual drive and sexual inititative.

The three steroidal hormones secreted by the gonads are closely related biochemically in molecular structure, and in the way that they are taken up into the nucleus of cells that use one or more of the sex hormones. Therefore, they are able to perform certain functions interchangeably. All three of them, for instance, are able to enter into a feedback partnership with the regulatory hormones of the hypothalamic-pituitary axis, and so govern the quantity of their own secretion from the gonads.

In various sexuoerotic centers and pathways of the brain, in addition to the hypothalamus, there are target cells that are able to take in and bind molecules of not only one, but two or all three of the gonadal steroid hormones. This ability of the cells to accept more than one sex steroid is put to therapuetic use in the antiandrogenic, hormonal treatment of paraphilic sex offending.

Steroidal Antiandrogen

An antiandrogen is any steroidal or steroid-like hormone that satisfies two criteria. When given in high enough dosage, it is able to compete with testosterone for entry into the nucleus of target cells, leaving no vacancies for testosterone. It is also an inert, or else an extremely weak stimulus with respect to inducing or activating a masculine signal from the cell.

Within the sexual brain, progesterone and its synthetic relatives, which are synonymously known as progestins, progestogens, or gestagens, probably do more than deactivate masculine signals from target cells. They may have a second and independent effect of being sexuoerotic tranquilizers (Herrmann and Beach, 1978). This proposition is conjectured on the basis of the knowledge that progestins, given in a large enough dose, have a direct effect on the central nervous system: they produce a short-lived anesthesia (Merryman, 1954).

Paraphilic men at the onset of antiandrogenic therapy with the synthetic progestin, medroxyprogesterone acetate (Depo-Provera®, Upjohn) typically report a relief of sexual tension and agitation. They feel less driven by their sexual compulsion, and their paraphilic fantasy imagery exercises less sexuoerotic tyranny in demanding to be put into practice. Male-to-female transexuals report a similar calming effect when first put on estrogen therapy.

The first use of medroxyprogesterone acetate (MPA) in the treatment of paraphilic sex offending was in December, 1966 (Money, 1968, p.

169; 1970b). Earlier that same year, another antiandrogenic compound, cyproterone acetate (Androcur®, Schering A.G.) had been used in treating two patients at the Institute for Sex Research under Hans Giese, at the University of Hamburg, West Germany. One patient was a severely mentally retarded adolescent with unremitting masturbatory exposure in public; and the other a heterosexual pedophilic farmer who needed help in order to avoid arrest and imprisonment. The treatment made possible the retarded youth's continued rehabilitation, and held promise for the pedophile.

Cyproterone acetate had not in 1965 been cleared by the Federal Drug Administration (FDA), for sex-offender use in the United States (and still has not been cleared). Therefore, it could not be used in the treatment of a transvestite father who had included his six-year-old son in a crossdressing "television game," and engaged him in oral-genital activities. Though this man was desperate for therapy of any type, including aversion therapy, no professional could be found to take on his case.

This was the point at which I consulted with my endocrinological colleague, Claude Migeon, M.D., and his Argentinian postdoctoral fellow, Marco Rivarola, M.D. The upshot was a trial period of treatment with MPA (Money, 1970b). This hormone was already known for its antiandrogenic effect in treating children with excessively early onset of puberty before age six.

When the success of treatment in this case became known, the demand for treatment grew, and a small investigative study got under way. By 1978, the demand for treatment had increased sufficiently to justify the setting up of an inpatient/outpatient clinic, the Johns Hopkins Biosexual Psychohormonal Clinic, for the treatment of paraphilic sex offending and related disorders.

Treatment Regimen

The ideal plan of treatment is one in which hormonal and talking therapy are combined. Hormonal therapy with antiandrogen gives the patient what can be called in the vernacular a vacation from his sex drive. Concurrent talking therapy assists him in the process of what may be called a psychic realignment.

Initially, the dosage of Depo-Provera is typically 5cc (500 mg) every week, though the dosage can be adjusted according to body mass, and to the pretreatment level of circulating testosterone. Contrary to popular assumption, sex offending is not caused by a high level of testosterone circulating in the blood stream. The average level in men is 500 to 600 ng/dl, with the range spreading from a low of 200 ng/dl to a high of 1000 ng/dl. In sex offenders, the average level of circulating testosterone has not yet been statistically determined. The range is the same (Gagné, 1981; Walker and Meyer, 1981) as in men who are not sex offenders.

The aim of treatment is to lower the testosterone level so as to approximate the very low level of prepuberty. At most, it should be no higher than 100 to 125 ng/dl. Especially in adolescence, the blood testosterone level fluctuates diurnally, which is one reason why the laboratory measurement is not the only criterion by which the dosage of MPA is regulated. Diminution of paraphilic behavior, and the subjective rating of diminished paraphilic fantasy also are taken into account. Individuals vary widely as to the maintenance dosage they require.

The size of the dose required to bring relief from paraphilic sexuoerotic excess does not automatically diminish genitoerotic functioning to the point of impotence, anorgasmia, or indifference. On an individual basis, the dosage can be regulated so as to permit a compromise between genital capability, on the one hand, and the risk that continued expression of paraphilic behavior would entail, on the other. In some cases, as for instance that of a young postpubertal adolescent seeking help to prevent the actualization of a paraphilic lust murder fantasy, complete sexuoerotic suppression may be obligatory, perhaps indefinitely.

Prior to treatment, preoccupation with paraphilic thoughts and imagery in many cases is unrelentingly perseverative and compulsively time-consuming. It may entail as many as six to ten ejaculations a day, either by masturbation, or with a partner, or both (see Chapter 16). During the sexuoerotic respite hormonally attained, there is a possibility that talking therapy will help to generate ways of filling up the periods of the daily schedule no longer occupied by the obsessive paraphilic fantasy rehearsals and their compulsive translation into practice. A pedophile, for example, prior to hormonal treatment, may have been, like Peter Pan who never grew up, completely inexperienced with people of his own age. Hormonal treatment alone, without talking treatment, does not ensure his social maturation.

Couple Counseling

Individual talking treatment may not suffice. When the issue is that of pairbondedness with a partner, it is necessary, on at least some occasions, to engage the two people in couple counseling (Money, 1981a). To be able to live with a paraphile over an extended period of time, married or not, the partner needs to have a lovemap that reciprocally matches his/hers, either because they started out that way, or because her/his lovemap adaptively accommodated to his/hers.

A girl with a childhood history of sexual abuse, for example, developed a lovemap in which she is an abused martyr. As a young woman, she married an older man newly released from serving time in prison as a pedophile. He was potentially more attracted to her young daughter than to her. The woman was thus exempted from coitus which, in her lovemap was equated with further victimization, as in childhood. At the same time, her abused-martyr role was not threatened, for his syndrome daily threatened her with martydom as a potential prisoner's widow. This relationship held together until he went on antiandrogen treatment, and was relieved of the threat of a pedophilic relapse. Then her health deteriorated, and she succumbed to an attack of anorexia nervosa. This was the juncture at which her husband's antiandrogenic treatment would have issued in failure, unless he and his wife as a couple were able to achieve a therapeutic realignment of their relationship on the basis of mutual health instead of mutually alternating pathology.

With respect to prognosis, it is a good sign if a patient becomes realigned in a limerent relationship, or in other words, in a pairbonded love affair. The first patient who reported this phenomenon was the one who first received MPA treatment. He described himself as if he had been a sexual automaton, prior to treatment. "It was just that I woke up in the middle of the night with a, with very stiff erections which I had to relieve by masturbation. And, this was very frequent . . . just constantly . . . Erections just seemed to come on automatically, with the slightest thought of anything in the sexual line. In other words, I could get an erection from just one of these wierd thoughts, and then have intercourse with my wife. It was just like having intercourse with her in those days was just like masturbation. It was a form of release. It was something to get rid of the erection, to have the orgasm. There was no real meaning to it. This was a hard realization to come to . . . that my wife was a form of masturbation . . . I think it was just sex for the sake of sex, uh, for a release. I don't think there was any real love motivation behind it . . . I think I had sex and love very confused. I didn't know the difference between the two. Sex was just a release to get an orgasm, and get it over with. Sex now is exclusively for my wife and I, for love. And that's the best difference."

Formerly, his wife had not been included in the content of his transvestic copulatory fantasies. She would literally have been correct had she said that he wanted her only for her body. During intercourse, they were psychically distanced from one another. After the change, his frequency of ejaculation became less compulsive and excessive, at three to four times a week, and he was able to realize, for the first time, that what his wife was experiencing sexuoerotically was in its entirety as important to him as what he was experiencing himself.

His wife was able to confirm the change. Indirectly, she thus endorsed the proposition that paraphilias are love disorders rather than simply sex disorders. They are a form of lovesickness.

Other Effects of MPA

MPA has, in addition to its androgen-depleting effect, a suppressive effect on spermatogenesis. Thus, it acts also as a contraceptive, so long as the treatment continues. After short-term treatment, fertility returns. After long-term treatment over a period of years, the outcome on fertility remains still to be ascertained.

Though there are exceptions, the majority of patients on treatment with MPA undergo a hormonally-induced change in the experience of satiation and hunger. This change is mediated presumably by way of the hypothalamus and the pituitary gland. It induces increased food intake and a weight gain of, typically, 20 to 30 pounds (9 to 14 kg). Posttreatment weight reduction can be achieved, provided a weight-reducing diet is adhered to.

Another hypothalamically-mediated and hormonally-induced effect of MPA, namely, increased drowsiness by the end of the day, is common though not invariable. Those affected sleep for upwards of two extra hours each night.

Increased eating and sleeping are, like decreased sexuality and eroticism, the only consistent effects of MPA treatment. It is possible that there may be other effects that occur inconsistently and sporadically, and only in predisposed individuals. For this reason, patients in treatment should be routinely checked, semiannually, for liver function, blood pressure, and blood-sugar level. A few patients have reported transient instability of thermoregulation with sweating and hot flashes at the outset of treatment. For those with acne, MPA induces major improvement.

One patient reported thinning of body hair, and arrest of balding. Gynecomastia has not been reported in published reports; in the clinic, there has been only one known instance since 1966, and that was of unilateral gynecomastia, moderate in degree.

Outcome and Followup

There are different criteria for judging the efficacy of MPA treatment. One criterion might be the length of time during which the patient remains free of a relapse into paraphilic fantasies and/or their enactment while continuing on hormonal treatment, as compared with after having been weaned off hormonal treatment. Another criterion might be the absolute and permanent disappearance of all signs and symptoms of the paraphilic syndrome while on hormonal treatment, and after its discontinuance.

This second criterion is the one imposed by society and its judicial system when the paraphilia is a sex-offending one. Society does not tolerate even a single relapse. In fact, even the word relapse is not tolerated, but is replaced with recidivism. Recidivism is punished; relapse is pitied. Paraphilias are among the relatively few syndromes in which a recurrence of symptoms is punished instead of subjected to renewed treatment efforts.

Equating relapse and recidivism impedes what can be done to evaluate the success of treating sex offenders whose paraphilia makes them dangerous to society. For the protection of society, dangerous paraphiles require some form of quarantine while being treated and tested to find out whether the outcome is successful or not.

The standard research design for a study of the outcome of treatment is the double-blind, crossover design. It requires trial periods of treatment with the hormone and, alternatively, treatment with a placebo and/or another type of medication. The successful outcome of hormonal treatment cannot be fully tested unless the patient is exposed to conditions of a real-life test. A prison, by definition, does not provide these conditions. The community at large does do so, but to the community it is absolute anathema to have a dangerous sex offender at large. There needs to be some compromise, an institutionalized protective quarantine of a type that society does not yet provide.

In the meantime, therefore, statistics on the outcome of antiandrogenic treatment will continue to be compiled on the basis of paraphilias that do not threaten the safety of others in the community. It will be feasible to include also the paraphilias of early adolescence that have expressed themselves only in fantasy, and that have not yet made the adolescent eligible for arrest. The more well known the availability of antiandrogen therapy, the greater the likelihood that pubertal and adolescent paraphiles will seek treatment.

At the present juncture, the best way to deal with the impasse in outcome research is to compare the situation with the treatment of cancer. In the case of cancer, the success rate is counted in terms of number of years of survival, as compared with the survival of those who remain untreated.

In individual cases of paraphilia, it is already evident that the number of years of unimprisoned survival as a functionally productive member of society is increased by combined antiandrogen/counseling treatment, whereas other prior treatments, including imprisonment, had failed. In fact there are some paraphiles who, without the antiandrogenic component of treatment, would have been destined for a very long period of imprisonment—a prodigious expense for the taxpayer.

No matter how long the period of a successful outcome of treatment, a person with a paraphilic history is, like his counterpart with cancer, in need of indefinite followup, so that a threatened relapse can be preventively treated. Paraphilia is a chronic condition. Its treatment, though rehabilitative, is not based on a reversal of etiology. As yet, therefore, it cannot be regarded as permanently altering the cause of the condition, but only its expression.

Treatment Comparisons

It is too soon to produce comparative statistics on the outcome of rival forms of treatment. The hormonal rival of MPA is cyproterone acetate which, though well established in Europe, has not, as aforesaid, cleared the FDA for the treatment of paraphilias in the United States. In Canada, as of 1984, both hormones have been cleared for comparative clinical trials, newly begun.

For comparative clinical trials, MPA might be matched with one of the pharmaceutical drugs known to have a direct action on the autonomic nervous system, the sexual autonomic system included. There are two major classes of such drugs, the antihypertensives and the antipsychotics, for example, guanethidine and thioridazine (Mellaril) respectively (Money and Yankowitz, 1967). Individually, the sexual suppressant effect of these drugs is inconsistent and unpredictable. They have not, overall, shown promise for the treatment of paraphilia. However, they do offer an alternative that is more than a placebo for those relatively rare patients who do not respond well to MPA.

As in psychiatry in general, there are rivalrous schools of thought regarding talking and/or behavioral forms of treatment for the paraphilias, ranging from exorcism and hypnosis to group therapy and psychoanalysis. No one of these methods has a good track record with respect to outcome statistics (Kilmann et al., 1982). There are no data to justify their use as exclusive alternatives to antiandrogenic therapy, instead of in combination with antiandrogenic therapy.

The outcome of antiandrogenic treatment may be subverted by the intervention of other concurrent pharmacologic products, medically prescribed, or self-prescribed. Thus, it is possible that anti-epileptic medication may sufficiently alter the state of consciousness so as to allow the break-through of paraphilic fantasy and action. Alcohol and tetrahydrocannabinol almost certainly do (Money and Bennett, 1981).

Treatment of Female Paraphilia

Since the blood level of androgen is normally low in women, and the progesterone level cyclically high, the paraphilias of women challenge both the theory and the practice of the effect exerted by a progestinic antiandrogen in the treatment of the paraphilias of men. Despite their relative infrequency in the clinic and the courtroom, the dangerous paraphilias of women parallel those of men in harm to the victim.

In one case of homosexual pedophilia, for example, a woman would baby-sit or befriend an infant girl. She would cuddle and caress her with her hands and tongue, and lick the genitals. Her own arousal would fail to climax in orgasm, however, until she inserted a sharp or red-hot object, like the burning eraser end of a pencil, into the girl's vagina. The child's screaming then triggered the woman's orgasm.

To avoid incarceration, and to separate herself from potential future victims, this women had herself admitted to a psychiatric facility. Her paraphilic fantasies persisted. On leave to visit her family, twenty-four hour supervision was imperative. She and the professional staff in charge of her case requested a consultation regarding a trial period of treatment with MPA combined with talking therapy. She was given intramuscular MPA treatment, 300 mg per week over a period of eleven months. Though she claimed to experience some relief, it could not be specifically attributed to MPA, as it became necesary to reduce the dosage, and then cease treatment for a test period, on account of an elevation of serum prolactin. Shortly thereafter, following discharge from the psychiatric institution where she had been in residence for four years, the patient was lost to followup.

Subsequently, in two other cases with a history of brain injury, paraphilia in women did appear to be responsive to MPA. Like so much else in women's sexual medicine, however, effective treatment of female paraphilias, dangerous or otherwise, remains neglected. Neglect ensures that the shibboleth of women as romantic and loving, but not, like men, erotic and sexual, will not be exposed as erroneous.

Self-Help Groups

Paraphilic women know better. Taking advantage of the new publicity and doctrine of sex as an addiction (see Chapter 5), they have begun to join with men in forming self-help groups. These groups have names such as Sexaholics Anonymous, Sex and Love Addicts Anonymous, and Compulsive Cruisers Support Group. All have a therapeutic philosophy and procedure modeled after Alcoholics Anonymous. Though there are no statistics as to the long-term efficacy of membership in these therapeutic groups, the positive testimony of individual members leave no doubt as to their value for some people who formerly were without hope. Men and women are equally accepted, including those who are concurrently receiving hormonal therapy.

18

Informed Consent

Crimes Against Nature

The medieval fires of the Inquisition finally burned out, but only as recently as the eighteenth century. In the preceding centuries, paraphiles had been burned at the stake. In colonial Massachusetts, William Hackett, an eighteen year old, was hanged in 1642 for sodomizing his penis into the vagina of a cow. Before he was executed, the cow was burned before his eyes (Bullough, 1976, p. 520–1). The deed had been espied by a woman detained by infirmity from attending the Sunday service. Thomas Granger, aged sixteen, met the same fate, also in 1642, for buggery with a mare, a cow, two goats, five sheep, two calves and a turkey, all of which were burned in a great pit.

Both boys were indentured laborers. Granger had been a herd boy in England. He said it had not been unusual for adolescent farm boys to have animal sexual contact. Farm help was in desperately short supply in New England. So also were farm animals. Nonetheless the boys and the animals all were condemned to death.

In the state legal codes, after the Revolution, bestiality continued to be subsumed under sodomy as one of the abominable and unspeakable crimes against nature. These crimes or perversions included, as a general rule, statutory rape, violent rape, child molesting, homosexuality, adultery, exhibitionism, and oral sex. In some states, there have been revisions of the criminal code regarding sex offenses. For the most part, however, today's sex offenses are yesterday's crimes against nature, and their treatment is by fine, imprisonment, or execution. For first offenders, and for lesser offenses, there is a greater likelihood of probation, subject to some form of treatment by a psychiatrist. Nonetheless, the system is imbued with a high degree of vindictiveness. Indeed, the scope of vindictiveness has in recent years expanded, because, under the impetus of the antisexual branch of the women's movement and the religious New Right, legislators have broadened the legal definition of rape, jurists have regionalized the judicial definition of pornography and, as of 1984, Congress has extended the age of childhood, as applied to nude photographs, from age 16 to 18 (Chapter 19).

Neither in the courts, nor among the public at large, has there been much of a disposition to regard the paraphilias as syndromes of illness that should eventually come under biomedical rather than penal jurisdiction. The predominant view is that they are degenerate crimes to be eradicated with punishment and death.

Homosexuality and Left-Handedness

Homosexuality, though it used to be, and in some cases still is punished as a crime against nature, stands in contrast to paraphilia. Earlier in the twentieth century, it became increasingly popular to reclassify homosexuality as not a crime, but a psychiatric disease. By the 1970s, the gay liberation movement had gained sufficient political strength to be able to shift official psychiatric policy away from classifying homosexuality as a disease. Instead, it was given the status of being, like left-handedness, a characteristic of a socially tolerated minority whose way of existing sexuoerotically, even so, is less than ideal in the eyes of the majority.

The trend toward the decriminalization of homosexuality, and then its removal from the list of official diseases points up the ethical issue of who has the authority to define what is and what is not a disease. In the age before germ theory, fever of unknown origin and fever induced by bacterial infection could not be differentiated with certainty. That certainty awaited not only germ theory, but also a test for infectious microorganisms in the bacteriological laboratory.

Illness Self-Defined

Since the cause of homosexuality still is not known (nor is the cause of heterosexuality), there can be no certain test for it. Therefore, the only test of whether or not to treat homosexuality is the test of whether or not the patient claims to feel wrong, bad, sick, uncomfortable, distressed, or in pain—for which the technical term in DSM–III (the third revision of the Diagnostic and Statistical Manual of the American Psychiatric Association) is ego-dystonic.

Any illness for which the cause is unknown is, in the final analysis, self-defined in terms of personal suffering, as has been the case since the days of Hippocrates. Physicians themselves have their own conventions regarding the symptoms they require before they accept a patient's self-definition of being ill, when there is no known cause of, or test for that self-defined illness. For example, the cause of transexualism is today still not established. That allows some physicians to express a very forceful objection to sex-reassignment therapy on the grounds that the patient's self-definition, or self-diagnosis as a transexual is a delusion. Some adhere to the doctrine that the delusion should be treated by psychotherapy and/or psychotropic drugs, despite the absence of systematic and statistical clinical evidence of the success of such treatment.

Paraphilia presents exactly the converse problem of self-definition of illness, insofar as the paraphile usually does not define himself/herself as feeling ill. Whether attained by the paraphilic or the nonparaphilic route, the feeling of orgasm is not a feeling of being ill! Nonetheless, the sex-offending paraphile is not unaware of the judgment of society and the law with respect to the consequences of orgasm by way of sex-offending. In fact, it is this judgment that creates the paraphile's distress, and which may precipitate the first request for treatment. The request may be prior to police intervention, while awaiting trial, or after conviction.

Because paraphilic sex offences are crimes, and because the sex offender commonly postpones the request for treatment until after being apprehended, there are those who, as aforesaid, refuse to construe paraphilia as an illness. They regard it as a moral choice or preference voluntarily embarked upon. For them, prison is the only form of treatment, the longer the imprisonment the better, despite the cost to the taxpayer, and despite the lack of systematic statistical evidence as to its efficacy.

Preference versus Status

As upheld by the American Civil Liberties Union, a currently popular argument for withholding any treatment other than incarceration for sex offenders has a sanctimonious ring of false piety. It is that a person who is eligible for arrest, or has been arrested, has lost the ability to give informed consent freely. He/she is already under duress and, therefore, must be protected from signing anything, in a bid for greater leniency, that might be personally harmful. The false piety of this argument is that it assumes that the offender gives informed consent to be incarcerated—or, at least, on the basis of a voluntarily chosen sexual preference, engages in sex-offending behavior despite the threat of incarceration.

The idea that sexual behavior is based on one's voluntary choice or preference has no more philosophical justification as a principle of explanation than does the idea that sexual behavior is based on one's sexual (or sexuoerotic) status which is neither voluntary, nor a preference, but the outcome of a developmental process. The idea of preference, voluntarily chosen, is of very ancient origin in religion and law. As applied to sexual behavior, it has many adherents. They believe in it with deep conviction. The idea of sexual status as a nonvoluntary outcome of development is of very modern origin in science and medicine. As applied to sexual behavior, it has relatively few adherents. They accept it not as a belief but as a hypothesis to be substantiated by empirical data.

The idea of sexual preference or choice does not lend itself to being scientifically substantiated by empirical data, for it is a belief or value judgment rather than a testable hypothesis. By contrast, the idea of sexual status is a hypothesis that can be tested against empirical data.

From the scientific point of view, a person with a paraphilic sexual status is the victim of paraphilia regardless of whether he/she is a candidate for arrest as a sex offender, though not yet apprehended, or has been apprehended, or has been convicted and imprisoned. Therefore, the issue that confronts him/her regarding treatment or no treatment, is not ethically or philosophically different in any one of the three circumstances. In this respect, paraphilia is no different than any other syndrome that, untreated, is likely to lead to entanglement with the law—the syndrome of temporal lobe epilepsy, for example, with rage attacks, or paranoia with violence against a delusional enemy. There is no serious argument that such syndromes should remain untreated, on the grounds that the patient's legal vulnerability has deprived him/her of the right and capability of informed consent.

Misuse of Power

The hue and cry against antiandrogen treatment for sex offenders is not only a pious justification of the continuance of vindictive revenge and punishment. It is also an alarm first sounded by social militants against biomedical science, and taken up by the sensation-seeking media, under the headline of chemical castration. Some paraphilic organizations, most notably man-boy lovers, have also taken up the alarm. The very term, chemical castration, is used because it evokes a return to the era of social eugenics, earlier in the twentieth century, when surgical castration was widely practiced on mental and moral defectives, as they were then called, in order to prevent their procreating and degenerating the race. This movement culminated in Hitler's "Law on the Prevention of Hereditary Diseases in Future Generations," which paved the way for his concentration camps and the atrocities of the holocaust (Pfäfflin, 1985).

Hitler's policies demonstrate the megalomaniacal misuse of power. There is no limit to the ingenuity of human beings in finding ways and means of misusing power. Any medication can, in fact, be misued by a megalomaniac. It is not the medication that is at fault, but the megalomaniac.

Antiandrogenic hormones are not, per se, dangerous medications. They are used other than for the treatment of paraphilic sex offenders. They do not castrate. They suppress testicular function. This effect is temporary and, after the completion of treatment, reversible. To equate the effect of antiandrogen with surgical castration is wrong—just plain wrong. It is as wrong as it would be to equate antiandrogenic treatment with amputation of the hand, the Islamic punishment for thieves.

19

Victimology

Antisexual Doctrine and Crusades

There is a deep vein of secular evangelism and moral crusading in American public life. Its origin traces back to the seventeenth century and to the politics of self-righteousness as practiced in the theocracy of the Puritans who colonized New England. Based on divine dogma, the legislated sexual morality of these colonial Americans claimed not to be democratic, but authoritarian and absolute. It became the basis of an implicit dictatorship of sexuality reenacted into the laws of the new states as America expanded. By extension, it became the criterion standard against which the banner of crusading protest is raised whenever, in the process of historical change, the authority of the old sexual dogma is eroded.

Historically, American moral crusades tend to have been paroxysmal. They build with great intensity and expenditure, and then fall into either disrepute or oblivion as they fail to attain their objectives. The funding of health research has often followed this pattern, to the detriment of effective continuity. The history of child abuse is an example.

In the 1870s, the public conscience was outraged when the extremes of brutality in child abuse in New York City were publicized in the New York Times (Williams, 1980). There was no social agency even remotely mandated to be funded for an investigation, so the responsibility was given to the newly formed Society for the Prevention to Cruelty of Animals. Within ten years, however, the flurry of prevention had dissipated. Official action against child abuse in God-fearing American homes was too much of a threat to America's official image of the sanctity of motherhood and of the authority of the family as the foundation of society. Child abuse was written off as a perversion of parenthood practiced by poor and ignorant immigrants, alcoholics, and the sexually depraved. It was a problem to be taken care of by crusades for education, for the prohibition of alcohol, and for the punishment of vice.

It required the best part of a century before child abuse was redis-covered and again brought to the public attention—this time by Henry Kempe and the pediatricians of Colorado (Kempe et al., 1962). It was named the battered child syndrome. Nationally, the ultimate aim of treat-ment became established as the reeducation of the parents, the return of the child to the home, and the preservation of the idealized image of the American family. The idealized image of the American mother was pre-served by underplaying her role as abuser, or by casting her in the role of second victim of the violence of her child's abusive father.

The term, battered child, insidiously has shifted and yielded to child abuse as the term of reference. With equal insidiousness, abuse has tended to be equated with sexual abuse, for even in the absence of force, sexual abuse is equated with enforced imposition of authority and power. This shift from general force to sexual force maintains the status quo of so-ciety's idealized morality. It preserves for parents and other disciplinar-ians the moral right and righteousness of punishment to enforce moral conformity—even if the outcome is total failure. Simultaneously, it pre-serves for society its ancient conviction that sex, not aggression, endan-gers the probity of its moral order, even though confirmatory evidence is lacking.

The shift toward equating child abuse with sexual abuse has taken place contemporaneously with the revival of antisexualism in the radical arm of the women's liberation movement. This revival has two doctrines. One doctrine extends the meaning of rape to any performance of sexual intercourse when, regardless of the proceptive antecedents, the woman was either reluctant or refused to capture the penis in her vagina, and the man was either insistent or coercive in putting it there.

The other doctrine, under the aegis of Women Against Pornography, extends the meaning of sadistic aggression in pornography to include not only all pornography, but also all explicit heterosexual depictions. Ac-cording to this doctrine, pictures or movies of women copulating with men are depictions of women as sexual objects exploited by the men on camera with them, by the men who run the industry, and by the customers who pay to view or own the product. The logic of this doctrine fails in the case of lesbian performers, women entrepreneurs, or women viewers; and likewise in the case of gay male productions for gay male viewers.

Among the militant radicals of the women's movement, antisexualism in the political crusade against rape and pornography is peripheral to the central issue of women's legal and political rights. Nonetheless, it paradoxically aids and abets the crusade of their New Right opponents, who, transported in a Trojan horse, have been welcomed into the besieged city of Equal Rights, and have set about destroying and conquering it from within. The New Right's antisexual crusade embraces the recriminalization of abortion, the censorship of sex education, "squealing" on teenagers who request contraception, the penalization of homosexuality, the expansion of the legal definition of rape and the exploitation of charges of sexual harrassment in the workplace.

The New Right crusade is also against pornography. Its antipornography strategy has been to focus on child pornography, because it is an issue that no politician dares to oppose, even if he/she does perceive in it the seeds of censorship and of the curtailment of constitutionally guaranteed freedom of expression. Legally, child pornography now includes taking and showing a nude photograph of anyone under the age of eighteen, your own baby included, regardless of how it is used. Moreover, Public Law 98–292, the Child Protection Act of 1984, signed by the President on May 21st, 1984, means that all Americans are now children until they are eighteen. Formerly the age limit was sixteen. The change was legislated as part of the crusade ostensibly to clean up child pornography.

The Dilemma of Privileged Communication

Twenty-five years ago, the legal recourse of pediatricians in cases of presumptive child abuse was so ineffectual that, instead of fighting for an abused child's protection, pediatricians commonly adopted a policy of legal inaction. In effect, they were retained by the parents to restore the child to them for the next round of abuse, in much the same way as army doctors restore a battle-impaired soldier to the military for the next round of battle; or, after a police shoot-out, prison doctors restore an arrested criminal for trial and possible execution. Even in dire cases of the battered child syndrome, the system condoned the return of the victim to the battering parents who would again beat, burn, cut, fracture, starve, dehydrate, isolate, deprive, or otherwise torture and in some cases, finally kill the child.

It is characteristic in such cases that the allegiance of the doctor is expected to be to those who retain his services, and not to the patient. The patient dare not rely on the privilege of trust and confidentiality in the doctor-patient relationship. In the battered child syndrome, children who are victims are unable to take advantage of privileged communication, even if it can be guaranteed to them. As in cases of the Stockholm syndrome (Chapter 5), they become allies of their persecutors. They enter into a collusional conspiracy with them, and do not report the facts of their abuse. In effect, therefore, the only confidentiality that an abused child expects, but does not verbalize, is that his doctor will maintain the secret of his guilty parents. The parents, in their role of being the wardens of abuse who have retained the doctor's services, expect also his hired complicity in not revealing their abuse. Characteristically, they always have their own self-righteous justification for what they do, not unlike the Biblical justification of Abraham's near slaying of Isaac.

It required new legislation to enable pediatricians, social workers, psychologists and others who come into professional contact with child abuse to be extricated from their potential status of hired complicity in child abuse. This new legislation made it mandatory to investigate child abuse which, in turn, made it necessary to set up a new investigative authority.

Policing

The new authority is a branch of children's protective services, officially charged with the humane care of children. Concurrently, it functions also as a quasipolicing authority for investigating parents, guardians, or others suspected of abuse, and for reporting them to the judicial system. Its agents are not only its own salaried employees, but also all professionals in medicine and its allied services who come in contact with cases of actual or presumed child abuse. Failure to report is a criminal offense! There is no longer a certain guarantee of privileged communication, should a parent or other person seek professional help for child abuse. All professional helpers are required to be, in effect, undercover agents of the law. The provisions for conscientious objectors are inadequate.

This violation of the Hippocratic oath has been taken up less enthusiastically by physicians than by social scientists, psychologists, and social workers. It has spawned a whole new branch of human engineering, the bastard science of victimology. It is a bastard science because it is not dedicated to finding out the cause and prevention of child abuse, but to victim ascertainment by means of enforced brainwashing of children to make enforced accusations, enforced confessions, and obligatory treatment by unproved methods. The confessions are put to use in what amount to heresy trials for the purpose of convicting offenders.

Guilt by accusation is more intensively pursued when the accusation is sexual rather than nonsexual abuse. Except in its more bizarre forms, child battering can relatively easily be passed off as legally sanctioned corporal punishment. Parents under investigation can be given the benefit of the doubt, and not charged with a criminal offense. Child abuse that involves an accusation or suspicion of sex, however, is altogether different. There is no mitigating circumstance. Child abuse laws are absolute in their criminalization of any kind of intimacy that can be defined as molestation of a younger by an older person, or as incest. For the suspected or accused offender who is male, the sanctions are more severe than for one who is female. In one case, an attorney said that the law made him fearful of bathing and drying his own daughter, aged six, lest his wife should ever sue for divorce and use child abuse as the charge.

The crusade against sexual child abuse tolerates no naysayers, and brooks no argument. To object is tantamount to exposing oneself to the suspicions of being a supporter of child molestation, child pornography, and child incest. To apply for a research grant to make an impartial study of sexuality and sexual abuse in childhood arouses the same suspicion. As in all crusades, the evil of the enemy is a foregone conclusion. All that is required is his conviction.

The Tyranny of Vengeance

For whatever reasons, personal or professional, social-work victimologists in the crusade against sexual child abuse, without thinking through its logical sequelae, say that their policy is always to believe the child. They are heedless of their professions's own profound acquaintance with severely disturbed children who do not distinguish fantasy from fact; and of others who, though legally still children, are delinquent liars, thieves, and sexual abusers themselves. They are heedless also of the fact that a delinquent at age fifteen, sixteen, or seventeen may also be as street smart as one of his or her own kind who at age eighteen is legally an adult in the techniques of sexual exploitation, extortion, blackmail, and revenge.

The stage is now set for youths who know the sexual-abuse system to exploit it for their own ends, as some already have done. A thirteen year old girl, for example, took revenge on her parents who forbade her dating a married youth of twenty, by reporting her father as having sexually abused her. She succeeded in having him imprisoned by testifying against him in a plea bargain that reduced the sexual abuse charges against her married boyfriend. Nonetheless, without the father's income, the family was disbanded. The girl herself ran away from her foster home placement, and then accused her foster father of sexual abuse. She was relocated in a reformatory for wayward girls.

Youth who have learned how to exploit the child-abuse system will circulate the information among their peers. Others will be coopted by unscrupulous adults to act as undercover agents instructed in how to entrap and blackmail the vulnerable. Thus, it is only a matter of time before victimologists will themselves be the victims of those they purport to help. It is often the fate of the zealot to be blown up with his own bomb. There already are cases of patients who accuse their therapists of indecent advances so that they can charge malpractice and collect a malpractice settlement. One woman collected out of court on the basis of a charge that her psychotherapist, a man, was getting personal erotic satisfaction from asking for and listening to her erotic fantasies. He was threatened with loss of his license to practice.

The greater malpractice vulnerability of male as compared with female victimologists is such that the victimology profession may become almost exclusively the province of women. Herein lies a fateful twist to the irony of history. A century ago, in the first round of women's fight for legal and political equality with men, their liberation from the economic and vocational burden of unrestrained childbearing was at the cost of female abstinence and continence. Women became officially asexual, and it was their responsibility to restrain the animal passions of their men (Mahood and Wenburg, 1980). Now, a century later, restraint has been changed to inquisitorial vindictiveness and vengeance against men.

This change was legislated by men who alone held the political and judicial power to effect it. It is a new version of feeding sop to Cerberus. It continues to deprive women of equal authority with men, by appeasing them, as in the myth of sacrificing Andromeda to the sea monster, except that the new Andromedas are men. The underlying assumption of the practioners of victimology is that "it could never happen to me." The sexual abuser, in the abstract, is always someone else, and never one's own brother, son, or husband, nor even one's own neighbor, or one's own self. Tyrants have always retained supporters on the basis of this faulty philosophy.

As well as being tyrannous, power may be beneficial. Thus the new source of power over adults that victimology gives to anyone under the age of eighteen may have an unexpectedly constructive outcome. To be confronted with the abuse of sexual power forces recognition not only of abuse, but also of the existence of sexuality itself. Thus victimology may, in spite of itself, lead eventually to the legitimization of the sexuality of youth, in exchange for the extortionate social costs of its enforced illegitimacy. In this way, emancipation of young people from the sexual tyranny that society imposes on them may move a step forward. As an example of how this emancipation may evolve, there is the nationally publicized case of Amy, a twelve year old girl from Solano County, California (*Time,* Jan. 23; *People,* Jan. 30, 1984).

After this girl had leaked information that her stepfather, a 32-year-old air force physician, had been fondling her, her parents and she went to a family therapist for counseling. As required by a 1980 state law, the therapist reported the case to the police. Subsequently, in the municipal court, the girl refused to testify against her stepfather, for "personal reasons." Judge De Ronde thereupon remanded her to the county Juvenile Hall, where she was kept in solitary confinement in a cubicle furnished with an open toilet, a washbasin, a thin mattress on a concrete slab jutting from one wall, a television and a radio. She was handcuffed each time she was returned to the courtroom. After eight days, a superior court judge ordered her release to a foster home. She maintained her refusal to testify against her stepfather, so that the case against him had to be dropped through lack of evidence.

Footnote

1. In Maryland, a professional is not legally required to report suspected child abuse unless the child has actually been seen and evaluated in person. Thus, an adult can claim privileged communication when requesting help as an abuser, but only if the physician or other professional specifically refrains from direct intervention with the victim. Some social workers circumvent this provision of the law and initiate a child-abuse investigation, even on the basis of hearsay, prior to direct contact with the victim.

20

Contagion, Degeneracy, and Pornography

Wholesome versus Dirty Sex

Erotography, in the Greek from which it is derived, means erotic writing. In Webster's dictionary erotography is not listed. The substitute term is pornography, which means harlot writing. Erotic writing, in other words, is equated with writing about harlots, or whores. By implication, they alone are entitled to be erotic and to be imbued with the sin of carnal passion. By contrast, respectable women—wives, sisters and mothers—are saintly and undefiled by the depravity of the flesh. Their husbands, sons, and fathers are the depraved ones who keep the harlots in business, and read and look at pornography. This is the stereotype that has shaped Western sexual ideals for centuries. The ideal, of course, does not always correspond with practice. An uncounted proportion of men are sexu-oerotically apathetic and inert. Conversely, not all women who are not harlots agree that they are lacking in eroticism and carnal passion. They know better.

Nonetheless, the ideal of asexualism as purity still seeds itself and spreads its roots broadly in the land, competing for growing space with sex as playful joy and ecstasy. Antisexualism invades the halls of congress, the pulpits of the clergy, the textbooks of the schoolhouse, and the benches of the courtroom.

In the courtrooms of the nation, the drama of antisexualism is repetitiously staged, with no public accounting of the prodigious cost to the taxpayer, on the issue of pornography. Every porno trial is bedeviled by the dictionary, and the Supreme Court, both of which have failed to give a hard-edged definition that differentiates wholesome sex from dirty pornography. This failure stems inevitably from the many centuries in which official doctrine stipulated that all erotic passion was sin, even in conjugal union, and that sexual intercourse was regrettably a procreational necessity, not to be indulged in for pleasure and enjoyment. Under the terms of this doctrine, any representation of the sexual act, in words or in pictures, qualified as pornography. The blanket of taboo stifled the explicit representation of sex completely.

Censorship of explicitly sexual publications first became a secular concern of the state as the rate of literacy increased, enabling more people to read erotic books; and, second, as advances in the mass production of graphics made erotic pictures more cheaply available. After the invention of photography in the middle of last century, and the production of movies early in the present century, visual portrayals of sex were not only explicit, but totally realistic.

Comstock's Sexual Dictatorship

More than any other person, Anthony Comstock was responsible for the legalization of antisexualism as it affects citizens of the United States today. He formed the Committee for the Suppression of Vice, and lobbied Congress in person. In 1873 his extremes of censorship became law (Commission on Obscenity and Pornography, Vol. 2, 1971). He had himself appointed as special agent of the Post Office, in charge of enforcing the Federal law. Until his death in 1915, he used his position to censor U.S. mail for whatever he classified as obscene or pornographic. All contraceptive information and merchandise were thus classified. He used his postal squad not only to confiscate materials in the U.S. mail, but also to stage raids directly on the premises of manufacturers. He was equally fervent in attacking both female nudity in art classes and obscene literature in retail stores. By obscenity, he meant anything that would suggest impure, or concupiscent and libidinous thoughts, especially to young men. Medical books, such as Russell Trall's *Sexual Physiology* (1881), were included.

Of obscenity he wrote: "The effect of this cursed business on our youth and society, no pen can describe. It breeds lust. Lust defiles the body, debauches the imagination, corrupts the mind, deadens the will, destroys the memory, sears the conscience, hardens the heart, and damns the soul. It unnerves the arm, and steals away the elastic step. It robs the soul of manly virtues, and imprints upon the mind of the youth, visions that throughout life curse the man or woman. Like a panorama, the imagination seems to keep this hated thing before the mind, until it wears its way deeper and deeper, plunging the victim into practices that he loathes. This traffic has made rakes and libertines in society—skeletons in many a household. The family is polluted, the home desecrated, and each generation born into the world is more and more cursed by the inherited weakness, the harvest of this seed-sowing of the Evil one'' (Comstock, 1880).

Degeneracy Theory

Victorian antisexualism was not invented by Comstock and his supporters in government, law, religion, and society. It was amplified by them. Its origins were rooted in eighteenth century sexual degeneracy theory (Money, 1985). The most articulate exponent of this theory was the Swiss physician, Simon André Tissot. By assimilating degeneracy theory into the medical teaching of the day, he gave it medical respectability and immense influence that persists even to the present. The first edition of his book, *A Treatise on the Diseases Produced by Onanism,* 1758, was in Latin. The first American translation appeared in 1832.

The two great cornerstones of degeneracy theory are the secret vice and the social vice, masturbation and prostitution, respectively. Both wasted the vital fluid, semen, which was believed to be made from the most precious drops of the blood. They also overstimulated and drained the nervous system with the erethism of concupiscent thoughts and carnal desire.

Like his predecessors long before him, Tissot knew that one of the effects of castration of the male is the drying up of the semen. From this he drew the momentously wrong conclusion that all the devirilizing effects of castration could be attributed to the loss of this vital fluid. Then, by one more step of logic, he concluded that similar degenerative effects could be prevented by conservation of the semen. The missing proposition in this logic, still undiscovered in Tissot's day, is that postcastrational degeneration of virility is caused not by loss of semen, but of male sex hormone secreted from the testes.

Tissot extended his logic of equating the effects of castration with semen loss by generalizing the effects of semen loss to include degeneracy in general. To justify this generalization, he pointed to the diseases attributed to the loss of semen by way of the social vice. They degenerated the health not only of promiscuous men, but also of the prostitutes who served them, and worse still, of the babies of prostitutes who became pregnant. The missing proposition in this logic, also undiscovered in Tissot's day, is that the degeneracies, so-called, of the social vice were caused by contagious venereal infections. Germ theory would not be discovered until a century later. In the eighteenth century, syphilis and gonorrhea were still considered to be one disease, not two; and the white discharge of gonorrhea was equated with the white fluid of the semen discharged in either self-abuse or coitus, or in the so-called disease of spermatorrhea (wet dreams).

Degeneracy caused by loss of the vital fluid applied also to marital coitus. In keeping with ecclesiastical doctrine, Tissot recommended continence, except for the duty of procreation. He also proposed the quaint notion that in marital coitus, vital humors, or *torrens invisibles*, are exchanged in the perspiration, so that there is no actual degenerative loss.

Even though the woman was included in this conceit, females really did not fit into degeneracy theory, since they do not lose a vital fluid corresponding to semen. Concupiscence saved the day, since women as well as men could degenerate themselves by harboring the thoughts and fantasies of carnal desire that drove them into the excesses of the secret or the social vice, awake or in dreams.

Degeneracy theory replaced its predecessor, demon-possession theory, as a multipurpose theory of disease. It dominated medicine without challenge until germ theory encroached upon it in the 1870s, and opened the 20th century door to scientific theories of the cause of disease. For over a century, degeneracy theory had been used to explain just about every ill except fractures and wounds—and even then it had served to explain defective or impaired healing. Degeneracy theory lingers on today in sexual medicine, almost exclusively. Especially in the popular media, those afflicted with a paraphilia are frequently stigmatized as sexual degenerates.

Abstinence Theory in America

In America, the first public crusader for degeneracy theory was the Rev. Sylvester Graham. The three big principles of his health crusade, in the 1830s, were food, fitness, and abstinence. He is the eponym of graham crackers, which being sweetened, would not have been included in his brown-flour diet.

Graham had many lesser-known followers. His most famous successor, who became a physician in the 1870s, was John Harvey Kellogg. A youthful disciple of Graham, he incorporated Graham's principles of health reform into the practices of the Battle Creek Sanitarium of the then new Seventh Day Adventist Faith. From there they migrated to Loma Linda, the Adventist medical school in California, where they still survive.

Kellogg's medical hobby was dietary health. He processed cereals and nuts as substitutes for meat, to suppress carnal desire induced by the eating of meat. Few of today's eaters of Kellogg's Corn Flakes know that he invented them, almost literally, as antimasturbation food.

Kellogg was degeneracy theory's most ardent antimasturbation advocate. For intractable cases of masturbation in boys he recommended sewing up the foreskin with silver wire; or, if that failed, circumcision without anesthesia. For girls, he recommended burning out the clitoris with carbolic acid. For fathers, he wrote detailed instructions of how they should silently encroach upon their sleeping sons and rapidly pull back the blankets. An erect penis was prima facie evidence of the sleeping sinner caught in secret vice.

Kellogg knew nothing of nocturnal penile tumescence. Whatever his wife might have told him about his own erection during sleep was forever unknown to him, because he saved his semen by sleeping alone and never consummating his marriage. Instead, he was a klismaphiliac who had his senior medical assistant give him an enema every morning, after breakfast.

As an abdominal surgeon, Kellogg was highly regarded profesionally. He kept up to date on developments in the new medical science of biochemistry. By contrast, he neglected germ theory and the new science of bacteriology founded by Pasteur and Koch in the 1870s. Degeneracy theory was too firmly entrenched in Kellogg's mentality to be dislodged, even though he lived until 1943 and was ninety-one years old when he died.

Concupiscence

There was no place for Kellogg's anachronistic antisexualism in twentieth century scientific theories of disease. Scientifically, it is easy to discredit the doctrine that loss of semen, whether by masturbation, wet dreams, or copulation, causes the full panoply of diseases attributed to it in degeneracy theory. The doctrine of concupiscent thought and carnal desire as a cause of the same diseases is also easy to discredit.

Beyond medicine, however, the antisexualism of degeneracy theory has continued its occupancy of religion, education, media, and law where it is too slithery for science to reach it. It has abandoned its physiological doctrine of conservation of vital fluids, and reinforced its moral doctrine of the social contagion of concupiscent thoughts and carnal desire. Its chief bugaboo is pornography, though the Comstockian phobia of any form of explicit erotic knowledge still persists.

Comstock's antisexual fanaticism had allowed anything to be defined as obscene and pornographic if it might suggest impure, concupiscent or libidinous thoughts. This definition embraced everything, from the least to the most exotic, from any part of the world or any period of history, that might ever prove sexually arousing to anyone of any age, experience, or mental type. Underwear advertisements in the Sears, Roebuck mail-order catalogue would have met the force of Comstock's wrath, had he discovered that farm boys could put them to use in masturbation fantasies. Indeed, by his own definition, Comstock had to condemn as marital purience the arousal a husband or wife brought on by their seeing one another, clothed or naked. It was sexual arousal itself that Comstock found morally repugnant and antithetical to the welfare of both the individual and society.

The Eye of the Beholder

Though society today no longer solidly endorses Comstock's complete brand of antisexualism, it has not been able to decide, legislatively and in the courts, where to draw the dividing line between permissible and forbidden depictions of explicit sex—that is between nonpornography and pornography. When the national Commission published its 1971 *Technical Report on Obscenity and Pornography,* it quoted (Vol. 2, p. 15) Supreme Court Justice Potter Stewart's famous dictum on defining hard-core pornography: ". . . perhaps I could never succeed in intelligibly [defining it]. But I know it when I see it . . ."

Justice Stewart was more empirically on target than he might have recognized in thus locating pornography fairly and squarely in the eye of the beholder. The best empirical definition of pornography is that it is explicitly depicted erotic and sexual material that generates in a viewer, reader, or listener who has access to it, a sense of being sneaky, surreptitious, and illicit, provided access to the same material by the same person at a younger age would have been prohibited, prevented, and punished.

In Asian culture, kissing is pornographic. Kissing scenes that children of the West take for granted in movies and on television are rigorously censored in the East. When Western children become adults, they do not join political action committees for the suppression of kissing in public as pornographic. Had they grown up as, say, Islamic fundamentalists, they would condemn permissiveness of sex above the belt as a sign of the moral degeneracy of the West. The contemporary change toward permitting topless exposure of female nipples on the beach and in bars would be proof positive of pornographic depravity, as indeed it is for some Christian fundamentalists, also.

Pornography in our Western culture applies chiefly to sex below the belt—to exposure of the nude genitalia to the public view, and to any strategy, even simulated, of their use in erotic practices. In the present age of xeroxed copies, polaroid photography and home videotapes, it is absolutely impossible for the agencies of society to impose totally effective censorship on sexual explicitness.

Outmaneuvered by technology, society has been afflicted with a case of double vision. Not only once, but twice, it recognizes pornography when it sees it, even though it may not be able to define it. Once is for youth under eighteen years of age, and the other for adults.

For youth the old Comstockian principle holds, namely, that they must be protected from moral degeneracy that would be induced by exposure to any representation of explicit sexuality and eroticism. Thus explicit description and depiction even of normal heterosexual intercourse is censored. With only sporadic exceptions, this censorship applies to the curriculum of sexual learning, whether at home, church, or school, despite the fact that normal heterosexuality is the official moral goal of the outcome of sexual development.

For adults, the old Comstockian principle has crumbled. Heterosexual intercourse, being by definition normal, falls short of qualifying as obscene or pornographic, even when shown in explicit detail on film. Nonetheless, the old Comstockian phobia of pornographic contagion and degeneracy haunts every public decision on pornography. Despite its false premise of contagion and degeneracy, this is the phobia that has paralyzed society into a state of obsessional indecision regarding that which qualifies as normophilic pornography and is permitted, and that which does not.

Phobia of Paraphilic Contagion

The idea that the activity depicted in pornography is contagious, and that having taken hold, the contagion descends an accelerating spiral of degeneracy, can be disproved empirically by almost anyone. Ordinary people who are not erotically aroused by, say, coprophilia or urophilia may prove to themselves that coprophilia and urophilia are not contagious if they watch a dozen times a dozen movies of people ingesting, spreading, and spraying feces and urine. At the end they will be indifferent or disgusted, but not capable of being sexuoerotically aroused by the products of excretion.

The pornography that most exacerbates society's phobia of contagion and degeneracy is, in fact, the material that depicts the imagery and fantasy of specific paraphilias. The illegal paraphilias incite the greatest threat. Paraphilic pornography, however, is able to stimulate sexuoerotic arousal only in those who already have the same type of paraphilic imagery built into their lovemap, which predisposes them to be responsive. For others, it is devoid of sexuoerotic appeal. It satisfies only intellectual curiosity, which rapidly becomes satiated.

The paraphilias that are not defined as illegal have their own pornography which society more or less disregards and is not threatened by. Paraphilic transvestite pornography is in this class, provided the genitals are not exposed. The same applies to the pornography of acrotomophilia in which exposure of the bare stump, rather than the genitalia of an amputee is the stimulus to sexuoerotic arousal.

The type of pornography that evokes society's greatest ambivalence is that which depicts sexuoerotic practices that are widespread, but are also illegal. Oral sex is an example. Fellatio and cunnilingus, even between husband and wife, are illegal in many jurisdictions. So also are sexuoerotic activities between two partners of the same sex; and likewise consensual bondage and discipline which might be legally construed as assault. The size of the population represented in the aforesaid activities is counted in the tens of millions. They do not become degenerates. Thus the contagion and degeneracy argument is often restated to apply only to youth: it is contended that, even though they may be predisposed to such sexuoerotic practices, they may stay "in the closet" permanently unless they are "brought out" by pornography. There are no empirical data to support this contention, and none to support the value of staying in the closet.

A rational way for society to deal with pornography is the antithesis of phobia and criminalization, and also the antithesis of unsupervised laissez faire. It is based on the analogy of death and the crucifixion. Millions of children learn in explicit detail, with vividly realistic models and pictures, how to perform a crucifixion. They learn also the moral principle involved, and they do not play crucifixion games with their dolls and playmates.

Explicit sexuality could be dealt with in the same uncensored way. It would require a new generation of society emancipated from the contagion and degeneracy theory of sex and eroticism, and capable of transmitting to youth the moral principles that differentiates paraphilic and nonparaphilic lovemaps. Positive moral endorsement of explicit sex and eroticism of the nonparaphilic type in the lovemaps of the young could, eventually, produce a society emancipated from centuries of futility in rolling the Sisyphus stone of paraphilia uphill, and never reaching the summit of success.

Bisexualism and Autassassinophilia in the Lovemap of a Male Hermaphrodite

Nosocomial Stress and Abuse

As everyone knows, very young children all too often anticipate a visit to the dentist or doctor, or even the barber, as an aversive experience. As early as six months of age, a baby, having become aversively conditioned to a white coat and needle pricks, cries upon entering the clinic for the next followup. For the infant, there is no ethic of informed consent. Decisions are adult-imposed, ostensibly in the best interests of the child, though arguably so in some instances. Neonatal circumcision is an example. In 1974, the American Academy of Pediatrics declared it an unnecessary operation. It is imposed without anesthetic. The afflicted infant's response is to scream, or to go into a state of silent shock. In either case, it is assumed that the reaction will be short-lived, and without serious sequelae. The same assumption is made regarding other aversive clinical procedures that are imposed on children, without their informed consent, as they grow older.

It is true, of course, that some aversive procedures, no matter how stressful, are a matter of life and death, for which a decision has to be made by adults acting on the child's behalf. In other instances, however, aversive procedures are elective, and can be postponed until the child has reached a state of being mentally prepared to deal with them. To impose such a procedure by edict, without adequate preparation, is tantamount to child abuse—nosocomial child abuse—and it is experienced as such by a child.

For some children, the experience of a clinical procedure as nosocomial abuse happens not only once, but intermittently over several years and multiple hospital admissions. In such cases, the effect is not transient but cumulative and the sequelae may be long-lasting. In fact, they may chronically impair the young patient's ability to cope with the ordinary exigencies of living over his/her entire lifetime. Such a chronic and deleterious effect of nosocomial abuse is a likely outcome of any severe birth defect that requires multiple hospital admissions and followup clinic visits. Birth defect of the genitalia is one such example. Masculinizing surgical repair of genital ambiguity may require not the initially projected two or three surgical admissions, but as many as fifteen or more, as in the case here reported.

One purpose of this present chapter is to put on record a case of male hermaphroditism in which multiple surgical admissions in childhood were experienced and assimilated as nosocomial abuse. One sequel in adulthood is a self-destructive, paraphilic coping strategy. It defeats in part the purpose of the program of masculinization of which surgery was a part. The case has been selected from among forty cases of male hermaphroditic birth defect, reared as males and followed in the Psychohormonal Research Unit. It dramatically draws attention to the fact that nosocomial abuse and its long-term effects, sexuoerotic and otherwise, have typically been overlooked.

For this report the patient's complete consolidated medical, surgical and psychohormonal record from age five to age thirty-five was indexed, and then systematically abstracted in sections as required for the clinical biography and coping strategies that follow. The psychohormonal segment of the record included reports from social agencies, as well as the results of psychological tests and transcripts of interviews tape recorded progressively across the life span. Interviews were conducted according to a systematic schedule of clinical inquiry for the purpose of obtaining developmental information (Money and Primrose, 1969). In addition, there were many interviews focused, as needed, on crisis intervention.

Clinical Biography

Information regarding the patient's birth was obtained retrospectively from the mother when she first brought him to Johns Hopkins for genital surgery at age five. She had lost one pregnancy prior to the birth of her first child, a girl. Twelve months later the patient was born, followed within the next two years by a brother and sister.

The mother was twenty-three years old at the time of the patient's birth, which was one month premature. It was a home delivery. Though a young physician had been in attendance, the mother did not know where the obstetrical record might be retrieved. She recalled having been told that the baby was a boy, and that she should seek a consultation at a nearby hospital. She had immediately recognized that the baby's genitalia did not look normal and that there were no testicles in evidence. Neighbors, she said, told her that the child was a morphodite. The term was unfamiliar to her. They said he was a freak whom she should put in a circus, for a side show. She recalled, though there are no records to confirm it, that she had taken the baby to the hospital because of swelling in the genital area, and had been recommended to give warm baths, which did reduce the swelling. There is a hospital record of two pediatric outpatient visits at age three, for tonsillitis and impetigo, respectively, with no mention of the genital defect.

At the age of three months, the baby and his mother went to live out of state with the maternal grandmother. The medical opinion that the mother recalled having received in her mother's home town was that "it looks like he is both, a girl and a boy," and that she should take the child back to Baltimore, and to Johns Hopkins. After about a year, she herself returned to Baltimore, but left the child with her mother. The child was aged 2 yrs. 3 mos. when she returned a year later, and was "wearing little dresses and ribbons tied on long, brown hair, all fixed up as a little girl." Dismayed at what the grandmother had done, the mother immediately arranged for a hair cut, put the child in boy's clothes, and brought him back to Baltimore not as a girl, but a boy. A quarter of a century later, the only memory of this change that the patient recalled was that, for the winter train ride north, he wore a new, blue snow suit—being blue, of course, for a boy.

By school age, the child's behavior at home was like that of "any other boy," except that sometimes he cried and asked his mother why he couldn't stand up, as his brother did, to urinate. She told him that he would have to have surgery. At school, his age mates would ask why he had to sit to urinate. He responded with elective mutism, social distancing, and self-isolation. A school medical officer initiated the Johns Hopkins referral and the first evaluation for treatment of the birth defect of the sex organs. The child was 5 yrs. 8 mos. old. For eleven weeks he was admitted for exploratory laparotomy and the first stage of hypospadiac repair.

The genital examination showed a hypospadiac micropenis, bound down with chordee (Plate 1). Insofar as it could be stretched, its stretched length measured 5 cm. and with width 1.5 cm. The urinary meatus opened, slit-like onto the perineum, without a urogenital sinus. There was a bifid labioscrotal structure, with "very mobile oval bodies" in the region of the inguinal canals. Rectally, neither uterus nor prostate were palpable. Urethroscopy showed a vestigial vaginal pouch entering the urethra near the neck of the bladder. The exploratory laparotomy confirmed the absence of mullerian organs internally. Surgery was not extended to include the inguinal gonads which, therefore, were not biopsied.

The progress of hypospadiac repair was not as expeditious as originally projected. There were postsurgical complications of severe keloid scar formation, recurrent urethral strictures, and urinary fistulas. Because of these complications, there were six different surgical admissions and eleven different surgical procedures in the two and a half years between first admission and age eight. At the end of this period standing to urinate still was impossible. Worse still, there was continuous urinary dribbling that created a social problem and prevented school attendance for a year at age eight. Because of sloughing of the left nipple and the skin-graft donor site below it, this region required its own graft from the left thigh, leaving the torso disfigured in two places.

The fifth operation done at the time the boy had his seventh birthday was a reconstructive urethroplasty. Three months later, there was a right-sided infection with epididymitis. This necessitated removal of the right inguinal testis. Four months and two operations later, the boy was again admitted, this time with acute urinary obstruction secondary to urethral stricture. After a suprapubic cystostomy had been performed, the urinary drainage tube became blocked one night. In the morning, urine had extravasated through the abdominal wall. The boy's calls for help had been ignored by the night staff. Two further operations during this admission corrected the urinary obstruction, but required that the boy sit to urinate from an opening in the perineum. The surgical correction of this defect required five more admissions and five more operations between the ages of eight and thirteen. The final operation was the fifteenth.

Upon discharge three weeks before his fourteenth birthday, the patient was at last able to stand to urinate, though not very well. As of the present, the urinary orifice opens into a ragged, funnel-shaped sinus on the shaft of the penis (Plate 2). From the glans penis to the urinary orifice, the skin of the constructed urethral tube has separated in the midline, thus forming an open gutter for a distance of one and a quarter inches. After the cessation of urination, urine has apparently backed up internally so that it then slowly leaks out through the funnel. There is a second source of leakage in the perineum, between the scrotum and the anus, where the former site of a postoperative, indwelling urinary catheter has failed to seal completely (Plate 3).

The patient did not tell anyone about his hygienic problem of urinary leakage for fifteen years, until he was twenty-six years old. At that time he opted against a surgical referral. His explanation was: "I didn't mention it until today because I don't want to go back in the hospital, not for that." On the same basis—"no more cutting"—he had at age nineteen opted against the implantation of a prosthetic right testis.

In the fifteen years between ages eleven and twenty-six, there had been three surgical admissions: at fourteen for severe urethral infection; at sixteen for tonsillectomy; and at twenty-four for repair of a left inguinal hernia. In addition to these three admissions, there began at age eighteen a long-continuing series of outpatient and emergency-room visits, punctuated by psychiatric and alcohol-detoxification admissions.

The presenting problem at age eighteen was premature ejaculation and copulatory erectile failure. Another problem was the onset, then recent, of acutely severe asthmatic attacks requiring emergency-room treatment. They have persisted until the present, with an annual average of three emergency-room treatments.

A third problem was brought to the fore at age eighteen, namely, increasingly severe and painful osteoarthritic contractures of the third, fourth, and fifth fingers of each hand, representing a worsening of a congenital phalangeal deformity. The knees also were subject to arthritic pain. The upshot of a plastic surgical consultation was to postpone intervention so long as the contractures did not become grossly incapacitating.

The first psychiatric admission was an overnight in the emergency room for depression and suicidal thoughts, and the second for exposure, frost bite, and facial contusions. The patient was twenty-six years old. Over the next nine years, in at least ten different hospital emergency rooms, psychiatric hospitals, and alcohol-detoxification centers within the metropolitan area, the count of ascertained admissions totaled twenty-five, and maybe more.

The typical sequence was that the patient would be brought to an emergency room, in several instances unconscious, suffering from wounds incurred either by accident or attack, while inebriated. After an overnight in the emergency room, he would be discharged either to outpatient or residential rehabilitative care, or to a psychiatric admission. There were six different psychiatric admissions of two to four weeks' duration, and two longer ones ordered by the court as a sequel to arrest and imprisonment for drunk and disorderly conduct.

Presently, at the age of thirty-five, the patient is again enrolled in a rehabilitation program, and again is on treatment with Antabuse for alcoholism. He is also on prednisone for asthma. From the latter he has a mildly cushingoid facies. He has also a problem of hypertension (blood pressure 140/94).

During a psychiatric admission at age twenty-eight, hormonal levels were ascertained as tabulated:

Hormone	Level	Norm
Testosterone	456 ng/dl	575 ± 150
Androstenedione	104 ng/dl	109 ± 20
Serum FSH	711 ng/ml	187 ± 89
Serum LH	158 ng/ml	50 ± 14

From a skin biopsy, the level of 5α-reductase was found to be only minimally subnormal. Intracellular androgen-binding receptors were normal in number, but subnormal in the level of androgen that they bound. The elevated levels of FSH and LH could not readily be accounted for, except in terms of an unidentified partial deficiency in gonadal function.

Karyotyping with the Giemsa and quinacrine banding techniques was read as normal 46,XY with a minor polymorphism, namely a large satellite region on chromosome 14.

The dimensions of the penis at age thirty-five were: stretched length 12.5 cm (5 inches); and base width 4.5 cm (1.5 inches). The one remaining testis, on the right, measured 3 x 3.5 cm. Distribution of pubic and axillary hair was normally masculine, though hair on the body and face was sparse, with shaving required once or twice a week. The voice was properly masculinized. The overall manner and appearance was unremarkably that of a male (Plate 4), except for an unsightly scar, the site of a skin graft, that partially obliterated the left areola and nipple. The scar on the left thigh was not so unsightly.

Recently, at the patient's own request, a sperm count was done elsewhere, and reported to him as prognostic of infertility because of sperms that are too few and malformed.

The risk of urinary infection is recurrent. The most recent attack was six months ago. It was treated on an outpatient basis with antibiotics.

First Coping Strategy: Elective Mutism

As a boy of four in nursery school, before his first hospital evaluation for hypospadias, the patient already was known for keeping to himself and not talking very much either to his teacher or other children. Some of the other children would ask the teacher why he was so quiet. They had probably watched him when he went to the bathroom, the mother speculated, because they had also asked why he had to sit down to urinate.

During the eleven weeks of the child's first hospital admission, the phenomenon of not talking became recognized as so extreme in degree as to qualify as elective mutism. The surgical housestaff were nonplussed by his failure to communicate and respond except, it was noted, to have "a psychogenic fit of monotonous moaning and wild screaming" when he got a needle or had a dressing removed. They wrongly inferred that he was mentally defective, and this stigma became perpetuated in the medical chart for several years.

One psychiatric consultant interpreted the reaction rather as apathetic listlessness, and another as a quasi-catatonic inhibition of social responsiveness, possibly related to disillusionment regarding surgery: he had expected repair of his penis, but had received only an exploratory laparotomy. Prior to discharge from this same admission, the first surgical stage of hypospadiac repair, namely release of chordee, was performed. Subsequently, beginning at age 5 yrs. 10 mos., there began a progressive lifting of elective mutism.

Ten months later, even though further surgery would be needed before standing to urinate would be possible, the boy surprised his pediatric endocrinologist by being able to talk to him. He explained that formerly he hadn't been sure what he was, a boy or a girl, whereas "I'm going to be all right now that I've had my operation." At home he told his brother the same thing. He was not modest when undressing or bathing with his siblings around.

The extent to which, at this stage of his life, he may have known about the year he spent as a girl is not on record. However, he did recall, at age twenty-six, that his cousins had told him that his grandmother had considered him a girl and called him "my little sweetheart."

He was not confronted with the concept of amphoteric genital anatomy until, at the age of nineteen, his mother was having a family talk about his operations. "She said I'm different," he reported, "because I had, uhm, a little female, and the male sex organs. . . . It really shocked me. . . . Medically, I wanted to find out for myself just what it was."

At this time, he was given a repeat explanation, illustrated with diagrams of fetal differentiation, of how the genitalia appear when they are "unfinished at birth" (Money, 1968; 1975). At his own insistence, he viewed also the presurgical medical photograph of his genitalia at age five. The visible evidence that there was no structure resembling a vagina at this preoperative stage was contradicted by the postoperative evidence, which he would still see and touch, of a slit in the perineum (at the site where a urinary catheter had several times been in place) that still allowed a seepage of urine. To him this slit had for years signified that he had once had a vagina. "It made me feel like a freak," he said.

From age seven onward, the boy did not ever again experience elective mutism globally, only episodically. There were some residual unspeakable things in his life. The persistence of urinary leakage was one of them, for to speak of it would risk additional surgery. Also, early in adolescence, at age fourteen, he was not able to talk about what he knew, or needed to know about sexual development either in general, or in reference to his own status as a genitally imperfect male.

With these exceptions, his coping strategy changed from the disengagement of elective mutism to active participation in the business of living and achieving success as a male.

Ambition and Achievement

One of the side effects of postsurgical problems with urinary leakage, already mentioned, was that the boy lost a year of schooling at age eight. Having the surgical confirmation of his sexual status as a male, however, he was no longer afflicted with elective mutism in the classroom. When he was able to attend school, he was academically an achiever.

Concurrent with this change, there was an upward shift in scores on the Wechsler Intelligence Scale for Children. The comparative IQs at age 5 yrs. 11 mos. and 7 yrs. 7 mos. were Verbal IQ: 68, 94; Performance IQ: 74, 106; Full IQ: 68, 99; respectively.

It was not until many years later that, as a young man of nineteen and a half, the patient explicitly formulated his academic ambition. In the context of talking about transcending ghetto poverty, and comparing himself with others, he said: "With me, I've always been different. I've always said, even as a child, that if I ever get, if I ever live to get older, I'm going to try to outstrive the conditions I'm in. I've always said that. No matter how much it takes, if it doesn't kill me, I'm going to try to better my conditions—better myself. . . . It's rough for any child who grows up in the ghetto. If you have a broken family, too, it's not easy; and I've had a lot of disappointments. I've had a lot of them."

He had been only three years old when his parents separated. His father moved out of state and thenceforth had only sporadic, brief contacts with his son. Because of the absence of "a male identification figure" in the boy's life, a social worker in the city's family assistance program referred him to the local Big Brother organization when he was nine and a half years old. The man who became his Big Brother sponsor worked in the administration of a local college and thus, by example, endorsed the boy's ambition to educate himself beyond the ghetto.

The course of his progress was interrupted when he began his sophomore year in high school. He changed from full-time schooling to working part-time and taking high school courses, part-time, at night. This change meant that his mother would lose family assistance funds if he lived at home as a wage earner. So he left home to live with an aunt and uncle.

Two other contemporary happenings were that his high school girlfriend broke up with him because her sex life with him was, in his opinion, unsatisfactory; and that he had the first severely acute asthmatic crisis, and the onset of arthritic joint pain. "Physically," he said, "I feel like I'm falling apart, but I'm trying to keep it all together, mentally."

Despite these challenges to his academic ambition, he continued working and studying. He was twenty-one when he obtained a high school diploma. In the fall of that same year, having just turned twenty-two, he enrolled as a freshman in a local college. He took courses on a full-time basis. He worked on a part-time basis, evenings and weekends, to support himself. The campus was within commuting distance of the home of his aunt and uncle with whom he resided. Lacking a family of their own, they had taken him in permanently so that he would have privacy and quietness for studying, which he would not have had in his mother's house.

He began his freshman year "on a high note, enthusiastic and confident," he said, and made the Dean's list for the first two semesters.

Then he began to procrastinate on assignments in favor of drinking and partying with uneducated and unemployed off-campus friends. Progressively, his ambition and achievement disintegrated. Those who stood by him became alienated, and his provocation of personal catastrophy and destruction became a way of life. This change did not prevent graduation, but it did delay it for a year. Then at the age of twenty-seven, when his college handed him a bachelor's degree, fate handed him a martyr's destiny of self-destruction. Act three of a Greek tragedy began.

Provoking Catastrophe

As an undergraduate, he had revealed a sign of self-sabotage for the first time when, at the age of twenty-four-and-a-half years, and after an absence of fifteen months, he requested a psychoendocrine clinic appointment—"because I didn't like the idea of being locked in the dark and doing something I didn't have any control over." His loss of control occurred when he came home drunk and unruly, foul-mouthed and violent toward his aunt and uncle who had shared their home with him. Once, late at night, when he became drunkenly torpid, he had left food to incinerate in the oven, thus endangering the dwelling.

Though, on this occasion, he effected a reconciliation with his aunt and uncle, the binges of drinking and drunken rage alternating with binges of remorseful repentance continued. After almost two years, there was a particularly violent blowup, after which he was homeless. "I want to destroy that rage in me," he said, "and I want to destroy me at the same time." His strategy was to get drunk enough to go out and rob someone, in the hope that the police would beat and arrest him, or better still, put a bullet through the back of his head as he tried to escape. "The idea of getting killed is a very potential thing, very strong," he said.

Four years later while once again in the clinic, and still showing the effects of a hangover, he reverted to the same theme: "I'm scared I'm going to go out there and buy me a gun, and just go somewhere, and start shooting people, and just let, let the police, just let the police end all this turmoil. I'm scared of that. I really am. I don't really want to hurt nobody, but at the same time I want somebody to hurt me. . . . I guess I'm talking a little foolish, but it's not foolishness. I can't find no happiness. I can't get nowhere. I can't, you know—I'm just tired. . . . I keep losing all the battles. And all the wars."

In the ten years of his life between the ages of twenty-five and thirty-five, there were literally dozens of times when the patient did get high enough to go out on the street, or into a gay bar or adult book store, and stage-manage an assault on himself. This pathological reaction required only the amount of alcohol that would make many people mellow. Rarely, he would smoke also a little marijuana or swallow a Valium or other sedative pill. Frequently he would pass out and have amnesia for how he had been injured, whether by assault, walking into a moving vehicle, or falling. He would also not recall how he had been rescued and transported to the nearest hospital emergency room.

Time after time, his pathetic plight would galvanize those who tended him into mobilizing all the resources of rehabilitation at their command. Dozens of people spent many hundreds of unpaid therapeutic and rehabilitative hours on his behalf. There were four occasions in particular when success was within his grasp, and he was placed in a salaried public-service job, teaching or providing social service for the underprivileged. In each instance he lost everything when he went on another binge of drinking and self-injury, and omitted to register for sick leave within the specified time limit. Reduced to penury, he would seek shelter in one of two inner-city rescue missions, or else live on the streets, until embarking on the next cycle of rehabilitative effort and its collapse.

Masturbation as Punishment

Shortly before he turned thirty, he disclosed that he had discovered using "masturbation as a form of punishment. . . . I've discovered I guess through trial and error, a new angle in trying to find other ways of relieving my anger than drinking and getting myself in trouble. I figured that now when I'm full of anger and frustration that I resort to masturbation, vigorous masturbation—even to the point of hurting myself in my pelvic region, and also around my abdomen. I do this practically all night long. It don't have to be night. I do it whenever I'm alone by myself, whenever I do get the feeling of frustration and anger; and I do it forcibly and sometimes continuously all night, off and on, to the point that the next day I'm sore, sore not in the penis area but around my joints and my pelvis area—also to the point where I think I strained myself, sometimes. To me it's a form of relief and a feeling, too, at the same time, I guess. Because, when I do it, I like the feeling I get from it. Not just the—it's a feeling of ejaculation, but also the alternate feeling, like a feeling that now you've done it you relieve that anger. It's just the fact of doing it and getting it over with.''

Masturbating in this way excluded erotic thoughts of having sex. "Maybe I'll start thinking about the last time Candy and I had a relationship. That's the initial thought. And I get an erection on, and then I start masturbating. But right in the midst of masturbation, thinking about sex is starting to fade out; and I don't think about anything in particular. But I may have in the back of my mind that I'm thinking about, you know, punishment for letting myself get into the predicament [of having no employment] that I am in. And to the extent that I can't do anything about it, you know, this is my way of saying it's what you expect from a child. . . . I think I use my penis because my penis is the only extension of me that—after all the operating I've been through, it's still ever present in my mind about the agonies I went through.''

This theme emerged spontaneously for a second time in an interview five years later. "Usually it happens," the patient said, "like when I feel depressed by loneliness and because I've botched up a relationship—as far as like trying to form a relationship with a female, or with a guy, a male; or if I'm in a mood, what I call just out of touch with what's really going on with me. I tend to, like, masturbate repeatedly and vigorously, over and over, to the point of exhaustion, and to the point of just beating my penis to death, you know. And when I do it, it's a form of punishment for being bad, or for botching up something, or for being angry. . . . The climax, it's a good feeling for the first five or six times. Then, near the end, it's a feeling of, of numbness. It's a feeling in terms of sore. It's not pleasure any more. That's why I know I'm punishing myself. . . . All the muscles in my groin and in my legs begin to tighten up, and they begin to feel tired and achey.''

Heterosexual Defeatism

After a hiatus of three years, he initiated a return to the psychohormonal clinic at the age of seventeen, as he had begun his sex life and was having a problem with the functioning of his penis. Earlier in boyhood, there had been, at age five or six, an episode of kissing his sister's girlfriend, and lying on top of her, both with their clothes on; and at age ten, with another girl, kissing and genital fondling. At age seventeen, he and his high school girlfriend decided to have sexual intercourse. It was his first attempt, and he felt inferior as she had begun her sex life at age fourteen with a boyfriend aged twenty-three. In the patient's opinion, she knew what to expect of a partner with a penis much larger than his own. His inferiority intensified with repeated failures to get a good erection, or having got one, to maintain it. If he was able to put his penis in her vagina, it would ejaculate immediately. Then it would not erect again. "What makes me feel so afraid," he said, "is because we've been going together for nine months, and doing it for nine months, and she only actually came with me once. . . . She don't never get no satisfaction from it." With variation in foreplay and afterplay, they tried accommodating to one another for a little over a year—"and then me and her broke up. . . . It was too much strain and too much worry and too much frustration—too much embarrassment. . . . I mean all we just had to scream about was about our sex life. That's all. . . . If I didn't satisfy her, and me knowing it—that she'd probably go to somebody else and get it, that would make me feel even worse."

Seventeen years later, recalling this girlfriend, he said, "That was the only true love, young love, of my life. . . . I couldn't satisfy her. I think that had a great impact, even to his day, on my life."

After the breakup, he began "playing around," with two other girls, "but I'm not getting involved," he said. With these partners, the problem of impotence "just went away. . . . Perhaps I was too much emotionally involved with the other girl," he speculated, by way of explanation. Subsequently, there was a recurrence of impotence in relationships of a casual nature, including two in which the partner was, ostensibly, a virgin.

The issue of deficiency in sexual performance faded in prominence, however, and was replaced by the agonies of adversarial fighting and reconciliation in two other long-term relationships. In neither of these relationships did the imperfection of the patient's genitalia evoke complaints from the partner. In each instance, the woman was older than the patient, by approximately five and twenty years, respectively.

The younger of the two women had known him since he was a small child. She and her husband became close friends with him when he was in college. A couple of years after graduating, upon release from a month of psychiatric hospitalization, he lived for a time in a rented room in their house. They needed the money, according to the patient. The husband had sickle-cell disease. Periodically, he had acute attacks, one of which killed him in his mid-thirties. The relationship between the three of them was one of pathological interdependency, punctuated by episodes of violent quarreling associated with drinking that began sociably. It was one of those relationships in which each of the participants had a different version of what had happened. The patient's own version was that the husband's disease rendered him impotent so that his sexually impoverished wife would, possibly with her husband's collusion when they all three were loosened up with alcohol, signal a sexual advance to the patient, and he would respond. The version of the couple themselves was that the patient ranted and raved in a quite irresponsible and crazy way when he drank too much. He also became, at times, unpredictably threatening and violent, which he himself confirmed (see below). After the husband died, the widow and the patient kept up a social, but not a sexual friendship.

The older of the two women with whom the patient maintained a long-term relationship was also a widow, an attractive woman who looked younger than her years. To earn a living, she took in lodgers, including one or two who were elderly or infirm and needed daily care. In his final student year, the patient became a lodger in her house, having first met her daughter who had dated him and had had sex with him on a few occasions. He recalled having been ''completely flabbergasted when Bernice [the mother] wanted to fuck.'' He was a student, and his reaction was, ''What the hell! If she wants some dick, okay, here's a good way to get some spending money.'' She was good-hearted in helping him financially. About a year later, their relationship began to change. It became ''more than just sexual,'' he said. They enjoyed each other's company, helped each other, and began to like each other. ''You could call it love,'' he concluded. His partner allowed that his penis was small. ''It's like a baby's,'' she said, 'but then it's not how long it is, it's how you do with it.''

When his status as a lodger terminated, presumably because of the irregularity of his rent payments, the relationship did not. It was sometimes harmonious, and sometimes fractious. Like all of the patient's close relationships, including those with members of his family, this one was contentious and strife-ridden whenever he was on a drinking binge.

Despite the turmoil of her relationship with the patient, Bernice was genuine in being drawn to him with a combination of protective care, erotic affection, and her own loneliness, as was evident in her contacts with the psychoendocrine staff. She visited him when he was psychiatrically hospitalized. During the year when he was twenty-nine years old, there were three such admissions. Because he had nowhere else to go, she took him in upon discharge from the third admission. Her daughter revolted against having him once more as a lodger in the house. The all too familiar pattern repeated itself: disruptive drinking, violent argument, and emergency-room treatment for beatings and robberies sustained on the streets while intoxicated. Twice police were summoned for uncontrollable strife within the house. After nine months, the patient departed for yet another psychiatric hospitalization, his fifth, followed by transfer to a residential alcoholic rehabilitation program and thence to a halfway house.

In subsequent years, Bernice continued to care about his welfare, and to see him once in a while as a friend, but fewer and fewer times as a lover. He did not again share shelter with a lover. He continued to be residentially unstable, and disputatious with other occupants of the places where he lived, until eventually he got an apartment of his own.

Homosexual Victimization

The patient did not mention the homosexual component of his erotic life until, at the age of twenty-two-and-a-half, he reported having been picked up in a gay bar by a man twice his age. This man was a business executive who made periodic business visits to the city. The two established a friendship that lasted until, six years later, the man died of a heart attack. As a young black college student, the patient particularly appreciated being on equal terms with this older, wealthy white man socially, as well as in the privacy of their sexual relationship. Ten years later he established a similar friendship with another older man. It also ended prematurely when, after a year, the friend had a stroke and died.

After the initial meeting with the first of these two older men, the patient said, "I felt guilty—like it's all right to experience that . . . but I got this feeling that maybe I'm homosexually inclined. . . . One thing I think I would have in my mind is that it's not really me. . . . I would always be wanting or wondering how it would be to have a heterosexual relationship, the same kind of ingredients, the compassion and the understanding, so I think I'll stick to women. . . . I want to be with a woman and be able to like, express myself through copulation or through emotions."

These statements disregarded a five-year, prior history of homosexual street cruising that had begun at age seventeen, and that the patient first disclosed only when he was twenty-six. "It happened the first time quite by accident," he said. "I was walking—as a matter of fact, I was going with this girl when I was seventeen, and it was late. It was in the summer time. So, she said, 'You're going to walk home this late at night?' It was only about one o'clock. So I was coming down to the Circle. . . . This real big tall guy was coming toward me. I was young, you know, but I guess I was attractive. I was dressed pretty flashy and neat. He said, 'Hi!' I say, 'Hi!' Then he took a cigarette out of his pocket, and say, 'You have a match?' I said I don't smoke. . . . He say, um, 'Would you like to take a walk for a minute? My car's right here. We can take a little drive.' I said, 'A little drive for what?' So that's the first time I heard the term, blow job. . . . He asked me where was I coming from. I said from my girlfriend's house. He say, 'Did you fuck her?' I say, 'Yeah.' He say, 'Did she really satisfy you? Would you want me to give you another way of having it? I'll give you a blow job.' Then I had to ask him what the hell was a blow job. I didn't know what a blow job was. So he say, um, 'I want to suck you off, you know.' So I say, 'Sure. What the hell if you give me some money.' "

In the urban culture familiar to the patient since boyhood, he was able to classify himself as a heterosexual who engaged in hustling, especially if he received money, provided his role was to pick up men whose turn-on was to perform oral sex on him or, much less to his liking, have him perform anal penetration on them. In his subsequent history, he became familiar with the section of town known to be a gay cruising area, and he would go there whenever he had the inclination to be approached by a homosexual seeking a partner. When he became old enough, he would hang out also in a gay bar and also in the peep-show section of an adult book store where pickups could be transacted.

By the time he was twenty-six, the already-mentioned ominous component of some of his homosexual ventures became evident. Primed with alcohol, they progressed to traumatic personal injury, possible unconsciousness, and treatment in a hospital emergency room. In some instances the patient had no subsequent recall of the details of what had happened, and in others his explanations were less than plausible. A likely formulation is that, after he became partially inebriated, ideas of being himself homosexually subjugated and raped engendered in him an acute attack of panicky belligerence. He would insult, rob, or threaten a would-be partner. Then he himself would be beaten up, wounded, and possibly left unconscious.

At age twenty-eight, there was one example of a panic attack which the patient did recall in detail, perhaps because it occurred one night in a city rescue mission where, because alcohol was forbidden, he could not have continued drinking until he blacked out. He was there because he had had a fight with Candy and Jimmy, his married friends in whose house he rented a room. He had accused them of stealing his money.

In the mission that night, he said, there were about forty young men whom he believed to have just been released from jail. "They were constantly masturbating," he said. "It was sort of like the raw bestial—like animal behavior of man in his sexual attitudes. . . . It was sort of like they had a code message, like this is their time to start, like to run a contest, you know. . . . It's as if they were in a training session, you know. They just kept on going, and all the slurping noise and, you know, whistling and moaning, and continuously on and on and on. . . . Well, they give this up, and I try to go to sleep. So I put my pillow over my head, because I was—the noise was bothering me and annoying me. I was curled up, and I kept hearing this one guy over in the corner saying, 'That guy over there sleeps like a faggie' and, um, of course I didn't pay him no mind, you know. Then this one guy kept on, persistent. So the guys that were in the place said, 'No, man, he's been coming here before. No, he's no faggie. Leave him alone. Let him sleep.' So, anyway, he kept on insisting, saying the same thing. And finally, by him hammering on the same thing, they all, you know, began. I guess it's their mentality. All of them are beginning to say, 'Hell, this is a piece of, piece of ass.' And they're all mixed up. They want their penis in a hole. They didn't care if it was a female or a male, you know. . . . They were ready to sort of like attack, you know. So they, one of them, a couple of them started for my bed. And I jumped up, you know, and I told the guy who was in front that if he came near me I would try to pulverize him. So he got back in bed laughing, and said he was only joking. And I laid back down, and the same guy started it all up again . . . masturbating, and they started doing it dangerously, you know. And several of them started howling about how much they wanted a piece of ass, you know, and I became more frightened. And they kept this up all night. Two of them tried to push me again. So I put a little blade [fashioned from the cap of his asthma atomizer] between my fingers, because the first one that touched me, I was going to use it, you know, to try to harm one of them, you know, before they hurt me. . . . One guy over in the top bunk said, 'I got something for that,' and he pulled out a switch blade and opened it up. And I became more frightened. . . . The night guard came with a flashlight, and wondered what all the commotion was about, and everybody jumped back in bed, just any bed, and made out like they was asleep.''

He was not reassured when the night guard told him, ''Not anybody there going to bother you; they're all gentle.'' Trying to go to sleep, he was sure he heard ''one guy sitting on a bottom bunk say, as he held up a gun, 'Hey, you're not going to get out of here alive today.' He was putting bullets in the gun. I was really scared, so I, you know, my water broke. I went back to tell the guard again that they're threatening my life. He still ignored me. So finally he got angry with me and told me to get my coat and just get out. It was about quarter to five in the morning. I told him I wasn't going anywhere unless he was going with me. So he went to the door with his flashlight, and I grabbed my coat, and he told me 'Go get your coat and get out.' ''

Running four blocks to a hospital, he fell and slit his leg, he said. In the emergency room, the people thought he was drunk, and the policeman on duty did not respond to his complaint about being threatened in the mission. He was being given treatment for an asthma attack when he thought he saw one of the men from the mission come in. So he rushed out of that hospital and to another one, nearby, where the emergency room people knew him and had previously treated his asthma attacks. There he rested until, later in the morning, he went to his sister's house.

A couple of months later, the patient had another similar experience. On this occasion, though he was at a different rescue mission, the men whom he feared would rape and beat him were, he believed, the same as before. He escaped to book in at a hotel. From there he went out drinking. His next recall was of being taken, cut and bruised, to an alcoholic treatment center, where he refused admission. On this occasion, he once again did not report for work, nor call in sick. So, once more, he lost his job. His married friends, Jimmy and Candy, whom he had reviled only a few months earlier, decided to give him another chance. They took him back to live in their house.

The next episode of alcoholic hallucinosis, half a year later, involved his friend, Jimmy. As the patient reported the incident on the phone, he got drunk and started messing around with Jimmy. ''Jimmy doesn't like me to go down on him in front of company,'' he said. ''He started to beat me up.'' After returning to his mother's house, the patient tried to leave with a screwdriver, saying that he wanted to kill Jimmy. His sister persuaded him not to take the screwdriver.

In the course of a long inverview four days later, the patient disclosed that he'd been having a recurrent dream of fighting with Jimmy and stabbing him with a butcher's knife: "I'm in there with Jimmy, and I'm just, I'm stabbin' him, just stabbin' him, and someone tryin' to pull me off of him, and he's already dead. And I just keep on stabbin' him. That's bad, bad, bad. I wanted—and I don't like that kind of feelin'. But in the same sense of dreamin' about that, at the same time I'm dreamin' of spendin' time in prison for killin' Jimmy. And I dream about Candy hating me. . . . And the part that gets to me, when the judge said so many years, I kep' thinkin' 'bout livin'—life in prison. I thought about what could happen to me—what, what, what would probably happen to me. And by me bein' so, the kind of person I am, I end up bein' a, a homosexual. Somebody gonna rape me and, you know, use me any kinda way you want to. And I, and in that dream also I, I figured that I couldn't take that. So I, I was, I probably end up killing myself."

Upon further inquiry, he said that he thought about this dream during the daytime, while not asleep. "I can feel it," he said. "It's gonna happen. It's gonna happen." When he was told that his friends had to be told about the jeopardy in which this dream placed them, his first reaction was indignant mistrust. Eventually, he felt relieved to have it out in the open.

Jimmy and his wife came to the clinic together for an interview. "When he's not drinking, he don't say nothing to nobody," Jimmy said. "All right. When he does drink, he curses me out, curses my wife out. He goes upstairs. He pulls his private out. He exposes his self. . . . I feel the man is very depressed. But when he's depressed—when he's drinking, I'm going to tell you, he goes into a female bag. And he tells me he loves me, and he does things, uh, like homosexuals would do. He try to kiss me. And he does all this while he's drinking. He even tried to feel my penis. And this, this has been gone on for about I guess in the last six years. . . . Oh, he even told me that—he said, uh, 'I'm getting ready to come on my periods.' He talk words like that. He said, 'You got, uh, a Tampax or a Kotex? Because my period getting ready to come on.' Man, we looks at him, you know." His wife finished for him, "And say, uhm, what's the matter with him?"

There was no recurrence of violence between the three friends in the few remaining months of Jimmy's life before he died in a sickle-cell crisis. In the ensuing six years the patient has mentioned only one other episode of alcoholic hallucinosis. It was not so dramatic as the three foregoing episodes. The risks of binge drinking continue, however. For example, after a very recent resolve to undergo surgical repair of the two persisting bodily stigmas of deficient masculinity, namely the meatal defect on the shaft of the penis, and the perineal fistula, the patient succumbed to drinking again. Thus, he circumvented a surgical consultation, and interrupted several months of abstinence as a member of Alcoholics Anonymous.

There was one occasion, only a week before Jimmy died, when the patient's behavior added an additional clue as to the character change that he underwent when embarking on a drinking binge. It began at around ten o'clock one evening when his woman friend, Bernice, telephoned, desperate to know what to do to restrain him from embarking on another bout of drunken injury. Only a few hours earlier he had had stitches removed from facial injuries suffered a week earlier. Now he was being abusive and demanding money for more alcohol.

He himself talked on the telephone. His manner was jaunty and defiant, and at the same time narcissistically wayward. He was about to go out on the town, and there was no stopping him. He'd had a pint of wine at 6 p.m. and now he needed two more good strong drinks. He would get them from Jimmy, or on the street. He needed "some happiness, not all this sadness around here—and dancin'. Jimmy always has some music."

He spoke as an addict on a euphoric high who was not about to be cheated out of his claim to a moment of joy by warnings about getting himself homosexually assaulted. "Never underestimate the human mind," he said, claiming Freud as his authority. He'd been preached at for twenty-nine years, and wanted no more of it.

In the content of the conversation, there was no evidence of vivid eidetic imagery or hallucinosis, but rather of an altered state of consciousness. The patient may very well have been in a dissociative, fugue-like condition. Such a condition is characteristic of the paraphilias. If so, it would explain the chasm between the patient's nonsexual life as a college graduate, and the pathological and ritual compulsiveness of his paraphilic, self-destructive sexual conduct with men.

In the present instance the patient was dissociatively indifferent to the injurious consequences of his paraphilic flirtatiousness as though he were a woman putting the make on a man. In the euphoric state of embarking on a sexual adventure, he disregarded the injuries that would be inflicted on him, possibly bringing about his death. There is something more here than ordinary masochism. It is a paraphilia of stage-managing one's own erotic death, the name for which is autassassinophilia.

Epilogue

According to the statistics of extremes, the value of a single case is not that it proves any particular hypothesis, but that it may require the revision of an established dogma that is too global and generalized. For example, in the present instance, the sexuoerotic biography demonstrates that knowledge in infancy of the patient's 46,XY chromosomal status and testicular gonadal and prenatal hormonal status was insufficient evidence on which to predict that his sexuoerotic status in adolescence and adulthood would be monistic and male. In fact it has turned out to be dualistic and bisexual. Thus, this one case alone indicates that a reductionistic hypothesis that attributes sexuoerotic status to a single determinant must give way to a multivariate hypothesis in which there is more than one determinant acting either concurrently or, more likely, in developmental sequence. One other potential determinant, biographically exemplified in the present case, is that of inconsistency within the family regarding the sex of rearing: there was a change from girl to boy by edict when the child was old enough to appreciate what had happened, but too young to understand its rationale, or to comprehend proposed plans of treatment. As he grew old enough to comprehend, there was a prolonged delay in explaining to him his genital status and its eventual surgical masculinization.

The heuristic relevance of this biographical document is not, however, restricted to its theoretical applicability regarding the determinants of masculine versus feminine in the sexuoerotic dimension of G–I/R (gender-identity/role). It is heuristically applicable also to the phenomenology of paraphilia, addiction (alcoholism), hallucinosis, suicide, homicide, and coping with stress. This chapter has been organized so as to expound paraphilia as an outcome of coping with stress, particularly stress generated nosocomially, that is by hospital and clinical procedures designed to be therapeutic.

As it affects children, nosocomial stress is experienced as a combination of nosocomial neglect and nosocomial abuse. Neglect ranges from delay in receiving appropriate intervention to lack of sufficient warning and explanation of what to expect. Abuse ranges from noxious and painful diagnostic and therapeutic interventions and deprivations, to humiliation and chastisement for conduct not befitting the ideal patient.

In the present case, nosocomial stress began as nosocomial neglect: society at large, not just its medical institutions, failed the child from birth until almost age six by neglecting the birth defect of the sex organs with which he was afflicted—a not uncommon consequence of the sexual taboo as it affects the practice of sexual medicine. The little boy's mode of coping with this stress was silence. In the hospital his silence became complete enough to justify its being called elective mutism. It was punctuated with paroxysmal screams when painful procedures were performed. This response led to a false diagnosis of severe mental defect, which in turn led to further neglect. The most pathological episode of neglect was an all-night failure of the ward staff once when, at age eight, he repeatedly called, in pain, for attention to a blocked urinary catheter. This neglect resulted in extravasation of urine from the abdominal wall.

From the child's point of view, the promise of an early and complete genital repair proved false. Instead he experienced as abuse the fifteen operations needed for correction of his birth defect and of the postsurgical complications arising therefrom. His left breast was permanently disfigured as the donor site of a large skin graft. His right scrotum was left empty, the result of a gonadectomy performed as a sequel to infection. The underside of his penis remains raggedy and ugly where the urethra has split open for an inch below the tip of the glans. Urine sprays from the meatus on the shaft of the penis, and also leaks from this site as well as from a perineal fistula at the former site of a urinary catheter. Even in adulthood, the patient interprets this site as a former vagina. He has evaded mention of urinary leakage so as to not be confronted with further genital surgery.

Despite the foregoing negative outcomes of polysurgery, at the time in childhood when the boy first could see the semblance of a pendulous penis, the silence of elective mutism lifted. At school he began to talk and to learn. His IQ elevated to normal. Academic achievement became his new way of becoming somebody worthwhile and of gaining self-respect. He had embarked on a second way of coping. It was the way that meets with social admiration and respect, namely encountering adversity by rising above it.

The early years of gender uncertainty followed by the experiences of nosocomial stress had, however, left a residual imprint of the trauma of neglect and abuse. This residual, like a stress line that renders a metal casting vulnerable to metal fatigue, rendered the boy vulnerable to the renewal of trauma. A new trauma did, in fact, emerge. It hit during the age of seventeen, when as a young man he had his only experience of limerence in a pair-bonded love affair. His genital capability with his girlfriend was for him a traumatic fiasco.

For the second time in his life, he had been a victim of the sexual taboo to which we all are heir. In initiating his sex life, he had essentially had to rely on trial and error in order to prove his genital manhood. Though sex-educational guidance had been available to him in the clinic earlier in his adolescent years, it had been threatening to him to break the taboo by talking explicitly across the age barrier about intimate sexual and erotic matters. The fact is, of course, that he needed much more explicit preparation ahead of time than do boys with a history of normal genital anatomy. Adequate services still do not exist. There is no specialty of either pediatric or adolescent (ephebiatric) sexual medicine with its own established principles and practices of preventive therapy for young people handicapped at birth by a defect of the sex organs. Until this very day, any sex therapist who might attempt to provide explicit preventive sex therapy for an adolescent would almost certainly be professionally ostracized, if not prosecuted for sexual child abuse, or for contributing to the delinquency of a minor under the age of eighteen. Sexologically, eighteen is the official termination of American childhood (U.S. Public Law 92–292, The Child Protection Act of 1984).

The disaster of the young man's first love affair and its genital expression marked the beginning of the impairment of the strategy of coping with adversity by overcoming it with achievement. The first response was to redeem his manhood by working to support himself financially, while continuing his high school education and then his college career on a part-time basis. Though the strategy of coping with adversity by overcoming it held up so as to permit graduation from college, it also became progressively eroded. It was punctuated by increasingly longer periods in which a socially condemned coping strategy took over, namely, that of addiction to abuse and the role of victim.

Over and over again the addict returned to the institution of his former suffering, the hospital. Emergency rooms were able to patch up his bodily wounds and bruises, but psychiatric, sexological and rehabilitation services had no corresponding success with the psychic wound to his masculine self, nor with the warring factions of homosexual and heterosexual in his G–I/R.

The phenomenon of addiction to abuse is not well known and is even less well understood. It occurs in a variety of guises and syndromes, for example, in children who have been rescued from extreme abuse and who behave in such a way as to instigate further abuse (Money, 1977b). One promising hypothesis, yet to be empirically tested, is that, in response to the pain of inflicted abuse, the brain releases an analgesic flood of endorphin, its own biogenic opioid. This hypothesis is based on the observation that children with the syndrome of abuse dwarfism become pain agnosic while living in the home of abuse, but not after rescue (Money, Wolff and Annecillo, 1972). Thus, in addiction to abuse, a repeat round of abuse may be the equivalent of a repeat "fix" of an opiate substance. It induces a reduction of tension and so, in a paradoxical way, is a means of coping with stress.

The only theoretical paradigm that has applicability to the phenomenon of addiction to abuse is that of opponent-process learning (Chapter 5). According to this theory, an initial reaction of panic and terror, for example in free-fall parachute jumping, becomes metamorphosed into a reaction of ecstasy and euphoria. After a few repetitions, ecstatic euphoria eradicates panic and terror. Free-fall jumping becomes no longer a scary stunt, but an addictive obsession. It is a way of getting high without extraneous drugs.

In the present case, addiction to abuse was closely correlated not only with paraphilic sexuality (homosexual autassassinophilia), but also with addiction to alcohol in binge drinking, even to the point of discontinuing Antabuse in preparation for a drinking binge or, on occasion, drinking despite the noxious effects of Antabuse. Addiction to alcohol rather than some other mind-altering substance may have been on the basis of a genetic predisposition, as the patient's father was reputed to be a chronic alcoholic, and one sister was alleged to drink too much.

State-of-the-art therapeutic and rehabilitative technique has so far proved inadequate to relieve this patient of the burden of self-victimization as a strategy for coping with the problem of impaired manhood and the war between the homosexual and heterosexual propensities within him. In terms not only of impaired personal well-being, but also of investment in medical and social services, one must, therefore, raise the issue of cost effectiveness, and of whether the outcome would have been more successful had the entire program of case management been directed from birth onward toward endocrine, surgical, and social habilitation as a girl and woman. In similar cases, unpublished and published (Money, 1970a, 1984b; Money, Mazur, Abrams and Norman, 1981), such a feminizing program has proved to be compatible with the establishment of a feminine G–I/R, sexuoerotically and in general. By reducing the number and frequency of hospital interventions, a feminizing program also limits the extent of what a child experiences as nosocomial abuse and, thus, prevents its potentially disastrous sequelae.

In conformity with Psychohormonal Research Unit policy, the patient whose case is recorded in this chapter was invited to read the chapter, to talk about it, and to make a written note of his reactions. What follows here is his written response.

"After reading your medical, psychological and biographical summary of my life, I feel that it will be of interest to respond appropriately. First, I'd like to say that the summary of certain medical and psychological aspects of my life was sad and yet gratifying to me at the same time. I had to do some metamorphosis, if that's the correct term to use in this analogy of what I interpreted from the report. To relive some of the things that I personally went through during my childhood, especially all of the trips back and forth to the hospital, Hopkins, for further corrective surgery every summer, and sometimes twice yearly was a strain on my psyche even up to this day.

"The personal ordeal really took its toll on me in a predictable fashion, affecting me socially, medically and mentally. I still believe that the surgeons, the medical staff, and hospital personnel could have been a bit more professional and considerate of this child who was subjected to this trauma annually for so long; for as much as 15 years.

"I remember somewhat vaguely that through much of this I suffered silently, meaning I didn't really complain or interfere with what was being done to me. Also, the saddest part was the different approaches people took in trying to explain what was happening to me to other people. For instance, the incident where my mother tried her best to relay to people that I was not a freak of nature but a child of God and more importantly that I was her child and a boy—born sickly through no fault of his own.

"The only thing that still appalls me the most is the insensitivity of some of the staff that dealt with me during this time in my life, especially the person whom was responsible for the accident that happened to me concerning the urine backup in my catheter, and subsequent poisoning of my system by this blockage.

"I don't harbor any bad feelings about this experience that I went through, only that I feel that some other child might be spared the undue strain to its psyche and maybe the child won't grow up feeling so inadequate and becoming as maladjusted as I have. I've gone through so many changes in my short life trying to 'fit-in' that now I'm beginning to feel some relief and that the torture is coming to an 'end.' 'I want to live' is my motto now."

Unhappily, his optimism faltered, and he embarked on another cycle of destructive drunkeness and job loss.

Summary

A patient with 46,XY male hermaphroditism of unknown etiology was reared as a girl through the second year of life, and thence as a boy. Since the first surgical admission for genital repair, at age 5 yrs. 8 mos., followup has been maintained for thirty years. The earliest strategy for coping with the birth defect and the stress of hospitalization, experienced as nosocomial abuse, was manifested as withdrawal into silence, or elective mutism. By age seven, when surgery had produced the first semblance of a pendent penis, the coping strategy changed to overcoming adversity by compensatory effort and academic achievement. This strategy disintegrated progressively when, after age seventeen, the first love affair ended in genital failure followed by heterosexual/homosexual ambivalence. The coping strategy that emerged was, by society's criteria, self-destructive. It manifested itself as provoking personal catastrophe, injury, and job loss; masturbation as a form of genital punishment; heterosexual defeatism; and homosexual self-victimization associated with alcoholic binges and, in at least some instances, episodes of hallucinosis. The change from achievement to self-destruction fits the paradigm of opponent-process learning, whereby an erstwhile experience of terror becomes transformed into one of euphoric compulsion or addiction that is reiterated irrespective of its disastrous consequences. It is possible that these consequences would have been prevented had the plan of case management been directed toward social, surgical, and hormonal habilitation of the baby as a girl from birth onward. In other similar cases the implementation of such a plan has proved more successful than the nosocomial failure here presented. It may have prevented the development of self-destructiveness embedded in a lovemap disfigured by homosexual autassassinophilia.

The Lovemap of Gynemimesis and Gynemimetophilia

Teminology

In the popular as well as the professional sexological literature there has always been, and continues to be, uncertainty regarding the nomenclature and the classification of the different types of gender-transposition, or gender dysphoria. This uncertainty is especially evident with respect to the phenomenon of the person who has the anatomy and morphology of one sex, and who lives in society as one who has the gender identity and gender role, that is the gender-identity/role, or G–I/R (Money & Wiedeking, 1980) of the other sex (see Chapter 14).

In the vernacular, such a person has been variously known as a drag queen, fairy, faggot, or effeminate homosexual, if morphologically a male; and as a bull dyke or butch, if morphologically a female. In the language of the popular stage, both have been known, respectively, as female or male impersonators or transvestites (in French as *travesties*). Legally and morally, both have been classified as perverts or deviants. Scientifically and medically they have been diagnostically innominate, except for being misassigned in an oversimplified way to the diagnosis of homosexual, transvestite, transexual, and sometimes paraphilic.

Such people do not belong exclusively in any one of the first three categories, but to a partial degree in each. They are homosexual insofar as they fall in love with and/or have genitosexual relations with someone of their own morphologic sex. They are transvestite insofar as they cross-dress and present themselves in public permanently as a member of the sex to which they do not belong morphologically, though they are not fetishistically attached to clothing for erotosexual arousal and orgasm, in the manner of the paraphilic transvestophiliac. They are transexual insofar as they may change their body morphology by taking the hormones of the other sex. But they are not transexual insofar as they live continuously with the genitalia with which they were born, rather than claim the right to genital surgical sex reassignment—even though they may claim the right to cosmetic transformation of other secondary-sexual parts of the body by plastic surgery.

There are no epidemiological statistics as to the incidence or prevalence of this phenomenon. The available clinical evidence indicates that its prevalence is greater in those born with the male than the female genital morphology. For these individuals it may be called the lady-with-a-penis syndrome. Using Greek etymology, the name for the syndrome is gynemimesis or woman-miming (Money, 1980). Its counterpart is andromimesis, man-miming.

The person who falls in love with a gynemimetic is a gynemimetophile. Gynemimetophilia is the erotosexual phenomenon of being attracted toward a gynemimetic lover explicitly and not inadvertently by misattribution of the gynemimetic as a regular female. The counterpart terms are andromimetophile and andromimetophilia (Chapter 14).

This chapter presents an illustrative case of gynemimesis followed for a period of ten years, from sixteen to twenty-six years of age.

Case Referral

At the age of sixteen years ten months, this young person was referred for evaluation in the Psychohormonal Research Unit by a Juvenile Services case worker in the urban Division of Social Services. At the time, the youth was registered as a boy, Gerald, who dressed in girls' clothes under the name of Geraldine, also known on the street as Regina. Geraldine claimed the right to be officially recognized as a female, to live full time as a female, and, like some of her cross-dressing companions, to be authorized to take female hormones in order to have a more feminine-appearing body.

Juvenile Services Biography

The patient (for this was Geraldine's status in the clinic) was born to unwed parents too young for parental responsibilities. The maternal grandparents took on the responsibility of their grandson's rearing. Contact with the parents of birth ultimately was lost. At age three, because of grandparental illness, the patient and a sister, twenty months older, were transferred to the permanent foster care of a distant cousin, in accordance with the tradition of the black community in which they lived (Money, 1977a). He established with her a bond of mother-child dependency that, with the knowledge of hindsight, appears to have been pathologically close because of child abuse. The foster father was alleged to have beaten him and his sister injuriously. This man died of a heart attack two days after the two children had been transferred to another foster home. In this new placement, the boy became enuretic, argumentative, and defiant, and ran away, back to his first foster mother. It required another eighteen months, however, before he was permitted to return to her permanently. Soon he was joined by his sister.

By the time he was eleven and the sister was thirteen, the sister's behavioral pathology led her into trouble with the juvenile authorities on charges of sexual promiscuity. She was put in juvenile detention.

It was while she was away that her brother began locking himself away in his room. He did not know that his foster mother would peep through a crack in the door and observe him primping in the mirror while wearing a woman's wig and clothing. Prior to this time, the foster mother recalled, she had not been aware of cross-gender signs in the boy's thoughts and behavior. Nor had she been aware of any juvenile sexual play. She considered herself a very religious person, averse to children's exposing their own nudity, and to their learning about sex.

At the time that he began cross-dressing, the patient also spent many hours occupying himself in feminine domesticities, helping his foster mother. Eventually, other children called him a fag and a punk, and there were complaints of his "fooling around" with other boys.

Shortly before his fourteenth birthday, he had six psychiatric appointments, without effect. The following month, he was brought home by the police wrapped in only a sheet. His alibi was that he had been abducted by a man and raped. Then he admitted that he had been visiting the man regularly.

He was sixteen when his sister was released from detention. The two of them sometimes cooperated, and sometimes feuded over his wearing her clothes or seducing her boyfriends. He regularly wore unisex styles or cross-dressed, with feminine accessories and cosmetics. In a girl's outfit, he was considered by some to be more femininely attractive than was his sister. He kept very late hours, and often did not come home at all. He was rebellious if censured or restricted. His poor school record made him ineligible for training in cosmetology. He had a short live-in relationship with at least one "husband." He had a record of arrest and detention for an "indecent sex act" in the men's room of a bus station, and was released under the continued supervision of Juvenile Services.

The case worker, recognizing the central role of the problem of gender identity, initiated the psychohormonal referral. The request was for evaluation with respect to hormonal sex reassignment, with or without a later possibility of surgical sex reassignment. The patient's own concern was specifically to grow breasts, not to undergo genital surgery.

Hormonal and Physical History

At the age of seventeen, and as a candidate for estrogen therapy, the patient was given a standard physical examination. The appearance was healthy. The height was 172 cm (5 ft. 8 in.), and the weight 71 kg (157 lb.). The body build and proportions were normal. Puberty, on the criterion of pubic hair growth was at Tanner Stage V (adult). The growth of facial hair was sparse. The penis was uncircumcised and 12 cm (4.75 in.) in length, flaccid. The testes were within normal adult limits in size (10 on the Prader scale). They were soft. This finding, together with that of a small nubbin of breast tissue, bilaterally, and everted, prominent nipples, was attributed to an undisclosed, prior use of a small amount of estrogen. Otherwise, the physical examination was unremarkable.

Serum FSH (follicle stimulating hormone) was 177 ng/ml (normal range 150–300); and serum LH (luteinizing hormone) was 102 ng/ml (normal range 30–75).

The consensus of opinion among endocrine, psychiatric, and sexological consultants was for hormonal sex reasignment as a transexual, but with surgical reassignment indefinitely deferred. The Juvenile Services supervisor, the foster mother, the birth mother, and the patient signed their informed consent. The patient was begun on Premarin, 2.5 mg once a day, for both its antiandrogenic behavioral effects, and its feminizing bodily effects.

After eight weeks, Premarin was changed to Depo-Estradiol, 1 mg each week intramuscularly, for ten more weeks. At the end of this time, the visible evidence of bodily feminization was negligible, and testosterone (normal range 425–725 ng/dl) was incompletely suppressed from 579 to 231 ng/dl. Depo-Estradiol was increased to 1.5 mg a week. Six months later, the breasts had attained the size of Tanner Stage IV puberty, with 10-11 cm of breast tissue bilaterally. In the next six months they did not enlarge further, nor after the addition of 10 mg daily of the synthetic progestin, Provera, to the hormonal prescription. They remain rather nonprotuberant. The nipples and areolae are small.

Subsequently, the same two hormones were prescribed on a maintenance daily dosage of Premarin, 5 mg, and Provera, 5 mg, both by mouth. Compliancy has been unpredictable, with at least two periods of several months of being off treatment, ostensibly for financial reasons. At the present time, the hormonal dosage is being reevaluated.

The patient is able to pass as a female in appearance, despite the small size of the breasts. Facial hair is scant and cosmetically controlled by shaving twice a week. The voice has a tenor quality and does not contradict the overall impression of femininity.

Body-Image Dimorphism

Throughout the ten-year period of followup, the patient's most consistent self-image has been that of an androgyne. At age seventeen, the androgynous balance was in favor of "a guy with tits," rather than "a girl with a dick." Whereas she said she wanted "to get titties on my chest," she disclaimed wanting to get genital surgery. Her ambition to have larger breasts has been consistent. She still would like silicone injections, or augmentation mammoplasty, but has not made a concerted effort to obtain the funds to pay for either procedure.

Over the years, her position on genital surgery has wavered from time to time, chiefly as a function of resenting financial hardship and abandonment by those on whom she depended for support. Once when she was seventeen, out of money, and not yet reconciled with her foster mother, she conjectured the possibility of deciding to live again as a man—though not for another fifteen years. More recently, at the age of twenty-six, in another crisis of abandonment, this time by a live-in boyfriend and provider, she resentfully blamed her fate on the boyfriend's discovery of her genital status, and on an economic system that failed to provide her with transexual surgery. In actual fact, there was documented evidence that the boyfriend had always known of her genital status, and found it acceptable. When the crisis resolved, her resentment at having not had surgery faded and disappeared.

She was again able to be content with herself "as a woman with everything," as opposed to a man with breasts, or a woman with a penis. At age eighteen, she made the following statement: "I'm making good money now. It's fun to freak out the straights, by pulling out my dick when I want to. I can tuck it in to dance, and fool everybody that way, too."

In an interview at age twenty-four, she was queried specifically about her self-image. "I could put myself into the category of transexual," she said, "or it could be bisexual . . . I don't consider myself as a drag queen . . . I still consider myself as a woman with ability to please everyone."

Projecting herself into the role of writing an autobiography, and selecting a title, she mused, ". . . the woman behind the man, or the woman in front of the man . . . and all the time you're writing about this woman, but in reality it's still a man. Let me see—He/She."

With respect to surgery, she said: "I don't want to be a woman. I just want to look like one . . . There are some things I want, some things I don't want. Like, I want bigger boobs. Nice big plush hips. I notice, as I've gotten older, my hips have sunken in, to take on that male form. And the buttocks, I want to fill them out. I would like to go through the whole process of electrolysis. And just be castrated, for the time being . . . After the castration, you know, you take on a more feminine form . . . You have to be castrated before you have the operation, anyhow."

When keeping a hospital apointment, the patient was groomed and dressed sometimes informally, sometimes formally, following the fashions of the day. One observational note, written by a woman medical student, when the patient was twenty-one reads as follows: "Looking very well. Neat and sedate appearance. Minimal make-up. Nails polished. Perfumed. Very convincing. Very feminine. Not overdone. Weight 165 pounds. Height 5 ft. 4 in."

Gynemimetic Community

At the time of the first interview, while still not quite seventeen, the patient had established contact with people like herself in the historic port area of the city. They worked as impersonators—night-club entertainers and hostesses, or bar girls, alongside regular hostesses, earning a living chiefly on a commission basis. Their impersonator status was traditionally one of the attractions of the bars where they were employed. In many instances, customers would patronize such a bar because of their presence. They were not, however, standard gay bars, but bars of mixed clientele where impersonators were to be found.

Despite changes of management and site, bars frequented by impersonators continue to operate in the city, catering to their particular clientele. There are also bars in which impersonators are not hostesses or entertainers, but patrons on the lookout for a pick-up.

Currently, some of the impersonators in these bars identify themselves as preoperative transexuals. Those who have had sex-reassignment surgery and still participate in the bar scene are referred to, somewhat disparagingly, by nontransexuals as "sex changes." Impersonators of the same type as the patient have no definitive name for themselves. They do not use the term, cross-dresser, nor transvestite, in self-reference.

They have no name by which to differentiate the men with a proclivity for impersonators from those without. In fact, an integral part of the credo of impersonation is not to make the distinction, the ideal of the impersonator being to attract ordinary heterosexual male partners.

A majority of the patrons at the bars are transients, interested in a casual relationship or one-night stand. Some, however, are regulars, and some maintain repeat engagements with the same impersonator. Rarely, a patron might establish a live-in relationship with a particular impersonator as her boyfriend and household provider.

Such a couple might break with the bar scene. More likely, the impersonator would regularly return, if not accompanied, then alone, drawn by her fascination for participating in the sexual lifestyle of the bars.

This lifestyle includes a loose-knit friendship or neighborhood network of impersonators. In the present instance, the patient participates in such a network. Several of them rent apartments in the same building. When times are hard, they share accommodations and help one another.

Though they socialize together, members of the network work independently. The patient, for example, has been solo when seen "working the bars" or "turning a trick" on the street. So engaged, she might signal one of her friends that she did not want to be recognized, lest it destroy her image of herself as a real lady. If she and her friends should meet together at the same bar, it would be for purposes of socializing, not picking up a partner.

The patient does not have a generic term with which to identify the network that constitutes her gynemimetic community. Their work might be "hustling," but they are not "hustlers." Their female wardrobes might be referred to as "drag," but they do not qualify as "drag queens." The patient disdainfully rejects this latter term as not having self-application.

For the most part, the gynemimetic community or friendship network is parochial. It has no organizational relationship with similar groups within the city, state, or region. They do not participate in the regional Gay Community Center, nor in the politics of gay liberation. They have no organization for defense against periodic police harassment, nor for the male sexual status accorded to them should they be held in jail for soliciting.

On the basis of individual contacts, the patient has known about the impersonator scene in other big cities. She has lived out of state twice—once for a few weeks with a friend in South Carolina; and once for a few months in New Jersey, with her live-in partner whose job had taken him there. Her knowledge of impersonation and impersonators in other countries was fragmentary.

Partner Affiliations

It became evident with the passage of time that there were two themes in the patient's sexual life. They corresponded to the familiar split between the madonna and the whore, and its reciprocal, the provider and the playboy (Money, 1980). On the madonna side of the split, the patient romanticized the idea of having an enduring partnership with a boyfriend who would be a husband-equivalent. He would be her provider, and would support her. She would delight in pleasing him. Erotosexually, her satisfaction would be achieved in satisfying him. He was idealized as being exclusively heterosexual in proclivity, blue-eyed, blond, and totally accepting of her as a woman, despite his knowledge of her genital status.

Romantic idealization of the partnership as a heterosexual one imposed a veto on permitting the partner to have a homosexual interest in the patient's own penis. Thus the sexual history, as reported in the patient's interviews over the years, tends toward being prudish with respect to genitosexual participation and erotic technique.

In the course of the decade under review, there was no period longer than a few weeks when the patient failed to have an affiliation with a boyfriend who was a provider. Whereas some of the affiliations lasted only a few weeks or months, two had a longer history. The first of these longer affairs began shortly before the patient was eighteen. The boyfriend was thirty-three. They lived together for eighteen months. Then the patient was arrested for soliciting. The boyfriend, now a diabetic, left town for job-retraining. Eighteen months later they resumed contact but did not begin living together for another year or more. They then shared an apartment in a distant city for nine months, after which they went their own separate ways.

The patient spoke endearingly of this partner. There was no evidence, however, that either of them had undergone the complete pair-bonding experience of falling in love. In fact this type of experience appears not to have been included in the patient's erotosexual repertory. Her partner affiliations have resembled rather the convenience of an arranged marriage. Each affiliation was not without fondness and affection, but it did not include the excitement of being love smitten. Excitement belonged less to the madonna, and more to the whore in her clandestine encounter with a playboy, or the call-girl with her client. No matter how well the provider provided, he could not compete with the challenge of "turning a trick" on the side, irrespective of either its monetary return or the danger involved.

The home visit made by two members of the Psychohormonal Research Unit for the purpose of meeting the first long-term partner did not succeed. It was the second such partner who gave an interview. He was a man in his late forties when the patient was twenty-three. He had been married for twenty-five years, and separated for four. His four children were young adults. He and the patient had known each other casually for several years before they started living together as a couple.

It was fairly well known that he was attracted exclusively to black transvestites and transexuals, one of whom had previously lived with him for a time. He himself was white. He had no attraction to gay men in male clothing. Though he rated himself as bisexual, he said, "I play the man's role only, and I got that straight with each of the girls before I started living together with her—that I would not play the feminine part. I would never dress up . . ." He said that he hadn't even heard the term, drag queen, until he was forty, and first met the one he eventually began to live with.

Of his partners' male genitalia, he said: "I don't know. I don't think that really matters. The anatomy, it doesn't faze me at all—period. It's just the feelings that I have for her, mainly . . ."

"I had more sex with my wife," he said, "than with the transexuals I've lived with . . . with my wife, we were having a lot more sex, and our sex life was great, and never had any problems." He could not explain why he had left his wife, apart from his fascination with the gynemimetics whom he referred to as transexuals. There was nothing unmasculine in his lean, gnarled, farm-worker appearance and manner.

Queried about love, romance, and sex in her relationship with this man, the patient said: "I don't know if it's love I feel for him, or just friendship, but I would say it's love . . . It seems like to me that it's something I can't do without. The feeling of being lonely. . . In my situation, I hate being alone. Just for him to call me on the phone from work, and say that he loves me . . . that makes me feel good all inside . . ."

"Romantic," she said, "to me is being in a little boat, just the two of you fishing with a bottle of Chablis and Galiano, and just sit there, and look out into the water, and tell each other your thoughts. That's romantic to me."

Sex, with body contact, was more elusive and problematic for her to define: "Sex is something that you would really like to have, to get into it, you know, heavily, emotionally, and, you have to put all your feelings into it." By contrast, playing around "is something easy, where you don't put all your feelings into it. You just do it, get it over with, and go to sleep." The playing around she referred to was having her breasts sucked, and her flaccid penis perhaps played with, as she played with her partner's penis until he ejaculated.

Genital-Erotic History

Inconstancy of memory and recall was characteristically typical of the patient's attempt to retrieve biographical information on different occasions. Thus it is not possible to give a juvenile erotosexual history with consistency or precision.

From puberty until the present, there has been no evidence that the wearing of female clothing served a paraphilic and fetishistic function of promoting erotic arousal and the achievement of orgasm.

The history of masturbation dated from about age fourteen. At that time, as a boy, he had become involved in gay life at school. While masturbating he would sometimes "concentrate on feelings," and sometimes on a boy who had been a sexual partner—"trying to reach the stage where I could be what I always want to be, a woman."

There was no early history of difficulty with erection or ejaculation when masturbating. In the role of a woman, in order to suppress erection so as to be more womanly for a male partner, she would think distracting thoughts. The idea of using her own penis for anal penetration of a partner was offensive to her.

A detailed inquiry into erotic practices took place in a recorded interview when the patient was twenty-four years old. At that time, she had recently resumed regular treatment with estrogen and progestin, with a resultant antiandrogenic effect on the genitalia, namely reduction of erection and ejaculation. "The last time I can remember getting an erection," she said, "was about a month ago. It was a very settled, cold feeling, not the way it used to be, real warm and cheerful . . . It was like, after I was done, I couldn't be bothered . . . don't touch me; leave me alone . . . So I just said, forget it . . . My penis doesn't really bother me. It's not even there . . . I'm just as happy now as I ever was."

At this time, she down-played having sex with anyone other than her regular boyfriend. "The only time I go to bed with another man," she said, "is when he's paying me some money. Other than that, I can't be bothered."

Of her own sex feeling, she said, "it's in my tits . . . only when Albert (my boyfriend) does it. It feels great when he does it, but when somebody else does it, it doesn't feel the same . . . It doesn't make my penis hard, or nothing like that, but it just feels good . . ." Albert himself reported more varied sexual activity including anal intercourse with himself as insertor.

Referring back to her previous boyfriend, and a period when she was not taking hormones, the patient said of orgasm, "Now that was a feeling that I could say really went over the top, the whole bit, because he made me feel . . . well you have to understand, at that point in my life, I was feeling unwanted, really down . . . and he brought back all these feelings I thought were never there." Their activities included sixty-nine, "and I always played the role of the women . . . or I would be very upset . . . I wouldn't fuck him in his ass; so that brought along some difficulty in the relationship . . ."

For paying clients, the patient had perfected her own technique for concealing her male genitalia. Eventually, in response to professional skepticism, she documented this technique, photographically. It entailed first pushing each testicle up through the inguinal ring so that it would not descend. Then the uncircumcised penis was stretched over the empty scrotum, backwards to the anus, and entrapped there, between the legs, by the tight clamping of the gluteal musculature. It was so firmly gripped that it would stay in position irrespective of vigorous movement, as in dancing or sexual intercourse. It was released by relaxation of the muscular grip, while in the squatting position—a trick which the patient had, on occasion, performed while showering postcoitally, as a joke, to surprise and dumbfound her unsuspecting customer. Previously, while having sexual intercourse, the customer's penis would have been thrusting, usually on the right side, deeply into a suitably lubricated pouch of scrotal skin, high into the cavity of the inguinal canal. To guarantee the complete success of this method, it was necessary that a client be sufficiently inebriated, and not too diligent in his pursuit of cunnilingus or digital-vulval activity.

Some clients did not require direct genital activity, but a paraphilic substitute. For example, one man regularly paid the patient to slowly chew dry hamburgers, which he provided. That was his erotic turn-on, until one day he discovered that the cook had put relish on the hamburgers. He left, and never returned.

Behavioral Health and Pathology

As a teenager known as a boy and named Gerald, the patient lived in an era when he might well have been given a diagnosis of juvenile delinquency, sexual deviancy, or antisocial personality disorder. The evidence adduced would have been: dressing as a girl, soliciting homosexual sex, having sex with an older male partner, not returning home at night, confabulating or lying about these activities, and underachieving at school.

A preteenaged diagnosis of the syndrome of child abuse or the battered child syndrome would probably not have been given because, at the time, these diagnoses were not yet in vogue.

Nonetheless, it is correct that, as a juvenile, the patient did have an undiagnosed case of child abuse. Thus, it now becomes possible to reconceptualize the subsequent behavioral development of puberty and teenage as the outcome of a developmental strategy for coping with the stress of child abuse. This strategy can thus be construed as a strategy of self-rehabilitation or self-healing. As a strategy, it needs a name for easy reference. Hence the term, gynemimesis.

Whether or not a strategy of self-rehabilitation or self-healing (Money, 1971) should or should not be equated with pathology should be a matter of officially endorsed nosological policy. In the present instance, those responsible for case management, especially the administration of hormones, did in fact need the support of a diagnosis to justify giving treatment. In the absence of the contemporary, generic terms, gender dysphoria, or gender transposition (Money and Wiedeking, 1980), they fell back on the term, transexualism. Transexualism, however, falls short of being precisely accurate. Hence the new term, gynemimesis. Gynemimesis is not by definition a pathology, but the term can be applied nosologically and diagnostically, as necessity dictates.

If that is done in the present instance, then the patient qualifies for only one diagnosis, namely gynemimesis. She has no other history of psychopathology, despite the fact that the law has disapproved of her sexual method of earning a living. Recently, even the latter has changed. Through the help of a friend, the patient has become employed as a woman security officer.

Epilogue

In the foregoing, the duality of Gerald and Geraldine may be considered in the context of the dual principles of identification and complementation (Money and Ehrhardt, 1972). These are the two principles according to which G–I/R differentiates in its postnatal, socialization phase. Under ordinary circumstances, identification is with persons of the same sex as that in which the child is assigned, and complementation is to the other sex. Parents usually occupy an initial role in identification and complementation, but they are not the exclusive representatives of their sex in a child's G–I/R differentiation. Eventually age mates assume a key position, also.

Analogously with the way that native language becomes implanted as a schema in the brain, so also do identification and complementation implant their gender schemas in the brain. Regardless of genital sexual status, everyone's brain carries a socialized implant of the gender schema of each sex, one by identification, and one by complementation. The identification schema carries the label, "This is me." The complementation schema carries the label, "This is not me, it is with whom I interact." Ordinarily, the identification schema, which is postnatally implanted in the brain, makes a conjunction with the erotosexual schema of the genitalia that precedes it, prenatally, and is phyletically preplanted in the brain.

Phenomenologically, it is the disjunction instead of the ordinarily expected conjunction of the phyletically preplanted and the socially implanted aspects of the identification gender schema which constitute the fundamental anomaly in the gender-transposition syndromes, gynemimesis included.

One consequence of this disjunction is that the observer frequently recognizes an element of theatrical play-acting in the gynemimetic, and of being on stage (Green and Money, 1966). Being on stage as an exotic dancer or entertainer is, indeed, a career favored by gynemimetics. The zenith is to seduce a man and entertain him erotically and sexually without being discovered. Multiply the number of men, addictively, and this strategy becomes synonymous with promiscuity.

As in all the gender-transposition syndromes, the etiology of gynemimesis remains obscure. In this present case, there were no retrievable prenatal hormonal or pharmacologic data that may have been significant with respect to subsequent vulnerability to an anomaly of postnatal differentiation of gender-identity/role (G–I/R). The retrievable data on childhood experiences relative to G–I/R differentiation are scanty. Nonetheless, these data do include evidence of child abuse which could be etiologically important. It is not uncommon to find such evidence in the history of a child with a G–I/R transposition. Parental abuse and neglect dislocate the parent-child alignment with both the mother and father, and that affects the early differentiation of G–I/R as masculine or feminine. In the present instance, the child became pathologically aligned with the foster mother, though it was the older sister whom he emulated as he became increasingly effeminate at puberty and thereafter.

The only information on the child's sexual learning, which affects G–I/R differentiation in childhood, was that it had been prohibited. As an adult, the patient had negligible recall of erotosexual rehearsal play in childhood, and referred to a childhood sexual experience only once—in an outburst of anger, this experience was claimed to have been rape by an older man, at the age of eight.

In the course of Geraldine's long period of followup, Gerald did not ever appear in toto. If he had ever alternated with Geraldine, in the manner of a patient with two names, two wardrobes, and two personalities (Money, 1974), then that alternation had long since ceased. Geraldine held center stage, and Gerald was incognito.

Only when Geraldine underwent a crisis of feeling that her status was being thwarted or destroyed, by the police, for example, or by the abandonment of a lover, might Gerald threaten to materialize. Then in a mood of depressive anger, Geraldine might make a reference to her penis, either to reinstate it, or to repudiate it completely by considering surgical sex reassignment.

Irrespective of etiology, duality in the G–I/R differentiation of Gerald/Geraldine might be ascribed technically to the phenomenon of splitting, if one uses psychoanalytic terminology; or to dissociation, if the terminology is that of Pierre Janet or Morton Prince. That which is split off, or dissociated is that which pertains to masculinity and its stereotypes.

The two components of the split or dissociation may or may not have equal status. The syndrome in which their status is more or less equal is the syndrome of episodic transvestism or transvestophilia, already referred to as two names, two wardrobes, and two personalities. This syndrome may be lifelong, or it may metamorphose into full-blown transexualism. When the two personalities alternate, they typically represent extreme exaggerations or travesties of the stereotypes of masculinity and femininity respectively. To be gentle, tender, and erotic, and to perform sexually, the episodic transvestite man has to become a woman by proxy, that is by wearing a woman's clothes. In men's clothes he is domineering and aggressive even to the point of treachery and violence.

In the syndrome of cross-dressing or transvestism which is not episodic but continuous, or in that which changes from episodic to continuous, the biography is one in which the split or dissociation becomes lopsided, so that one part of the split predominates at the expense of the other. Thus, the boy who grows up to live and cross-dress full time as a girl and woman becomes increasingly convincing as a gynemimetic. He is able to give a well-rounded impression of femininity that does not seem exaggerated or grotesquely stereotyped. Conversely, he becomes increasingly unable to give a convincing presentation as a man.

In some cases, gynemimesis becomes attached to an abiding obsession to demasculinize the body to become a eunuch by castration, or to demasculinize by hormonal feminization, or by hormonal and surgical sex reassignment. The latter has become known as the syndrome of transexualism, though, more accurately, transexualism names the method of treatment and rehabilitation, not the syndrome.

The syndrome of gynemimesis without transexualism is probably the same as what sexologists earlier in the twentieth century called passive or effeminate male homosexuality, or in some instances, male transvestism. However, gynemimesis is not a synonym for male homosexuality, nor for transvestism, per se. By far the vast majority of males who are defined as homosexual are not gynemimetic, and are not transvestitic.

Some males are defined as homosexual erotosexually only. They are able to fall in love only with another male. Otherwise their G–I/R is masculine. They may have been able to copulate with a female and may have produced offspring.

Other males who are defined as homosexual should more properly be defined as partly bisexual. They are males whose love affairs are, or have been exclusively with a woman. Situationally, as in prison (Money and Bohmer, 1980), they have proved capable of relating genitally to a male whom they cast in the role of female.

There are some 50/50 bisexuals. However, most people who have had bisexual experience are more likely to fall in love with only a man, or only a woman, not both.

For most of the general public, gynemimesis may be construed as a medical or psychiatric condition, though more likely as an egregious insult to common sense, a defiance of the social definition of male and female, a conspiracy against sexual morality, or a criminal offense to be apprehended and punished. Conversely, the general public also condones gynemimesis provided it is institutionalized within the entertainment industry on stage, in the movies, or on television, where the impersonation does not need to be unmasked because it is advertised in advance.

Summary

Gynemimesis is a subtype of gender transposition or gender dysphoria in which a person with male anatomy and morphology lives in society as a woman without genital sex-reassignment surgery, and with or without taking female sex-hormonal therapy. The lover of such a person is a gynemimetophile. The corresponding terms that apply to the female are andromimesis and andromimetophile. In most large cities of the West there exists an unnamed gynemimetic community that corresponds to the social institution of hijras in India, and xanith in Oman (see Chapter 14). Clinicians can contribute to the rehabilitation and welfare of gynemimetic youth in society, by providing overall health care, including endocrine treatment and mental-health counseling.

23

The Lovemap of Acrotomophilia

Unsolicited Biography

The tragedy-into-triumph formula that is characteristic of all the paraphilias celebrates the triumph rather than laments the tragedy. Thus, the triumph is apt to be pictorialized, written about, or publicly proclaimed, often in pedantic detail, despite the potential risk of self-incrimination. Some paraphiles catalogue their records, including the addresses of paraphilic acquaintances, with a librarian's precision of filing and retrieval. They may lapse and be indiscreet in their self-revelations, or they may be self-propelled to betray themselves. More likely, they unburden themselves only to those whom they expect they can trust. Among those whose paraphilia is a crime for which they have already been apprehended, the extent of self-disclosure may be astonishingly complete. Indeed, among those who share the same paraphilic diagnosis, it is not unheard of for one to claim another's crime, even though he was not responsible for that particular criminal incident. Understandably, however, the range of trust is wider among those whose paraphilia does not qualify as a crime.

It is from members of this latter group that the professional specialist sometimes receives unsolicited biographical material by mail or on the telephone. The following is an example. It was enclosed with a personal letter in a three-part mailing that included xerox copies of all the published material that the sender had obtained from a library computer search, or by exchange, with respect to his own syndrome, acrotomophilia, of erotic fascination with amputee women. Highly trained in his own high-tech profession, he sought equally high-level information about his paraphilia, though without having to adopt the role of patient applying for treatment. He readily gave permission for his personal biographical recollections to be published. The prologue was written, its author noted, "before I had read any of Prof. Money's articles on paraphilia." The epilogue was written after reading the articles.

Prologue

The existence of amputee paraphilia is not as rare as it may seem. Most of those whom I have met and with whom I have discussed the subject keep their feelings hidden in a closet. None that I am aware of is willing to publicly announce his/her preference for amputees as the emotional source of erotic arousal, since only negative and derogatory comments are presented about this subject. There is a large underground network of "devotees" who spend occasional time seeking, locating, and meeting amputees, and socializing. The full extent of this fraternity is not truly known just because the activity is denounced by society as sick, and the closet devotee cannot bring himself to be open about his feelings. There are an uncounted number of devotees hiding their true feelings in fear that it is not normal to feel such emotions. Such disclosures in fact bring about severe emotional turmoil in others. Even those amputees who could greatly benefit from the unusual attraction that they offer do not readily accept the attentions of someone who "finds them attractive because of the missing limb." They are told that anyone who might be attracted to them must be sick, and that they should not have anything to do with someone so sick. One woman amputee has stated: "I wouldn't go out with anyone who would go out with me!!" This attitude helps to keep the devotee from disclosing his real feelings, and requires him to hide his true feelings towards the amputee.

This paraphilic attraction is deeply rooted in childhood emotional development, and cannot easily be erased by just understanding the cause. I know, I was a closet devotee for most of my life, thinking that I was the only one experiencing such feelings, until I found out about the underground fraternity, and learned that there were others that actually felt the same way as I did. At that time I actually met with some amputees who were aware of this attraction and who were trying to bring the subject out into the open so that it could be legitimized and thereby be accepted so that the effect could be used beneficially by both sides. I have discussed the subject with many devotees (a term coined by the amputees) and since then I have been trying to learn and understand how my own feelings developed along this line. I have managed to recall many of the happenings of my childhood that relate to this development. I want to relate how I was brought up, and how my attraction towards amputees developed in response to that upbringing.

I need to begin this narrative in the third person because the story is prior to my own memory of events or emotions. As it moves into my own personal emotional remembrances I can then shift to the first person. Some of this is difficult to remember without again experiencing the emotions of the moment.

Early Family Life

Let me tell you a sad story. Fifty-six years ago, a child was born to a woman who was happy to become a mother. The woman was already 39 years old, and had been married for ten years by the time this child was born. Another child, a baby girl, had been born five years earlier but was a "blue baby" and died soon after birth. This child, a boy, became the replacement for the lost girl. There was heavy conflict between the mother and her husband, and six months after the birth she separated from the father and moved home to live in her parent's house. Now the grandmother had never approved of this marriage in the first place. In fact, she never approved of any one of her four daughter's choice of husband. This was the family attitude that the child was to grow up in.

Eventually the mother became divorced, and the child was never to see or know his father. Any mention of the father was made or couched in derogatory terms. The mother was more charitable, but the grandmother always let it be known that the father's side of the family was all scum. Although occasional visits were made by the mother and the child to the home of the paternal grandfather, such visits were soundly denounced by the maternal grandmother. These visits were probably made in an effort to keep trace of the father who had fled to an adjoining state to avoid alimony payments.

The maternal grandparents were quite old, this being their youngest daughter. Other grandchildren had already grown up and married. The child had second cousins his own age. The grandfather was always ill and the child was always being told to stay out of his way. There really was no man in the house. When the child was six, the grandfather died. The two women were now the only family. The mother worked. The grandmother kept house. In effect, the grandmother became the house-wife/mother, while the mother became the working husband/father. The home was strong in religious beliefs. The church activities were foremost in the social efforts. Heavy religious (Methodist) training was instilled in the child. Charitable activities were encouraged. The attitude of feeling sorry for the less fortunate was taught.

For the most part the boy received only the women's viewpoint of life. As a means of control he was always being instructed: "Do as you are told," and "Don't argue." He developed feelings of inadequacy since men were always being put down as no good. Confrontations created fears of rejection. Control was obtained by developing a sense of shame and guilt. The favorite critical admonition was: "What will the neighbors say or think?"

The boy was under constant pressure to excel in school. This pressure produced in him a feeling of need to escape the requirements. By chance, from the adults, he overheard expressions of pity for an amputee. He developed feelings that being an amputee would reduce the pressure. After a humiliating experience he would go to bed hoping to wake up as an amputee. Amputees became people to admire for overcoming adversity.

Childhood Social Life

I was that child, that boy, and as this tale moves along the memories become more real, more personal. I was raised in a small coal mining and foundry town in Appalachia. The small town atmosphere provided a means of control. Everyone knew everyone else and their kids. There were several men amputees in the town, but no women amputees. The grandfather of one of my running mates was BK (below the knee amputee) and his uncle was an AK (above the knee). I spent many days in their house and was quite familiar with the gait of an artificial leg. The uncle was a mechanic who worked in a car service shop, and drove a truck and delivered coal on weekends. He demonstrated to me that an artificial leg was no big handicap. So, later my dreaming about an amputee girl friend did not seem to be too bad.

I would not see that first woman amputee until I was 20 years old, a long way in the future. I was required to stay in the yard, and not permitted to "run the streets" with other kids. I learned to play alone and did not develop comfortable interplay with others. I developed my imagination to help amuse myself at play. Most children employ imagination in their play, but I used it to also keep from being lonely. I would dream up fantasies to provide playmates, and those same fantasies were used to solve problems encountered in reality.

Discipline was enforced. Both mother and grandmother believed in the motto: "Spare the rod and spoil the child." And a rod was applied generously for any infraction, at least until I reached teenage and "got too big to lick." The rod was a thin switch of a tree branch, not heavy enough to injure, but stiff enough to sting when applied on a bare rump. I got licked for many things, such as getting in a scrape with other kids. "Nice boys don't fight," I was admonished. And even when I just stood my ground against someone trying to pick a fight, I was punished when I got home for being in a fight. The word was: "It takes two to make a fight," and I was guilty of being one of those two. So even if I won the fight I lost when I got home, because my mother would have been called by another mother to report my crime.

I learned to tuck in my tail and walk away from any form of confrontation or encounter, for fear of the retribution awaiting at home. I still have that panic fear reaction to any encounter situation. I became known as "the coward of the county," and kids would pick on me knowing that I would not fight back. I also grew taller than other kids, so I was also admonished: "Don't pick on kids smaller than you." They were all smaller than me, and when they picked a fight with me they were being brave for picking on the big guy. They also knew that they were safe because I would not defend myself. It became a game with them. In many instances the frustration became so great that I wished that I could have blown their heads off with a shotgun.

As a consequence of this absolute suppression of such strong inner emotion, I also suppressed any desire for competition, athletic or other. I was a complete pacifist, with raging internal turmoil. I never got involved with sports in high school since that involved competition. It was not "nice" to be a winner because winners were punished. When I came home with a report of winning at marbles, I was greeted with: "Shame on you." Even when I would win at a board game, I would feel guilty for taking advantage of the other players. I would sometimes cheat to lose, and thereby salve my conscience. I did not want to win, but I don't like to lose either. A real Catch-22. So I avoid confrontations. Confrontations or encounters raise strong fear emotions. I enjoy challenges but not competition. And although I was one of the tallest kids in high school I wouldn't play basketball because I was self-conscious and "ashamed of showing my bare legs."

For the most part, I was an outsider, a loner. Except for my fantasies. I did have some friends, so-called running-mates, but there was always the sense of distance, no camaraderie. I never developed a feeling of confidence about myself until I later entered the Navy. Everything that I did seemed to be wrong and criticized. I was an avid reader, preferring a book to playing sand-lot baseball. I roamed the country hillsides with my dog, preferring to be exploring by myself. I also excelled in school, an intellectual outlet that pleased me. But by the time that I was in high school I was beginning to rebel, too late.

I was distinguishable from the other kids in town also by the clothes that I wore. Up until about eight years of age I was dressed in short pants and long heavy stockings. Those stockings were held up by a garter belt or harness. I am just glad that I didn't have to wear a dress. Then I graduated to knickers, the only kid in town to do so. I was always the laughing stock of the other kids, but my mother thought it was nice. She "always liked the look of a man in knickers." I did not get to wear my first pair of "long pants" until after I was in high school. I can remember that big day in the store selecting those first "grown-up trousers."

Teenage

As I approached teenage I was constantly being told: "Keep away from the girls," or "Just leave them alone." No problem at first; but as the urges of puberty approached the conflicts began. The natural development of sexual attraction to girls produced strong feelings of guilt. The shame that accompanied these guilt feelings required a mental sanctuary as a means of escaping the guilt. At some time I overheard a comment of concern and admiration regarding a young girl amputee. It provided the needed idea. I developed the protective trend of thought that I would be "permitted" to be attracted to a girl if she were an amputee. Thus the erotic thoughts of a girl amputee were introduced to my sexual fantasies. I used that fantasy to avoid the guilt feelings.

Now I had additional reason for thinking about being an amputee myself. What would it be like to be missing a limb, an arm or a leg? I thought about it a lot. The lack of any women amputees in the town allowed the fantasy to grow without the interruption of reality. I developed deep curiosity about the mystery of being an amputee. Through my own feelings I developed an empathy with those imaginary girl friends. I knew just how they must feel. And I wanted to help them. Occasionally I would read stories in the newspapers or magazines about a girl who had lost an arm or leg due to an accident or disease. These stories always represented the girl as strong and courageous and deserving of consideration and compassion. I was intrigued and sympathetic to her situation. She became my heroine.

My heroines have always been amputees. I have admired them for their strength. From my own feelings of inadequacy and insecurity they represented the courage and strength that I did not possess. They became my idealized girl friends. I hoped that someday I would actually meet that amputee dreamgirl. SHE would understand me. SHE would not find fault with me. SHE would not criticize me. SHE would accept me for what I am. SHE would be the close friend that I needed. SHE became my ideal girl.

Through this process the woman amputee was placed on a pedestal to be admired. As a result, I could avoid attraction to other girls. I felt then that I could be attracted to a girl only if she happened to be an amputee. Since none ever was, I was safe from being attracted, and avoided any guilt. I was safe in my sexual sanctuary, immune from the local girls. My defense was the thought that only an amputee could be attractive. That defense kept me away from the girls, and them away from me, through my teens. I avoided developing any closeness to girls, although I was friends with many in school. There was never any dating. I hid behind my shield, quite asexual outwardly but burning inside with hidden desires. I avoided the feared confrontation of my own sexuality.

I did once actually pretend being an amputee. That was in my mid-teens, and due to an accident which happened to the father of one of my buddies. He worked in a local foundry, and one day an iron casting fell on him and crushed his lower leg. The leg was amputated below the knee. He lived just two houses away from me and I could see him walking around their yard on crutches. Now I was no stranger to someone on crutches. My grandmother had a "bum" leg from a fall many years earlier, and I had grown up with her occasionally using crutches to favor the leg. I had played with those crutches at times, pretending a bad leg. But here was a real amputee, albeit a man, getting about on crutches.

He eventually did get an artificial leg, but before that I got the idea to pretend having his amputation. Somewhere, somehow I had read about how knee-bearing peg legs were fabricated, and I decided to make one. So with a few strips of wood I fashioned a means of strapping a peg leg to my bent up leg. At first I just used it to walk around in the basement workshop where I mostly played. Then one night I ventured out and walked all around the block on that peg leg. The awkwardness was a lesson in reality. I don't remember ever trying to use that peg leg after that.

I was safe in my sexual sanctuary throughout my teeange. I still had no use for girls. They were just someone to be avoided. But I also felt a strong sense of oppression that I wanted to escape. I realized that somehow my life would always be tied to my mother if I stayed in that town. After high school I got a job, but still I felt the need to get away from the people who I felt were the cause of my oppression. I had a lack of self-confidence and self-respect. I lacked assertiveness and decisiveness. I was never demanding; always agreeable. I was a "nice boy." I didn't outwardly demonstrate my sexual needs, but I had been exercising my fantasies in secret. The "Wish Book" was my substitute for Playboy and Penthouse.

The Sears-Roebuck Catalog was where I learned what a woman was all about. A woman was make-up and high-heeled shoes, with nice clothes. Nothing erotic except that I could imagine that the women models were really amputees, and then I could accept them as a model of the girl friend that I wanted to meet. I adopted several, and followed them through many annual issues of the catalog. Occassionally, a particular pose would present itself, and a razor blade could transform the woman into a convincing amputee. I had a small secret scrap-book where I kept these transformed beauties. Then I grew up and ventured out into the world. I had to get away. So I joined the Navy. Before I left home I destroyed the scrap-book. I felt that I wouldn't need it any more.

Fantasy Realized: Panic

Then I experienced my first real woman amputee. The sight of that woman walking on an artificial leg there in front of me created such a sense of panic in me that I cannot adequately describe it. It was a combination of fright and erotic arousal, and held me captive for ten minutes, before I could finally leave the scene.

Half a year later, I was traveling to a new duty station, and had paused for the weekend to see the big city of Oakland, California. I had just gotten off a bus and was walking along a downtown street, when I noticed this girl in the distance coming down the sidewalk towards me. She was a LAK [left above the knee] on a limb and was using a steady but awkward loping gait. The next thing that I noticed was her mother marching along beside her. Her mother was wearing a large heavy coat, and looked as mean as a Sherman Tank. GOD!!! What can I do?? Under these circumstances?? This being only my second encounter, I went into a mild sensation of shock!! I couldn't think straight. I became confused and befuddled. I tried quickly to invent some reason for speaking to her. Nothing was produced.

As they drew closer I could see that the girl was just my general type, about eighteen years old, tall and slender, about 5'8", a very pretty face, and long blond hair. OH!!! How I wanted to meet her!!!!! But I was afraid of that mother riding shotgun! I could imagine that if I stopped her to say hello, that her mother would beat me off with her umbrella, screaming: "Stay away from my daughter, you weirdo!!" What else could I expect?? These were all my own secret fantasies. What could I say as an excuse for stopping and engaging her in conversation? So all that I could think of at the time was to pause and feign interest in an item in the store window.

I do not remember what item, because I really concentrated on watching them pass me in the reflection of the glass. From the profile view I could see that the girl was using a lot of pelvic and hip motion to thrust the limb forward for each step. She may have been a HD [hip disarticulation], but at the time I did not think of that possibility, and I assumed she had a short, barely functional stump. My excitement was growing. As they passed I reversed my direction, and walked behind them for half a block hoping that they would turn in somewhere, a store or whatever, where I might have the opportunity to press a meeting. As I walked watching her from behind, my mind raced through all the previous fantasies that I had ever had. The anticipation of possibly actually meeting someone like her created a nervous emotion to swell through my system.

My fantasies raced into the future. What could I say??? What excuse would I employ?? I was not at ease talking to a girl in any situation. In this case I would have been tongue-tied, if I didn't faint from the excitement produced by the anticipation. I really began to shake from the effects of the excitement of the moment. Then I began to recover from the initial shock, and I realized that I was in no condition to try to meet anyone. I knew that I would have made a quivering fool of myself. And for that reason I stopped, and watched for several minutes as she loped away, out of my life, unaware of my quandary. Then I turned and continued on my original course.

It took about an hour for me to relax from the excitement I felt towards her. I had blown my big opportunity. I had faced the encounter and had failed the mission. I did a lot of introspective analysis of my feelings, emotions, reactions, and actions for years to come. But I have never forgotten her and that day. For many years she was the object of affection in my dreams and fantasies. She was that until I began dating other girls. Then her memory faded a bit as I shifted my attention and fantasies towards a real girlfriend. But in quiet moments of recollection, her memory will come forward. Was it love or just merely fascination? I often wonder who she was, and where she is now. She made someone very happy.

Visual "sightings" or encounters still grip me in an initial hackle-rising, fear response. There is a feeling of concern, and I am pleased if the amputee is with a man escort. After the first two encounters, later sightings did not have such a devastating emotional response, although the arousal feelings always developed in a mild sense. Eventually, I managed to meet girl friends, but I was always on the lookout for that special amputee girl to whom I could be attracted. When I did see her she usually was with someone else. I was too shaken by the thought of encounter to approach the ones who might have been available.

Eventually I did manage to meet a few women amputees on their own ground, with them accepting me and my attraction without question. That acceptance helped to eliminate my concern about my paraphilia. They did understand me, and I was not criticized for having those feelings. In fact they welcomed it. It made them feel special. And that is what they needed. That acceptance removed any guilt about my feelings. I could feel good about myself. It is for that reason that I am relating this story. I hope to remove the sense of guilt that surrounds this subject.

Epilogue

This unusual desire to associate with women amputees has not greatly hampered my life. I never managed to meet an amputee woman who appealed to me in a personal way, one whom I found attractive in the many other personal areas. Eventually I married a nonamputee and had children who are now grown. My marriage broke up over the usual disagreements. It was during this interim that I learned about the devotee fraternity and so was able to actually socialize with a group of women amputees. It was a great experience, being able to discuss my most secret feelings.

The more I socialized with the women I did meet the less I needed to sexualize. The novelty of the situation vanished, and I realized that there was still a real person attached to the stump. The more acquainted I became with her I came to appreciate the person, and the desire and lust faded to be replaced with remorse. Finally the person became the saint, and I felt guilty for having felt as I did towards her. After visiting with and dating quite a few of these amputees I was no longer so strongly attracted to them. They were just ordinary persons with special physical problems. Their personal problems and personalities became important, and I decided to avoid any further involvement. The entire fantasy was satisfied and dissolved. But, later as time passed the fantasies began to grow again, probably through the absence of real experiences to keep them down. Finally I had to scratch the itch again. That has caused marital problems that I don't like. Confrontation again! Now my problem is what to do.

I know that my present wife is not at all comfortable with my paraphilia. She says that she cannot accept my "sickness," nor allow it to continue. Otherwise, "I would have to be as sick as you," she believes. She likens it to adultery, in that my thoughts drift to anonymous women amputees for erotic arousal. She has gotten on my case so heavy that I can no longer get aroused with her, so she now charges me with impotency. In my efforts to submerge my natural emotions I have inhibited all arousal capabilities. I now feel so guilty about my feelings that I can't allow myself to think sexy thoughts about her. I used to be able to caress her and become aroused with full performance, but now I can't bring myself to try. And I don't think that any more explanation will help. I need to feel good about myself. How can I manage to achieve that?

Apart from the handicap that paraphilia imposes on our sexual life, I have a good relationship with my wife. But on occasions, especially at times when my wife is being difficult or critical, I revert to thoughts of that dreamgirl, I resign myself to the thought that she wouldn't treat me that way because she is an amputee; or the equivalent thought that if my wife were an amputee, she would be more understanding of my feelings. So my fantasies continue to make life more acceptable. "I have always been crazy, but it keeps me from going insane."

24

The Lovemap of Asphyxiophilia

Telephonic Biography Taking

Through an intermediary who knew his mailing address, I requested a second telephone call from the young man who has contributed his case to this chapter. "What I thought of doing after we put the bulk of your first call on tape," I explained, "was to use that as an example to show people how that help can be given on the telephone. In fact I think—and you may be able to confirm this for me—that sometimes it's actually easier to talk on the telephone than it is face to face, with eye contact."

"It is," he replied. "It is, because I told you all kinds of stuff on the phone I wouldn't er, that it would take me much longer to er, to, to open up in front of a person."

"That's a very interesting thing, isn't it?" I commented by way of endorsement. "I've seen it before. I think everybody does it up to a certain extent."

"Yes," he agreed. "In fact it helps too that you, that you're, what—two thousand miles away?"

"Yes," I said and added: "If I have your permission to do so, I will write up the conversation, edit it, and cut out a few parts that made it too long-winded."

"Okay."

"I expect you'd like to see a copy when I get finished, would you?" I offered.

"Sure. Sure. That'd be nice," he said.

The history of the first phone call began with a television talk show in Baltimore, on the subject of autoerotic death. Two bereaved mothers appeared on the show, their purpose being to forewarn and prevent more deaths like that of their own sons, aged fifteen and eighteen. Each had been found dead from self-strangulation by hanging. The fact that they had hung themselves as part of an autoerotic, paraphilic ritual seemed incomprehensible to their families. Their parents had believed that their boys had been protected from sexual immorality by the strength of their Christian rearing and devotion. They had always seemed to be model sons, sexually modest and virtuous, and not sullied by contact with obscenity or pornography. The only local person with sufficient knowledge to be able to explain the autoerotic nature of both fatalities was a retired coroner. It was through him that the two families met.

After returning to their home state, one of the women at last succeeded in persuading the local media to carry a story, again by way of warning and prevention. As a sequel to this story, a young college student applied for help against his own potentially lethal autoerotic activities.

Not knowing what to advise him, nor where to refer him, the mother whose newspaper story he had read wrote to me. I had been the sexological participant on the Baltimore talk show with her and her friend. One of my recommendations was that she act as intermediary and tell the young man that he might set up an appointment with me for a consultation by telephone—without charge, since as a student he had no funds.

I Don't Hang. I Choke.

It was late when he called one night, and identified himself as a survivor. The courage to make such a call is fragile, so I decided to protect it by dispensing with an appointment, and talking there and then. At the outset, the caller was concerned about privacy, especially to protect his parents. "They don't know," he said, referring to his sexual ritual, "and they can't find out, because it would kill them."

My response was that he was in a very awkward situation, since they would probably be even more devastated if they found him hanging, dead. "I don't hang," he replied with alacrity, "I choke. I put, usually, nylon, a woman's nylon leotard around my neck, and pull."

I made handwritten notes: He would stand in front of a mirror, wearing tight bikini underwear, with his butt end to the mirror, his head turned at a 45 degree angle, so as to get "a half-assed side view." It would turn him on to watch himself struggling, with his hips and every-thing wriggling like a harem dancer's, as he would knot the leotard more tightly around his neck. Although he would actually be choking himself, in his imagery someone else, nameless, would be supposed to be stran-gling him. This other person would be someone strange, someone like John Wayne Gacy, a homosexual lust murderer of adolescent youths, who had been arrested in 1978, in Chicago, and convicted and sentenced in 1980.

This part of the ritual would end when the self-appointed victim couldn't hold his breath any more. Exhausted, he might then masturbate manually, though sometimes he would just get a "hunger to do it," with no erection. He would sometimes get an erection while self-strangulating, and sometimes not.

Dial M for Murder

To explain how he could get an erection while masturbating, he began by having me confirm that I had been on a Phil Donahue television show on serial lust murder, a few months earlier. He particularly re-membered that I had mentioned the paraphilic phenomenon of replaying a "mental tape" of a paraphilic ritual instead of performing it in actuality. "I do that constantly," he said.

His mental tape would be borrowed from a television movie, like Alfred Hitchcock's "Dial M for Murder," 1954, with Grace Kelly in the role of victim. Scenes in which the woman met death by strangulation or drowning were the ones he found most effective for arousal, erection, and ejaculation while masturbating. He then would be no longer a gay boy being homosexually murdered, but a straight boy being turned on by the imagery of a woman being murdered. The scene of her murder in the movie was, however, nonerotic. No censor could ever delete as pornography the murder imagery to which he masturbated, because no one in the movie was either sexual or naked.

Taking written notes retarded the telephone dialogue too much. So, at this juncture, I requested and obtained permission to tape our conver-sation. The transcript, edited so as to protect privacy and avoid redun-dancy, is as follows.

I want to backtract a little. You mentioned "Dial M for Murder" and other TV shows. I'll give you a list of the shows: "Strangers on a

Train.'' There's a girl that gets strangled in that. Did you see that one?
No. "Frenzy.'' That's about the necktie strangler. "Blood and Lace.''
You saw that one? *No.* There wasn't any strangling in that one. There
was a drowning in that one. Drowning turns me on too, I told you that,
didn't I? *Yes.*

Paraphilic Drowning

I've tried to drown myself in the bathtub. I put a mirror in the
bathtub, and I put little goggles on, and I pretend I'm getting drowned.
But that's not really that dangerous because I'm just holding my breath
and I get practice at it. Then I swim better. But I don't do that much.
I tried to do like they did it on "Blood and Lace.'' After she was drowned
in a bathtub, the killer took a knife and slit her wrist. I tried to do this.
I used fake blood, food coloring. I put that in the water. But that didn't
turn me on at all. It just made one big mess to clean up.

Do you do this at home only, or can you do it at school too? I do
it in the bathroom. At school, I have an apartment. So I just, you know,
do it in the bedroom and in the bathroom. It's a totally private thing.
Nobody knows. I don't do it in front of people either. I don't do it at
school or anything. I've done it at home, yeah. It started at home. Then
I thought I had kicked it when I went to school. But it came back.

It comes back in the winter time. I don't have any problem in the
summer. When it's hot I don't have any problem. In the spring time I
don't have any problem either. But the months of December, January
and February are my worst months. *How often does it happen then?*
Sometimes once a week. Sometimes two days in a row I do it.

[Subsequently, this self-strangulating survivor learned that one of
the two local youths who had died from it had done so on Christmas
morning. He then speculated that the seasonal intensification of his own
asphyxiophilia might have more to do with the agitation and excitement
of the celebration of Christmas than with the winter climate. The feelings
in his stomach imploded. He likened them to the feelings of riding on
a roller-coaster. They drove him to repeated acts of self-strangulation.]

Self-Strangulation versus Masturbation Murder Fantasy

*How do you space the self-strangulation scenes and the masturbating
to murder fantasies?* How do I space? *That's two different things, isn't*

it? Oh, yeah. But I strangle myself in a mirror. After I've been strangled and killed and everything, then I have, er, masturbation and that's—and I have a fantasy, totally different fantasy after that.

The thing is, for some strange reason, after I choke myself, I have found the er, I have then found that I have a better orgasm. *That's common, that way. At least it is to my knowledge.* What's common? *That you get a better orgasm.* Oh, yeah. It's much better. Then you feel a lot relieved, more relaxed. *Uhumm.* It squirts out better.

Do you have any fantasies just of the women being murdered without strangulating yourself first? Oh, do I have masturbation fantasies by itself, you mean? *Yes.* Oh, yeah. *With masturbation too?* Oh, do I have—ask the question again. I'm confused now. *Do you sometimes masturbate, and all that's happening is not strangulation, but thinking and playing the mental tape of the murder, the woman murdered?* Oh, yeah. All the time. Yeah, I was doing that before I started strangling myself a year and a half ago. *The self-strangulation began only a year and a half ago?* That's correct. But, I mean, ever since I've been ten years old I've been masturbating myself.

How often these days do you masturbate? Every day or every week? Uh, six a day. *Six?* That's right. *And I guess that's sort of something that's just very demanding and you have to do it?* Uhumm. Right. *Do you space it across the twenty-four hours?* Sure. Sometimes, usually, it's pretty ritual. Usually when I get up in the morning, then when I go to bed at night, and in the middle of the night, like that. And then, if I'm home in the afternoon, in the afternoon. And if I'm home in the morning, in the morning.

How long does it take for each session of masturbating? As long as I want it to. Usually, I might have a plot, or a movie in it. *So it takes a long time?* It takes a long time sometimes. Sometimes I let it take a long time. When I'm about to ejaculate I might stop it, to make more build up in the mental picture. To make it more exciting, more glamorous. And then, then I let it go. *So, give me an estimate of the time. Is it five, ten, twenty minutes, an hour or what?* Sometimes—the most it's gone is thirty minutes. Usually it's about five minutes, but sometimes it goes ten, fifteen, or twenty. I think they've gone thirty minutes, too. Sometimes I have trouble getting the ejaculation, too. It doesn't want to come. So it takes a while.

When you're doing just only masturbation without the strangulating nylon around your neck, do you do any replay, mental replay of strangulating yourself? Or do you do that only for real in front of the mirror? No, I do that in my fantasy too.

The underwear has to be just right. It has to be 100% stretched nylon; and it has to be white, so that you can see through it. And it looks kind of neat. And sometimes a light blue color. *Do you know how blue and white stretched nylon got into it?* No, I don't know. Probably because—no, I don't know. I think it started with my pajamas a long time ago. I had nylon pajamas, those tight kind. And that's how it started. I discovered myself in front of a mirror. So that might be how it got started. *That would be age what?* Oh, I don't know. Fifteen, fourteen.

Puberty and Fantasies

What age did you get your puberty, do you remember? How do you tell that? When you first ejaculated? *Yeah.* I think that was around—how old are you when you're in the sixth grade? *Twelve or thirteen?* Around there. In sixth grade, that would be about twelve.

Did any of this fantasy stuff get into your first masturbation? Sure. Yeah, I've always been strangling, and stuff. *So it was in fantasy back there, but not in reality, or how was it?* In fantasy. No, I didn't start in until a year and a half ago with the strangling part done on myself. And when I was about fifteen or sixteen I discovered myself in the front of a mirror. I started playing in front of the mirror. *What were you doing then in front of the mirror?* Well, I was pretending I was being strangled without strangling. *I see. Holding your breath, or what?* Nothing. *Just the fantasy?* Well, in front of the mirror, I was just struggling like I was being strangled. I didn't hold my breath, and I wasn't pulling anything. *But you had a fantasy of somebody strangling you?* Right.

Okay, I wanted to ask you: Did this sort of stuff come in your first wet dream? I never had a wet dream. *You started out with masturbating, straight off?* Right.

Have you figured out where it originally came from? Where what originally came from? *The fantasy. Each part of the fantasy. The strangling of yourself and the strangling or drowning of the woman.* The only thing—the drowning with the woman, you mean? *Well, she drowns sometimes, you said, in the movies.* Right. Uh, the, I don't know where I got it from. Uh, it seems I've always been fascinated with asphyxia, you know. Newspapers, you know, when people are killed, strangled or drowned, by asphyxia, specifically young people, women, and—that's, that's always fascinated me. It's sad, but, I mean, it fascinates me anyway. You know.

Do you think this goes back to before you got your puberty, or don't you know? I don't know. I'd have to, you'd have to analyze my whole life story. I can remember way back to when I was three years old. But I'm not quite sure how the idea got in. *Sometimes I find that people actually had the experience in their childhood. Sometimes in play, where someone was threatening them.* No, I've never been strangled or anything like that, or drownded, or nothing.

When it first came to you in early teenage, did it scare you? No. No. No, the only thing I can think of is I got the idea from the movies. I mean I was masturbating before, anyway, but I think I got the idea from movies, somehow; from TV shows about strangling murders, uh, because it's the theme in the movie that I pattern the fantasy after. You know, I'm not original at all, in the fantasy. It's always patterned after a murder in the, that I saw on TV.

You said something about you were masturbating before that. Do you mean in childhood, before you could ejaculate, that you masturbated? Yeah. I was masturbating in fourth grade, third or fourth grade. *Do you think you had murders in them?* Ah, it seems like I was just masturbating. Uh, there wasn't any strangling. I don't think, at that time. There was some violence though. I think it did start off from pretending I was being killed, or something.

I wonder if you were pretending you were being killed for doing something bad like masturbating? Hmm. Ah, I come from a Catholic family and sex is not the thing to talk about. So there's little (pause). *I always think to myself that some of these fantasies, like yours, are a sort of formula for being able to have your cake and eat it too. As long as you get punished for what you're doing, you can get by with it.* Right. *Does that make sense to you?* Sure. Sure. Yeah, I read your lovemap article. *Oh, I mailed that off, too, didn't I?* Yeah. Yeah, it says on the top here, "for the young man to read." *Did that make sense to you?* Uh, yeah. It sure does. Uh, yeah. I've never been punished for it, though, but I've been told that is not the thing to do. *Yeah. The church does that very well, too.* Yeah. They're a bunch of dummies. I did have a lot of problems during childhood. I don't know. But, but the church started somewhere. I'm hearing impaired to begin with. *Yeah.* I had a lot of school trouble. *A lot of which?* School trouble.

And I don't get along—I had problems with girls. I had girl troubles. They didn't like me. *Way back?* All the way through. All the way up to now. They don't like me. I never had a girlfriend; I've never dated. I'd like the girl, and they'd never have nothing to do with me, because

I always wore braces, and I had a hearing aid, and I had glasses. I was the ugliest person in school. So they pretty much didn't like me. They always went out with the football players and basketball players, so I never had much of a social life. *And you haven't found a way of making one for yourself now?* No. I haven't tried either. I just figure it isn't going to work.

Well, you might change your mind eventually. I always say there's somebody out there for everyone. Yeah. I have crushes, but it's always a disappointment, because the crush would never like me. Yeah. So I don't know what else you want to know or anything.

The Bisexual Factor

Well, I do have another thing I've been thinking about and that is: what have you tried to figure out in your own mind about the bisexual factor that's involved here? You've been a victim of a homosexual murder, but when your other fantasy comes, it's always watching a girl being murdered. Right. *Have you tried to, sort of fit that together?* You mean, you mean am I both a woman and a man, do you think? *Well, I'm wondering. I don't know what you're thinking about yourself.* Oh. Well, I'm a man, and, uh, and a woman is a woman. And I don't, no, I don't think I'm bisexual. I, I'm just turned on by my butt, because I think it's girlish. Looks like a woman's butt.

I even thought of shaving my legs. But then if I do that I won't get my pubic hair back. *What?* I won't get my pubic hair back. I shaved a little off once, and it hasn't come back yet. *Really. When did you do it?* Oh, four months ago. *It usually comes back.* No. There's a spot, I have a little spot there. I was careful, I tested it first and I shaved it off, and it won't come back. So, I don't want to lose my pubic hair because—on my legs, on my legs I mean. I don't want to lose the hair, you know, because it's supposed to be there.

Where did you shave it off that it didn't come back yet? Around my uh, around the thigh. The upper part, the upper, higher part. Right below the pelvis. *Did any part of it come back?* No. *It's gone completely smooth?* Yeah. Smooth. *It's not like shaving on the face?* No. *Where you see the stubble?* No. No, it's gone. I think I shaved about three or four inches off. A circular area. And it just won't come back. So, see, I was thinking of shaving my legs, and I could put nylons on. And then they'd look exactly like a woman. *Yeah.* Then I could strangle myself in the fantasy much better. *Then you would sort of be strangling a woman?* Well, I'd be the woman, I mean, be the person. I would be strangling myself, but I would be pretending that someone was strangling me. *Yeah.* As a woman, in front of the mirror.

Well, is that part of your mirror fantasy, now, that you're being strangled by a man and that you are a woman? Well, if I was to do that, if I shaved my legs. *No, I mean right now without being shaved.* Oh, right now? No. I'm a man. I'm gay in front of the mirror. But I'm not gay in real life. But in front of the mirror when I'm being strangled I'm gay. The guy is someone like John Gacy who is killing me. *Well, that's sort of interesting in a way, isn't it? That you're now a man who's being killed by a homosexual killer, but with the nylons on your legs you could be a woman killed by a nonhomosexual killer, right?* No. It would be a homosexual killer. I would just be a homosexual dressed in woman's nylons, for some reason. It just turns me on to have the nylons on.

On Being a Survivor

Let's change the subject somewhat. Was it of any help to you to read the newspaper story of autoerotic death? Oh, yeah, I guess so. You know, I was wondering how I was going—I was wondering, you know, if there are other people like me. But what I don't understand is why they hung themselves. Because I know, common-sensewise, if I hang myself, my neck will snap. Or something. You know, it's just,—

Have you ever come close to dying? No. *Because you opened this conversation by saying you're a survivor.* Well, I don't know, that's what they—that's what it says in this article, newspaper article, written about the coroner that doesn't hide the facts about sexual dying. He talks about survivors. You know, families, the families are survivors, too. So, I just, I'm a survivor. So I didn't die or nothing, yet. *You haven't come close to it?* No. Because I just, as far as I've gone is maybe a little dizziness. Then I let go right away.

That's a point I haven't had much chance to find out about—whether the dizziness is an important part of what increases your orgasm. No. The dizziness pretty much causes me a headache. Uh, that's pretty much what cuts it off, right there. I get the warning and I immediately break, I break off immediately. Because then it gets uncomfortable and starts to hurt. Then, of course, I start gagging, because I'm not getting any air. But it gets uncomfortable and then I pull away, right away. *Uhumm.*

Have you tried to take a reading on the future and see what the ending of all this is? Have I ever tried what? *To take a reading on the future and see how this is going to be, what its ending is going to be.* How do you do that? *Well, just guessing.* Guessing what will happen to me? *Yeah. You're twenty-two now, aren't you?* Uhumm. *So what about when you're thirty-two or forty-two or fifty-two?* I'm hoping I won't be doing it then. *Uhumm.* But, I don't seem to have much luck. See, because I thought I'd broken it off last year, I mean, yeah, last year, last summer. I wasn't having any problem in September. I wasn't having any problem in November, or October. But then in December I just got that urge again. The colder it gets, the worse it gets.

I see. That's only for the strangling? It's not for the other masturbation fantasy? It's for the masturbation fantasy, too. Yeah. I don't masturbate as much in the summer. The orgasm just isn't there. I don't feel good at all. I don't feel anything at all, except hot, sticky, it comes out, and I just can't get the feeling. *Uhumm.* So, it pretty much subsides in the summer. *So you don't even have to masturbate?* No. Oh, I do, but very infrequently, not six times a day. *And do you use the fantasy at all in the summer?* Oh, yeah. I use the fantasy. The fantasy's still there.

Have you got any explanation other than climate about the seasonal change? No, I can't think of anything. It just seems to be the seasonal change, you know. And of course, I have the hardest time, my hardest problem is usually in December, January, or February. *Uhumm.* And I have a difficult time, you know, because I keep saying I'm not going to do it, I'm not going to do it, but next thing you know I've got my tight underwear on, and I'm in front of a mirror choking myself to death. Then I have the orgasm. Then after I do it all, I think, I say to myself: What the hell do I do this for? You know. Next time I won't do it. And the next time, you know, a week later, I'm doing it. *Uhumm.* So, it's just a battle. In most cases I fail. Until, of course the springtime comes. Then, for some reason the urge disappears.

Do you have any theory about why you started strangling yourself just a year and a half ago? I don't know. *There wasn't anything special happening in your life at that time?* All kinds of stuff were happening, all kinds of confusion. I was finding out that I was not, that I was not—you see, I went to high school labeled as emotionally disturbed; and educably retarded, because I was hearing impaired, and the IQ tests were bad, my IQ tests were bad. You know, I had a low IQ; below average. So I was put in the emotionally disturbed. And er, well, I didn't know what to do with myself. I wanted to work with handicapped children. I'm a cinema student right now, and I wanted to work with handicapped children. But I couldn't, because I couldn't get educated because I was not prepared for college education, because I got screwed up in this, in school, through the hearing loss. I didn't get a hearing aid until I was nineteen. And I had a hearing loss since I was four. *Nobody found out about it?* Oh, they knew about it, but they didn't do anything about it. See, I could talk. You know, and, with, in a hearing culture—so they just figured that it wasn't a serious thing; but it was a serious thing, because it was very easy for me to misinterpret things and hear words wrong. *Uhumm.*

And so, about a year and a half ago I was seeing a counselor, er, who was a jerk because, I think, he was just an excuse to cover up the school's mistake; because I was pretty upset about it. And I was trying to get educated, trying to get some financial aid, and I was having trouble with that. And I was at a tutoring center at the University, and they were trying to get me educated, while the counselor was trying to get me to move out on welfare. And so, huh! That's when I started out. Strangling myself. And my sexual fantasies were going crazy. Uhh, that had to be in October or November or something like that. That's when it started. And then I, then I was getting so carried away with it that I called Hot Lines. The girls at the Mental Hot Line at the psych ward thought I was making passes at them, telling them what I was doing. So I didn't get any help there.

Then I was sent to the psych ward at the University. *Who did that?* My counselor sent me there. For a week evaluation. And that's when they wanted me to move out on welfare. *Uhumm.* Because it (welfare) pays for "social skills." And I was having a problem with that, because that doesn't make sense. And they were saying that I was doing this strangling stuff for attention. *Who was saying that?* These psychiatrists that evaluated me at the psych ward. *They'd never heard of this condition, I guess.* No, no; I discovered it in the newspaper article about the retired coroner who told the two families how their sons died accidentally with autoerotic hanging. It tells about the boys that were found hung.

Why are you researching this stuff? *Why am I doing it?* Yeah. Because no one else will? *Oh, I guess that's as good an explanation as any. Also because there isn't a proper textbook describing all of these difficult and different problems people get into with their sex lives. I have one that I'm working on right now. It's actually all written; I'm doing the glossary—you know, definitions of terms. It's going to be called* Lovemaps.

So, the book's all finished, then, and none of my stuff will be in it? *Not unless you want me to write a new chapter.* Did you want to write a new chapter? *Not really; I'm tired of writing.*

When you were on the Phil Donahue Show about serial murderers—have you interviewed serial murderers? *Yes.* Did you interview John Gacy? *No, I didn't.* Yeah, you seemed kind of sad on the Phil Donahue Show. *Did I?* Yeah, you weren't getting research money. *Well it's true.* And some of those women there were misinterpreting you. You know, they thought you were—I don't know what they thought. But they were thinking that you were supposed to—that they thought you were rehabilitating serial killers. And one thought they should be eliminated and everything. It was weird. I videotaped it.

See, that's what really started me ticking because you said, er, that the murderer plays a tape through their mind. And, I'm not a murderer, but I play a tape through my mind all the time, and I said: Wow, that sure sounds familiar. You know, and no one else seems to be aware of that.

Everyone else wants me to live on welfare, and it's all my fault, I'm sure; you know, psychologists, I've—and then they're covering up the school system and their screwups. The school system I came from does not have their act together as far as handicapped children are concerned. Like I said, the way they labeled me, hearing impaired, they put me in the emotionally disturbed where there is no education, because the emotionally disturbed educational thing, uhm, don't have any education because the teachers of the emotionally disturbed are too busy battling the teachers that teach regular classes. So it's just a battle and nothing gets done. So, you either leave or drop out of school, the students do, or else, they just graduate or something, I don't know.

There have been millions of things going on and there's probably thousands of things that have been going on in my life. You know, I have theories of where I could have started this autoerotic stuff but that could go on. I could be here all night. We could go through all that. And I've got already a big phone bill as it is. *Well, next time you want to talk with me, you can make an appointment and I can call you back and pay for it at this end.*

Childhood

Let me ask you a couple of things before we hang up. Do you have brothers and sisters? Sure. Sure, but I didn't grow up with any of them.

I am number six of six children. And number five is fifteen years older than I am. So they were all grown up by the time I was born. *So you've essentially grown up as a lonely, only child?* Uhumm, and I wasn't allowed to have any friends either. No one liked it when I played with friends.

I was, I was, I was always chasing after girls even when I was four or five years old. No, that's not true. Six, about six or seven, I was chasing after girls. It seemed like that wasn't the thing to do. I got into trouble. I wanted to play with them, you know. I didn't know anything about sex at the time, just that I got into trouble all the time. And I was a sissy, being called a sissy and everything, and I was never able to talk to girls. I mean, I was never able to have any friends. I, you know, I was always after the girls all the time because I wanted a girlfriend. You know, not as a girlfriend, going, not dating, I didn't know what dating was. It's just that I was attracted to girls at a very early age, and it just seemed like, um, they, they didn't like that. My mother and father didn't like it, nobody seemed to. They thought I was abnormal or something.

Well, parents often do that; adults do that with kids all the time. That's kind of dumb, don't you think? *Absolutely. I've made a big point of that in my book. Antisexualism on children has terrible consequences.* That might be part of my problem because I had—it's normal, I assume it's normal for a boy to like a girl and er, I didn't wait until puberty before I started developing an interest in girls. I was always chasing after girls when I was six or seven. And um; you know. *So you got into trouble no doubt?* Yeah, I don't know, my sister always got, interfered and er, they would, they would either make excuses, somehow, they would, you know, the family. Don't play with that girl because their family, they're snobs, or their family are trash. You name it, they came up with an excuse so I could never play with girls or anybody.

Was your family more wealthy or what? More wealthy? No, not really. *Did your father have a trade, a business or what?* He worked at Chrysler, as a, er—in fact, he was my stepdad since I was four. My real dad died when I was two. He worked at Chrysler for over forty years, and so he has a pension. And my mom's on Social Security right now. *And she was always a housewife?* No, I think she—well, she was most of her life, and then she used to work at a mental institution. And now she teaches crafts. She has her own small studio right here at the home.

You got along okay with your stepfather or not? No, I had a lot of trouble with him. I get along with him fine now; that's because I'm grown up. No, he didn't like me much when I was a kid. In fact, he didn't like any kids, except his own. *He had another family?* Yeah, from a previous marriage. And his grandchildren could do anything they wanted to do. Just his.

Well, that's awkward when that happens, very much so. Yeah, it seems like I've been in sort of like a crossfire. It seemed like no matter what I did, it was always wrong. I couldn't do nothing in, right in school because of the, er—I went to a Catholic school for eight years. Ah, and being hearing impaired complicated things because I just didn't hear nothing straight, misinterpreted everything, so I just, you know. I was always accused of everything else but what I really was, the problem, what the problem, it was. Like being lazy. I was always accused of that, like, and I was having trouble at school. I could get, could get nothing right and I, I've had, on account of the hearing loss, I had a tendency to hear things backwards. And so I just had a lot of problems with teachers; and so I just went into my own private life, private world, by myself most of my life.

Prevention and Treatment

I want to backtrack to fantasies. Have you ever had any premonitions from movie fantasies that you might actually kill a girl one day? Ohh! Sure I've had that. I've had a scare, a feeling, what happens, what'll happen to me, will I turn into a murderer? I've thought of that. *Then, what's your answer? Do you get an answer to it?* You mean, when I ask myself that? No. *Do you think you might turn into one or not?* No. No, I don't; but it used to scare me. But no, I've pretty much found that I don't think, I don't want to kill anyone.

I want to bring to your attention—I guess you got that information sheet I sent to you about the treatment program that we use here, with the hormone, did you? Is that a shot? Or is that pills? *You can take pills or a shot. The shot is better because it gets right into your bloodstream.* Umm. Yeah. Ah. That would be something to do, but I suppose I'd have to see you for that, wouldn't I? *No, you don't have to. I have arranged with some other patients who live far away to find a local doctor who would get the instructions and then give the shots.* Do they hurt? *No.* They're just like ordinary shots, huh? *Yeah.* How many times a day? *You take one a week.* I hate shots, I used to have to take four shots a week. *Well, I have a patient who decided to try the pills, and he said he's finding them very helpful. I'm thinking that when you get the worst of it coming in the winter, you might take the pills for about four months, to see if they help.* Oh, you mean I don't have to have the shots? *Well, I was thinking at school, you might find it easier to take the pills.*

You know, I'm afraid of shots, afraid of needles, stuff like that. You know, I don't like cutting-up crap. I've had, I've tried some bloody fantasies but they're not successful. All they do is make my stomach turn. Uh, I don't like sharp things.

The pill, would my family doctor, would he have to get in contact with you? *Yeah, that would do.* Okay; okay. Well, I can do that, give him your number, and stuff like that. *Uhumm.* But you'll have to know who I am, won't you? *Well, I would think so, yeah! I told you you can trust me.* Uhm. Although I gave my name, Strong. *You did.* Don. Well, then you got it. [Actually, this was an alternate name.]

Also, you can write to me if you want to. Yeah, do you want me to write more detailed stuff? *Yeah, why don't you do that? Sometimes people have found that it's very helpful to put all this stuff down in writing; it helps them to gain control over it.* Well, I write a lot of stuff but I find that when I write a lot of stuff, that turns me on. *Uhumm.* But I can still write anyway.

Do you have any stuff that you've written that you might Xerox and send me? No, I have some er, some stuff here. Uhumm, sure. I got a lot of junk. It's pretty dark. I even made out my own coroner report. *What does that mean?* Well, I followed a coroner's report. You know how a coroner, they have a report after somebody dies. *Yeah.* And I made out my own report of my own death, that someone strangled me to death. *Uhumm. Well, anything like that would probably be useful, helpful, and interesting to me to understand your situation better. So, I would be glad if you send it, and I will return it to you at the address that you want.*

[My attempt to conclude the telephone call at this point was superseded by the introduction of an unfinished agenda. First the young man wanted to know about telling his story on television. Then he asked about the two youths who had hung themselves autoerotically.]

Autoerotic Hanging

It must have been quite a shock for the parents to go down and see their sons hanging, huh? *Uhumm. Absolutely.* What's it look like, in real life, when someone is strangled to death. Are their eyes open like they say on TV? *Well, it's variable. Do you use the stories of these two boys who hung themselves as fantasies, masturbation fantasies?* No I've never—I don't even know them. It was just the parents' article, and I called them up. I actually had a hard time getting a hold of them. You know, I mean, in the article I got a lead, and it took a lot of work to even get a hold of them. I mean, and what gets me in this city, most of the counseling centers don't even know this problem. You'd think they'd know. *That's true.* You'd think they'd know by now, but they don't know. After all this.

The hanging part I don't understand because I can't get turned on by that. It scares the hell out of me. *Well, everybody's got his own special thing, that's the remarkable part of it.* And it gets me that they use the rope. I can't use the rope because it hurts. It leaves burn marks on my neck. See, the other, the nylons, not nylons, leotards, not regular nylons, leotards, they're thicker, and you have pretty much a lot of control over what you're doing, then, as far as squeezing is concerned. And I could have, I could choke myself and, really choke myself and er, and then come out of there, and go to school, and no one would ever know because there's no marks on my neck. I will know of course because I will have a headache, and I'll be tired. Exhausted. But er (pause)—

The coroners, they don't like to write them off the way they're supposed to be either. Isn't that true? *Yeah?* Coroners will think—how come they won't write them off as autoeroticism when they're supposed to? *Sometimes they don't have enough knowledge.* You mean, it's not that they're being bullheaded and they won't do it. They just don't want to—I mean they just don't know any better?

[There was still another item on the young man's agenda that further extended the conversation, namely, the relationship of his own paraphilia to those listed in the reprint, already mentioned, that I had sent him (Money, 1984a).]

Differential Diagnosis

I ran off some copies of this article and was giving them to this counselor that I'm seeing. I showed him the list of all the philias. The amputee part is gruesome. Do they actually get turned on by cutting themselves apart? *Some arrange a hunting accident.*

Now, what's the next one after asphyxiophilia? Autass—*There's one where you arrange to get yourself assassinated by someone else. That's a bit similar to you, isn't it?* Uh, yeah, except no one else is involved but me. *Yes, well some people do actually get into big heavy masochistic stuff.* Do they actually get a hired killer and everything? *No, they don't hire them, they just pick up some hustler kids and*—And the kids kill them? *They do sometimes.* Do they pay them for it? *Usually not.* Then, why do they do it then? *That's a very good question.* That's weird.

And this other one, on stage, what's that? *Oh, putting on a live show so somebody can see you doing it, usually with a partner. You get turned on by having an audience watching you.* Yeah. No. That's totally opposite of me.

Fabrics, do fabrics have anything to do with me? What's a "high philia"? *Hyphephilia. That's a bit of fetishism.* What's fetishism? *Well, the fabric fetish, the feel of fabric. Taken all together the fabric fetishes are called hyphephilia. The "touchy-feelies."* And does that have something to do with me? The nylon? *Well, a little but, not much. It's very minor in your case. The loss of breath and strangulation and self-punishment are more important.*

What about the penile "exhibition?" *Exhibiting the penis? Well, you don't have that. That's where you go out in public and do it to girls who freak out.* (Chortling)—Girls who freak out? *Yeah, because they don't expect to see a guy with a hard-on in the ice cream parlor, showing it. They get panicky and frightened.* The guy has a what on, a hat on? *A hard-on, an erection on his penis, playing with it in public.* Ha! Ha! The girls freak out. Ha! That's pretty good, er—*Well, you've got your own one, you don't have any of these other ones.*

Yeah, I was wondering, see I've had masturbation fantasies, I've experimented where I was on a stage as a sex dancer or something on stage, but in a fantasy, masturbation fantasy. And then I was strangled after that. You know. *Uhumm.* But that's, that's why I was asking about these other, things about fabrics, and what I'm wearing, penile "exposition."

I've had, I've had some homosexual fantasies. I didn't say that, did I? I've had some homosexual fantas'—Are you still tape recording? *Yes, it's still going.* I've had some homosexual fantasies, too. You know, the homosexual peter in the butt and all that stuff, you know. I've had those fantasies too. And then killer, the, the—then the strangler strangles me. That's the only exposition [exhibitionism] I can think of.

And the erotic, the "narrarotic," what's the narra—the erotic talk, that's talking to people about this stuff? *Narratophilia. Telling dirty stories, while you're having sex, to get excited and roused up and keep your erection.* While you're having sex or while you're just talking to anybody. *While you're having sex with your partner.* No, that's not me either.

Yeah, that's pretty good when you said that none of them, it's very rare that they overlap or that someone has more than one. Mine is just the asphyxiophilia, huh? *That's it.* Okay. Well, I guess I got that cleared up then.

You haven't had any actual homosexual friendships or experiences, have you? I've never had any experience, friendships. I've had no friendship at all. *Would you be able to have one if somebody got interested in you, or would it be not attractive to you?* What? If it was a man? No. *You couldn't turn on to a man.* No. No, even though I've had fantasies with—well, when I have fantasies, I don't really have fantasies really with men. Though, when you think about it, I have some with men, maybe; but a lot of times I have fantasies with boys. You know, before their puberty. The boys have to have a girlish look. *Yeah.* So, if they're boys, they're girlish, sort of cute and a nice butt, pretty eyes, and all that stuff. But they're boys.

That's about it, but that's, you know, 2 percent. The other 98 percent is with girls drowning and strangling. And er; yeah, I still manage to attract toward the girls. Anyway, uh, you know, even if I was to say, well I'm not going to have anything to do with girls anymore, I'm just going to forget them and go chase after boys, uh, just; uh, I'd still end up attracting towards the girl, because I'm not attracted to boys at all, really. You know, still I'd want to have a relationship with a girl. Uh (long sigh). But then you have to have money to go out with girls. *Yeah.* I can't get, I'm busy going to school right now.

I wish I could make a movie about my autoeroticism, that'd be neat. *Well, you're a cinema student. You'll probably do that one day.* Yeah. *It'd be very good for teaching medical students. The public would be interested in it too, I guess.* Do you think I would be able to go, to, to give speeches or maybe give lectures on some of my problems to medical students? *Yes, I'm sure you could. If you were here, I'd let you do one next year.* Maybe, I could next year. *All right, we'll keep in touch and maybe you can come and talk to my class.* Well, that'd be neat because it makes me feel better. *I have to see my class on the 6th of March. If you could get down here on that day, I could let you talk to them.* The

6th of March? No, there's no way I could get out there now. *Uhumm.*
I just don't know why everything is so far away from me. You know.
Because it always helps when I'm with a group of people or with somebody that is interested and, er, you know. It always helps to talk it out
with somebody, or to talk out to a class, and everybody. I sure as heck
couldn't do that here. *Alright, well, I'll remember that for next year.*
Yeah. *Just in case it's a possibility.*

You haven't got any last minute things, have you? I can't think of
anything. *We've had a pretty good long talk.* Yeah. *Okay. So why don't
we sign off now? And I'll be waiting to get something from you in the
mail.* All right, then. *It was good to talk to you and I'm so glad you gave
me a call.* Yeah, I'm glad I did too.

Epilogue

As a sequel to his telephone interview, the young man embarked
on writing an autobiography, presently completed up through the age of
finishing grade school. He dated his sexual fantasies back to nursery
school. "I was only four years old and I just used to think and imagine
girls' panties in my mental mind pictures," he wrote. "I would make
mental pictures in my mind about the yellow and pink underwear on
girls; and then I would wish I could have a pink underwear to wear."
Already at this early age his imagery included borrowings from television
serials, like *Lost in Space,* that he watched. "I would dream about Angela
Cartwright's green tights and panties," he recalled. "There was another
girl on the show, too, and her name was Marta Kristen. She always had
yellow tights and panties in my dreams. I used to dream and think about
them over and over again. And I watched *Lost in Space* all the time, and
would wait for Angela Penny Cartwright to come on. She was my favorite,
and so were her legs and panties. Even though I could never see the
panties I would always imagine them in my head. And I loved it when
something on the show would scare her and she would scream. I loved
it when both girls screamed; or at least I was fascinated by it."

His specific fascination with "asphixia" [he spelled many words
in phonetic approximation] dated from around age eight, in the third
grade: "There was one girl who I fell in love for sure with. She had
brown hair and brown eyes, and I started loving her when I saw her go
to the bathroom in the rasberry bushes behind the garage. When me and

a neigbor girl somehow got into a fight with these other neigbor girls, and when I grabbed this eight year old beauty by the arm and wrist and tried to hold her in place, and she screamed, I just went loving mad. I started to breath heavy and I felt her warm soft wrist, and I wanted her; and I didn't want to fight her anymore, and so I let her go and she ran away. Finally we all made friends and there we were building a fort together. This happened in the summer of 1971, and me and the neigbor girl and the three sisters from the other part of the block built this fort; and it was the youngest sister that I had touched and started to like. Started to love. It was wild.

"One of the sisters was trying to teach us how to smoke a ciggerate and blow the smoke out of our nose and ears, but I choked to death, so I didn't. The neigbor girl did it real good, but the girl I fell in love with couldn't, or wouldn't try it. But the two oldest sisters were experts at it and it turned into a joke. Especially when the one tried to teach us how to do it. They were smoking all the time. But I don't think she liked me because she didn't have a chance to, because I got in trouble with my sister. She cought us smoking, and I got yelled and yelled and yelled at that night for playing with such a trashy bunch of girls. But when I saw the eight year old crush I couldn't help but look at her. She didn't go to the bathroom outside anymore and the so called trashy family moved.

"And then the girl who I thought was my sweetheart hopeful drowned while swimming at the beach; and then my fascination of the word asphixia came into play. I used to sit and try to imagine her nude body drowning underwater, and I wondered what it was like to drown; and I started having dreams while sleeping about swimming underwater and drowning, and then swimming like a fish where I didn't need any kind of air tank. But I could swim and watch other people drown, mostly girls. Then I started to masterbate. But I'm not sure exactly when or what the first fantasy was, if there were any at all, with the first orgasm. But it was sometime after her death. But it just had an effect on me ever since I saw her wiping her cute little butt with the leaves off the trees."

The loss sustained by the drowning of his girlfriend was exacerbated when, within a year, he was separated from a second girlfriend. Recalling this separation in adulthood, he gave specific biographical prominence to the fact that he had been humiliated in the girl's presence by being whipped for playing with her.

"Somewhere around this time," he wrote, "I fell in love with an eight year old blonde-haired, blue-eyed, deaf girl who was beautiful. But she couldn't talk, and she acted too wild for my sister who made me miserable because I wanted to play with her. The deaf beauty and myself were friends for real, but not for long. You see, when I first fell in love with her she slapped me in the face because she thought I was going to hit her, but I didn't; and my sister balled me out because she was still my favorite person and I wanted her. So I had to sneak off and play with her in the fields in back of her home. We didn't talk to one another because we couldn't understand, so we just chased each other around the fields and the junk that was lying in the yard. She fell down and I was looking at her scab on her soft wrist. I touched and looked it over and she let me examine it. I was hoping she didn't cry. She didn't cry. She never cried. She was tripping and falling around all the time. She was a maniac sometimes. She always rode her bike all over the neighbor-hood—and trying to talk to people. And she couldn't. She only made all those love noises that I just loved to hear. She did a lot of soft sqeels and hums and her words were all snug and musical notes with no lyrics to them. She was beautiful! My stepdad whipped me with his belt right in front of her, so that took care of that. She had a funny look on her face when he hit me. That was the last time I ever saw her because she moved away. But after that one embarrassing day, that same night I cried all night long, and I never forgot her. I loved her so much. But for a ten year old boy that was silly and rediculus, I would be told—and that I should think more about my mom and be more concerned about my school work then that dumb deaf girl they, my family, would say. My brother even took me to the deaf girl's new house, but I was afraid to stay and play because of getting into trouble and all; and I just had had enough. And she lived too far away anyway. But then my sister made fun of me because I didn't stay. So I just said: 'Well there was some kind of smell in the house that I didn't like, so I wouldn't let him leave without me,' and that lie seemed to satisfy everyone. I always remem-bered however, when the deaf beauty and I sat on the old mattress that was in the junkyard in the field in the back of her home. She always wore orange. Everyday she wore orange."

These autobiographical memories are etiologically significant, for they illustrate the principle that a paraphilia has its onset early in child-hood, before puberty; that it flourishes in the sexual vacuum created by being deprived of normal sexual learning and normal sexual rehearsal play; and that it is not "caught" from viewing or reading commercial pornography. The author of this autobiographical writing was raised in a morally strict and religious household, and was educated in a Catholic parochial school. He was deprived of access to sexual knowledge in print because of misdiagnosed hearing and learning problems as a child. His hearing impairment and eccentric behavior deprived him also of sharing the sexual knowledge of his peer group. He was sixteen before he knew how a baby is made.

The ultimate indictment of the family, church, and school system under which he was reared, however, is yet another deprivation, namely, deprivation of the possibility of disclosing the nature of his paraphilic fantasies during childhood and adolescence. He was obliged to live with them in solitude until age twenty-two. Only then could he dare to reach out for help. The experience of talking, writing, and approving his own story for publication seems already to be proving beneficial in bringing about a change in both the imagery and practice of autoeroticism. In addition, there is the promise of hormonal help, which is already being negotiated.

The two youths who, indirectly, made help available to this third one, had paid for it with their lives. They, too, had the paraphilic lovemap and the syndrome that go by the name of scarfing in vernacular nosology, and asphyxiophilia in professional nosology. They had died the victims of autoerotic fatality.

Motherhood Encumbered by a Nepiophilic/Zoophilic Lovemap

Paraphilia in Women: Ascertainment

The prevalence of paraphilia in women is unknown. There are no census statistics covering even a small regional population, and there has been no epidemiological survey. Clinical statistics are artifacts of gross underreporting because there are no specialty paraphilia clinics for women to which those in need of help may be routinely referred. Only a limited number of cases is ascertained from existing clinics, usually psychiatric clinics, where the women have registered, usually with a complaint other than paraphilia.

Like clinical statistics, court statistics also are biased either because the syndromes of paraphilia that afflict women seldom are prosecuted as criminal; or because the law, adhering to the Victorian stereotype of woman as asexual, does not ascertain women's offenses with the same frequency as it does men's.

Paraphilic women in need of help either must turn themselves in to the authorities if their paraphilic behavior warrants, it, or they must themselves discover where there is an agency or service that proffers help. Having located a source of help, a great many paraphiles lack the financial resources to pay for it. They must search again for free help. Some of them phone-in a question about their problem to an expert on a radio or television talk show. Some attend a public lecture on sex and covertly solicit help by approaching the speaker afterwards with a question or comment. This latter tactic was the one employed, in the era prior to the popularization of sex therapy, by the woman whose paraphilia is here reported.

Her husband was beside her as she talked. Simultaneously, several members of the audience were within earshot. Neither they nor her husband inhibited her from being very loquacious in revealing intimacies regarding the problems of her sex life and marriage. The hour was late. She and her husband both accepted the offer to continue the conversation in private and by appointment at a later date.

The Mask of Middle Class Normalcy

The lecture had been sponsored by the parents of children enrolled in a kindergarten cooperative, on the topic of issues in the home related to pornography. There was nothing that distinguished this woman and her husband from the other married couples seated in the audience. Both were of average height. He was of average weight for height. She was about 20 lb. (9 kg) overweight for height. She wore her hair modishly short. Her makeup was applied sparingly. Both of them were conservatively dressed.

The couple were in their early twenties when they married. The pregnancy history included eight miscarriages interspersed with three live births, a boy, a girl, and a boy, with five years between the oldest and youngest.

Juvenile Biography

The husband and wife were seen separately and together during the period of initial contact and again during the followup contact after eight years. For the period prior to marriage, the wife's biography was obtained by self-report exclusively.

She had been born out of wedlock when her mother was twenty-one years old. In a family of working-class, Irish Catholic stock, the disgrace of illegitimacy was so great that the pregnant mother was "put away." At birth, the baby was put into foster care until, at age two, she was adopted by the maternal grandparents. She called these people her mother and father. At first she lived alone with them. Later, their two sons, whom she called brothers, not uncles, married and returned home with their wives and infants. The woman she called her sister (actually her birth mother) by then married, lived elsewhere. Her birth father's whereabouts were unknown.

In retrospective recall, the actual age when she first ascertained the true history of her birth is fuzzy. It was around the age of twelve. The occasion was a traumatic one. Cut and bleeding, she had fled to find sanctuary in a neighbor's house, after her mother (grandmother) had beaten her with an extension cord for procrastinating over a Coke with friends, instead of returning directly home from the library. Other people then told her she "did not have to take it," because she was adopted.

Subsequently she accused her grandmother of not being her real mother, and was told her actual history. Besides the grandmother, only two people knew the true story—her birth mother and one of her brothers. The grandfather died without knowing that his adopted child was actually his daughter's out-of-wedlock baby.

His marriage had been marked by wrangling, fighting, and cussing. He often would stay away from home, working late. Unlike his wife, he was not abusive toward his adopted daughter; but he was neglectful insofar as he failed to intervene to prevent his wife's role as a cruel stepmother abusing and exploiting her Cinderella child, and depriving her of opportunities for playing and socializing with age mates.

The availability of sex education in childhood was zero. "I really don't know how I found out about sex," the woman said in a volunteer interview before a medical student class, "because nobody ever talked about it. But somewhere through the grapevine the children in school, or kids next door, I guess, I picked it up—because, believe me, I had it." Whatever she may have picked up before puberty was not recalled. Her memories of sex dated back to a time that could be only diffusely specified as pubertal.

Pubertal and Adolescent Biography

Because of the diffuseness of memory, it is not possible to date biographical experiences at and around age twelve in exact chronological sequence. This was the age when the girl first discovered the truth of her birth. It was also the age when she began to masturbate very frequently, and when she first arranged to have a genital rubbing experience with a boy, the son, approximately aged four, of her married brother (uncle) who lived in the same house. In addition, it was the age when she and a middle-aged brother-in-law of her mother (grandmother) established a noncoital, petting alliance which continued for some years before she terminated it.

In adolescent psychosexual development, it sometimes happens that a child exonerates a parent's or older person's former transgression by replicating it. The covert principle involved is that the more prevalent the transgression, the less abnormal it becomes in the eye of its recipient beholder. Thus, it may well be that, in the present case, having learned at age twelve of her own birth as a product of her mother's sexual transgression, the girl embarked on exonerating her mother by way of being a sexual transgressor herself. Her first sexual transgression, as she called it, if not solo masturbation, was with her brother's (uncle's) four-year-old son.

"Now, I'm sure it began with this child," she said in her talk to the medical student class, "and from there it went to other little boys [never girls] in the neighborhood, as I got to be twelve to fourteen, where I could baby-sit. I love little children, but something would just happen, like the chemicals within you would just completely change, and this is all you could think about. I don't know whether you would say molest. I never hurt anybody. And I always used very small babies that couldn't tell."

What she did with a young boy as partner was genital rubbing. She would position the child between her legs so that his genitalia and hers were in juxtaposition. Then she could rub her vulva up and down on his body. Vaginal penetration was not included. She described her sexual climax as "a tingling numbness that starts at the toes and goes up the body . . . energy release and tension relief . . . very pleasant."

Using dogs for genital rubbing had the same age of onset as the use of small boys. It was "by my own imagination," she said, that dogs became substituted for boys. "I invented it. . . . We had a dog at home but it was female. . . . The first dog I used was this boy's. . . . I'd go over and take care of his younger sister. . . . I don't think there could have been any penetration, probably just rubbing," though she might masturbate the dog afterwards. Usually, she recalled, she kept her panties on.

A student asked if she had been molested sexually as a small child. "That I wouldn't know," she replied, "but now that you've mentioned it, I can remember an uncle [great uncle], though I didn't come into contact with him until about twelve. . . . I can remember him doing it—not actually having relations with him, but making me feel his penis and stuff like that." He would ejaculate in her hand, never in her mouth, though there was some oral sex.

In later life the woman was not able to formulate either temporal or causal explanations of the origin of her paraphilic history, nor to relate either to early masturbation, or to encounters with children, animals, or adults.

Biography of Parenthood

The topic of motherhood first came up in the medical student interview. The woman's response highlighted the phenomenon not infrequent in cases of pedophilia and nepiophilia, namely, of the child who herself/himself never grew up. "I always played with dolls," she said. "I was very, very old and still played with the big, real-life doll babies. I still have one. Even though it's packed away, I don't think I would ever part with it."

Of her own children, she said: "You know, I hoped to be a good mother, but I do notice that I'm always pushing them away. I don't want to get too involved. My best relationship is with my youngest child who is four. But I was having all kinds of emotional problems with the others and, you know, I sort of blame that."

She spoke of her fear when her first child was born. "I just knew I was going to have a girl. When I found out he was a boy, I just about died, because all I could think of was that I am going to do the same thing to my child that I'm doing to these other children. At this point I was still doing it. I had been married three years and I was still doing it to children of friends of mine that I was babysiting for. Like I said, you're one person one minute, and then something happens within you. I can't explain it.

"There wasn't anybody I could go talk to about it, to find out why this was happening. The thing of it is that you go within yourself, because you don't want anybody to find it out. And my God if I had ever been caught! I guess it was my obstetrician that I went back to, probably for my six weeks check up, and I said I am petrified of this boy baby. I vaguely told him what had happened. All I can say was that his advice must have really been the turning point of my life. . . . Many a time the temptation was there, but I held tight and I never gave in."

The void was filled by dogs. "I don't want to dwell on it," she said, "but as far back as with the babies, in high school, right after high school, and in the apartment when we were married, I remember taking dogs and using dogs when I couldn't get a baby. And I thought oh my God, if anybody would ever catch me, you know, I'd be ruined for life. But the drive is so great to satisfy this need. . . . I would sneak dogs in the house, and get them up there some way. It's ridiculous when you think about it—filthy, dirty, germs—but you don't stop to think about it."

It was not feasible to find relief in solo masturbation. "Oh the guilt feelings," she said, speaking of dozing through an erotic fantasy culminating in masturbation. "I was just sick inside. . . . What is worse? Walking around with all this horrible tension inside of you, that you had no control over, and didn't create, or the guilt feelings from trying to release it?. . . . I'd walk around like paralyzed for days, because I couldn't have relations, and this is when it would end up in masturbation, which then went to guilt and sick feelings from that. . . . You had work to do and other things to think about, but you just couldn't do them. I would just walk in circles and I just couldn't think of anything else."

This was no idle exaggeration. The woman was, indeed, immobilized and unable to do her share of the domestic and child-rearing chores. They devolved largely upon the husband. In the mornings, he was the one who got the children off to school, as his wife was unable to rise and face the day. The children suffered. All three of them had severe behavioral pathology for which minimal help was available owing to the lack of financial resources throughout the extended period of their father's unemployment. He had been laid off as a sales representative when his firm's business declined.

There was no relief from this paraphilic pathology by way of ordinary sexual intercourse. When it was attempted, the wife experienced acute stomach pains. "When we first got married," she said, "I had a spastic colon. The only thing I could do to relieve the pain there were these deep burps that start way down in my stomach, and I work them up until they would come up. . . . Now it's gotten to be not really a joke but, instead of being angry about it, I'll say to him: See, I still love you. . . I'd have to interrupt him in the process of marital relations maybe three and four times in one evening, because I couldn't breathe. I'd have to get this thing out. He's very kind and loving, and he puts up with a hell of a lot of stuff from me. I know that the average man just wouldn't. They would have walked out on me a long time ago."

The husband knew about his wife's paraphilic disability, at least to some extent. He did not complain, but rather took on a martyr's role. Since boyhood, he had been plagued by fear of failure, and had his fear confirmed by the loss of his job. For years, despite retraining, he was afraid that a new job would end in another failure. Eventually he took janitorial work, far below his occupational level. He could not afford to admit that his marriage might end in failure. He was able to hold on either because he had entered the marriage with a high degree of sexual phobia or inertia, or because, confronted with the fact that his wife did not turn on to him sexually, he became apathetic. Whenever his wife turned for help, he faithfully followed—in an attempt to get family therapy, for example, at a local mental health facility. Some years later they jointly attempted to find "deliverance" in a charismatic renewal movement with which their Catholic parish was affiliated.

After the birth of the third child, they decided on family planning, and the wife went on the pill. Addressing the medical students, she led into the subject spontaneously, but obliquely: "Let me say that one of the biggest helps for me was after this third child was born. Now, I had had seven pregnancies at the time. I had a lot of emotional trouble. I had been to several psychiatrists, and things—but the sex part was never treated. I just didn't want any more children. I didn't want the third one because the other little one—they were like nineteen months apart, and I just wasn't ready for this baby. So the doctor put me on the pill. After I got on the pill, it relieved all these pressures and anxieties. Within three or four months I was a completely different person. That was a big step in my being able to function properly, because it relieved all of these big tensions, and this desire for so much sex. And, you know, nobody ever tells you that this is an effect of the pill."

At that time, the program initiated in the Johns Hopkins Psychohormonal Research Unit for the treatment of male paraphiles with a progestinic steroidal hormone, medroxyprogesterone acetate (Depo-Provera, Upjohn), was in its infancy. It is only with the knowledge of hindsight that one infers that the beneficial effect that this woman found while on the pill came from its progestinic component. A comprehensive and systematic study of progestinic treatment of paraphilia in women still remains to be carried out. It will be complicated by reason of the monthly fluctuation of ovarian progesterone secretion in synchrony with the mentrual cycle. In the meantime, there are a few anecdotal reports of women paraphiles who have benefited from Depo-Provera. In the present instance, the woman's own serendipitous discovery of the beneficial effect of the pill on her paraphilic fixation was the first indication that a pro-gestinic hormone may be of value in the treatment of paraphilia in both sexes. "Whether it is or whether it isn't," she speculated, "that was how the pill affected me."

Continuing she said: "I've had several more miscarriages since then, and I just go panicky when I think I'm pregnant, because I just feel like I can't cope with another child. I'm seriously thinking of going in for a tubal ligation. . . . My biggest fear is what is going to happen when I go off of these pills, you know, if these emotions come back and I don't know how to handle them."

After the tubal ligation, the sexual relationship with her husband continued to be perfunctory and lackluster. Sexually, with him, she felt "like a limp rag," she said. Simultaneously, she developed an increased interest in masturbation, up to two or three times a day, for which she reproached herself. Her fantasies began to include other young men, especially those in swimming trunks on the beach. She had dreams of "big lovely penises," which she attributed to her thinking that her hus-band had "too small of a penis" to be able to get her sufficiently aroused and interested in copulating with him. The big penis imagery backfired four years later when, while her husband was away, a convicted rapist entered the house and, stabbing her with a knife when she resisted, raped her. The assailant was a heavy-built black man. When she felt him push his large erected penis against her back, she began to think "this is the greatest thing that happened to me, one of the greatest fantasies of my life." Then the Lord miraculously helped her "to resist temptation," she said. The temptation did not, however, let up in her dreams of being molested and running around with someone else. They recurred, off and on, for several years. To some extent they relieved the fantasies of sex with children and with animals—in addition to the male dogs, she had tried also a male cat.

The full extent of the relief was not disclosed. At the time of the last contact, some years ago, the woman was deeply committed to finding a cure through her participation, with her husband, in charismatic "re-newal." Nonetheless, their marital lovemap pathology continued to be unremittingly debilitating, and the problems of psychopathology in the children had yet to be resolved.

Vocabulary of the Paraphilias, A to Z

acrotomophilia: a paraphilia of the stigmatic/eligibilic type in which sexuoerotic arousal and facilitation or attainment of orgasm are responsive to, and dependent upon a partner who is an amputee [from Greek, *akron,* extremity + *tomé,* a cutting + -philia]. An acrotomophile is erotically excited by the stump(s) of the amputee partner. The reciprocal paraphilic condition, namely self-amputation, is **apotemnophilia.**

adolescentilism, paraphilic: the paraphilia of impersonating an adolescent and being treated as one by the partner. *See also* **infanitilism; juvenilism.**

agalmatophilia: a fictional paraphilia, not a syndrome, in which the sexuoerotic stimulus is a nude statue or model of a human being [from Greek, *agalma,* image + -philia]. *Synonyms,* **statuophilia; Pygmalionism.** *See also* **pictophilia.**

amelotasis: the condition of being an amelotatist.

amelotatist: one who is attracted to amputees [from Greek, *an-,* not + *melos,* limbs + *tasis,* irresistably drawn toward]. *Synonym,* **apotemnophile.**

andromimesis: a syndrome of male impersonation in a natal female who is able to relate sexuoerotically exclusively with women, and who may be hormonally, but not surgically sex-reassigned. It is a syndrome of gender transposition, not paraphilia. *See also* **andromimetophilia.**

andromimetophilia: a paraphilia of the stigmatic/eligibilic type in which sexuoerotic arousal and facilitation or attainment of orgasm are responsive to, and dependent upon a partner who is an andromimetic or, in some instances, a sex-reassigned, female-to-male transexual [from Greek, *andros,* man + *mimos,* mime + -philia]. The paraphilic counterpart in men is **gynemimetophilia.**

apotemnophilia: a paraphilia of the stigmatic/eligibilic type in which sexuoerotic arousal and facilitation or attainment of orgasm are responsive to and dependent upon being oneself an amputee [from Greek, *apo,* from + *temnein,* to cut + -philia]. An apotemnophile becomes fixated on carrying out a self-contrived amputation, or obtaining one in a hospital. The reciprocal paraphilic condition in which the partner is an amputee is **acrotomophilia.**

asphyxiophilia: a paraphilia of the sacrificial/expiatory type in which sexuoerotic arousal and facilitation or attainment of orgasm are responsive to and dependent upon self-strangulation and asphyxiation up to, but not including loss of consciousness [from Greek, *asphyxia,* no pulse + -philia]. When the ritual is autoerotic, split-second failure to release the noose or gag at the onset of orgasm results in death. There is no technical term for the reciprocal paraphilic condition which is subsumed under the general category of **sadomasochism** with the dominant partner supervising, or presiding over the ritual. *See also* **autoerotic death.**

autagonistophilia: a paraphilia of the solicitational/allurative type in which sexuoerotic arousal and facilitation or attainment of orgasm are responsive to, and dependent upon being observed or being on stage or on camera [from Greek, *autos,* self + *agonistes,* principal dramatic actor + -philia]. The reciprocal paraphilic condition is **mixoscopia.** *See also* **troilism.**

autassassinophilia: a paraphilia of the sacrificial/expiatory type in which sexuoerotic arousal and facilitation or attainment of orgasm are responsive to, and dependent upon stage-managing the possibility of one's own masochistic death by murder [from Greek, *autos,* self + assassin + -philia]. The reciprocal paraphilic condition is **lust murder** or **erotophonophilia.**

autoerotic death: death from self-strangulatory asphyxia or electrical self-stimulation as part of a paraphilic masturbatory ritual. Release of the asphyxiating noose or reduction of the electrical current requires split-second timing at the critical moment, before blacking out. The autoerotic ritual may be repeated for years before the occasion when the critical moment is miscalculated and death ensues. *See also* **asphyxiophilia.**

autonepiophilia: a paraphilia of the stigmatic/eligibilic type in which sexuoerotic arousal and facilitation or attainment of orgasm are responsive to, and dependent upon impersonating a baby in diapers and being treated as one by the partner [from Greek, *autos,* self + *nepon,* infant + -philia]. Autonepiophilia may be adjunctive to masochistic discipline and humiliation. The reciprocal paraphilic condition, namely having an infant as sexuoerotic partner, is **nepiophilia.** *Synonym,* **paraphilic infantilism.**

bestiality: *see* **zoophilia.**

biastophilia: a paraphilia of the sacrificial/expiatory type in which sexuo-erotic arousal and facilitation and attainment of orgasm are responsive to, and dependent upon the surprise attack and continued violent assault of a nonconsenting, terrified, and struggling stranger [from Greek, *biastes,* rape or forced violation + -philia]. Acquiescence on the part of the partner induces a fresh round of threat and violence from the bias-tophile. Biastophilia may be homosexual as well as heterosexual, but is predominantly the latter, whether the biastophile is male or female. There is no term for the reciprocal paraphilic condition, namely stage-managing one's own brutal rape by a stranger, which probably exists only in at-tenuated form and rarely gets transmuted from fantasy into actuality. *Synonym,* **raptophilia.**

bisexualism: other-sex and same-sex contacts, either concurrently or sequentially in the course of development, and either in genital acts or as a long-term sexuoerotic status [from Latin, *bi,* two + sex]. The distribution of heterophilia and homophilia in bisexualism may be 50:50 or, more likely, in unequal proportions such as 60:40 or 20:80. Bisex-ualism is not a paraphilia, though paraphilias may exist in association with bisexualism.

bondage and discipline (B & D): in the vernacular, **sadomasochism** involving constraint with rope, chains, or other equipment, and abuse, punishment, or torture with various forms of equipment to enforce obe-dience, servitude, or enslavement.

bottom: sadomasochistic vernacular term for the submissive, masochistic partner.

buggery: a pejorative vernacular term and a legal term for anal copulation, chiefly between males, or with animals [from French, *bougre,* a corruption of *Bulgarian* derived from the medieval belief that Bulgarians were Manichean heretics who practiced anal copulation]. It is not a paraphilia. *Synonym,* **sodomy.**

chrematistophilia: a paraphilia of the mercantile/venal type in which sexuoerotic arousal and facilitation or attainment of orgasm are responsive to, and dependent upon being charged or forced to pay, or being robbed by the sexual partner for sexual services [from Greek, *chremistes,* money-dealer + -philia]. There is no technical term for the reciprocal paraphilic condition of forced charging or robbing.

chronophilia: one of the paraphilias in which the paraphile's sexuoerotic age is discordant with his/her actual chronological age and is concordant with the age of the partner, as in **nepiophilia, pedophilia, ephebophilia,** and **gerontophilia** [from Greek, *chronos,* time + -philia].

coprolagnia: *see* **coprophilia** [from Greek *kopros,* dung + *lagneia,* lust].

coprophilia: a paraphilia of the fetishistic/talismanic type in which sexuoerotic arousal and facilitation or attainment of orgasm are responsive to, and dependent upon being smeared with and/or ingesting feces [from Greek, *kropos,* dung + -philia]. There is no technical term for the reciprocal paraphilic conditions of defecating in the mouth or over the body of the partner. *See also* **urophilia.** *Synonym,* **coprolagnia.**

dendrophilia: love of trees. It is not a paraphilia.

displacement paraphilia: one of the paraphilias in which an intrinsic element becomes developmentally dislocated and repositioned in the lovemap, thus changing it from normophilic to paraphilic.

dominatrix: a female in the sadomasochistic role of total domination and discipline.

drag queen: vernacular term for a gynemimetic.

ephebophilia: a paraphilia of the eligibilic/stigmatic type distinct from **nepiophilia** and **pedophilia** in that the age of the partner is postpubertal and adolescent [from Greek, *ephebos,* a postpubertal young person + -philia]. The technical term for the reciprocal paraphilic condition in which an older person impersonates an adolescent is **paraphilic adolescentilism.** *See also* **gerontophilia.**

erotophonophilia: a paraphilia of the sacrificial/expiatory type in which sexuoerotic arousal and facilitation or attainment of orgasm are responsive to, and dependent upon stage-managing and carrying out the murder of an unsuspecting sexual partner [from Greek, *eros,* love + *phonein,* to murder + -philia]. The erotophonophile's orgasm coincides with the expiration of the partner. The reciprocal paraphilic condition is **autassassinophilia.** *Synonym,* **lust murder.**

exhibitionism: a paraphilia of the solicitational/allurative type in which sexuoerotic arousal and facilitation or attainment of orgasm are responsive to, and dependent upon evoking surprise, dismay, shock, or panic from a stranger by illicitly exhibiting an erotic part of the body, including the genitals [from Latin, *exhibere,* to exhibit]. The reciprocal paraphilic condition is **voyeurism,** also known as being a Peeping Tom. *See also* **peodeiktophilia.**

fetish: an object or charm endowed with magical or supernatural power; an object or part of the body charged, for a particular person, with special sexuoerotic power [from Latin, *facticius,* artificial].

fetishism: a paraphilia of the fetishistic/talismanic type in which sexuoerotic arousal and facilitation or attainment of orgasm are responsive to, and dependent upon a particular talisman or fetish object, substance, or part of the body belonging to the partner. There is no technical term for the reciprocal paraphilic condition in which the fetish, for example, a uniform, must belong to the self. *See also* **fetish.**

fetishistic/talismanic paraphilia: one of a group of paraphilias characterized by triumph wrested developmentally from sexuoerotic tragedy by means of a strategy that incorporates sinful lust into the lovemap on the condition that a token, fetish, or talisman be substituted for the lover, since lust irrevocably defiles saintly love.

formicophilia: a specialized variety of **zoophilia** in which sexuoerotic arousal and orgasm are dependent on the sensations produced by small creatures like snails, frogs, ants, or other insects creeping, crawling, or nibbling the genitalia and perianal area, and the nipples [from Latin, *formica,* ant + -philia].

frottage: *see* **frotteurism.**

frotteur: one who has the syndrome of **frotteurism.**

frotteurism: a paraphilia of the solicational/allurative type in which sexuoerotic arousal and facilitation or attainment of orgasm are responsive to, and dependent upon rubbing especially the genital area against the body of a stranger in a densely packed crowd [from French, *frotter,* to rub]. There is no technical name for the reciprocal paraphilic condition, namely being sexuoerotically dependent on being rubbed by a stranger. *Synonym,* **frottage.** *See also* **toucheurism.**

gerontophilia: a paraphilia of the eligibilic/stigmatic type in which the partner must be parental or grandparental in age [from Greek, *gēras,* old age + -philia]. Its parallels are **nepiophilia, pedophilia,** and **ephebophilia.** There is no technical term for the reciprocal paraphilic condition in which a younger person must impersonate a parent or grandparent.

golden shower: a vernacular term for **urophilia.** *See also* **water sports.**

gynemimesis: a syndrome of female impersonation in a natal male who is able to relate sexuoerotically exclusively with men, and who may be hormonally but not surgically sex-reassigned. It is a syndrome of gender transposition, not paraphilia. *See also* **gynemimetophilia.**

gynemimetophilia: a paraphilia of the stigmatic/eligibilic type in which sexuoerotic arousal and facilitation or attainment of orgasm are responsive to, and dependent upon a partner who is a gynemimetic or, in some instances, a sex-reassigned, male-to-female transexual [from Greek, *gyne,* woman + *mimos,* mime + -philia]. The paraphilic counterpart in women is **andromimetophilia.**

heterophilia: a condition of being in which sexuoerotic arousal and facilitation or attainment of orgasm are responsive to, and dependent upon a partner of the other morphologic sex [from Greek, *heteros,* other + -philia]. *See also* **heterosexualism.**

heterosexualism: other-sex contact, either as a genital act or as a long-term sexuoerotic status [from Greek, *heteros,* other + sex]. It is analogous to right-handedness in being in conformity with the norm and, therefore, not pathological in itself, though subject to other pathology. A heterosexual person is able to fall in love with, and become the pair-bonded sexuoerotic partner of only a person of the other morphologic sex. Paraphilias occur predominantly in association with heterosexual pairing. *Synonym* **heterosexuality.**

heterosexuality: *see* **heterosexualism.**

homophilia: a condition of being in which sexuoerotic arousal and facilitation or attainment of orgasm are responsive to, and dependent upon a partner of the same morphologic sex [from Greek, *homos,* same + -philia]. *See also* **homosexualism.**

homophobia: pathological fear of homosexualism [from Greek, *homos,* same + *phobos,* fear]. It is not itself a paraphilia, but may be associated with one, as in homophobic lust murder.

homosexualism: same-sex contact, either as a genital act or as a long-term sexuoerotic status [from Greek, *homos,* same + sex]. It is analogous to left-handedness in being not pathological in itself, though not conforming to the norm and not being exempt from other pathology. A homosexual person is able to fall in love with, and become the pairbonded sexuoerotic partner of only a person of the same morphologic sex. Homosexualism is not a paraphilia but a gender transposition, variable in extent and degree. Paraphilias may occur in association with either homosexual or heterosexual pairing. *Synonym,* **Homosexuality.**

homosexuality: *see* **homosexualism.**

humiliation: one of the variable components of sadomasochism.

hybristophilia: a paraphilia of the marauding/predatory type in which sexuoerotic arousal and facilitation and attainment of orgasm are responsive to, and dependent upon being with a partner known to have committed an outrage or crime, such as rape, murder, or armed robbery [from Greek, *hybridzein,* to commit an outrage against someone + -philia]. The partner may have served a prison sentence as a convicted criminal, or may be instigated by the hybristophile to commit a crime and so be convicted and sent to prison.

hyphephilia: one of the paraphilias of the fetishistic/talismanic type in which the sexuoerotic stimulus is associated with the touching, rubbing, or the feel of skin, hair, leather, fur, and fabric, especially if worn in proximity to erotically significant parts of the body [from Greek, *hyphē,* web + -philia].

inclusion paraphilia: one of the paraphilias in which an extraneous element becomes developmentally incorporated into the lovemap, thus changing it from normophilic to paraphilic.

infantilism, paraphilic: the paraphilia of impersonating an infant and being treated as one by the partner. *Synonym,* **autonepiophilia.** *See also* **juvenilism; adolescentilism.**

juvenilism, paraphilic: the paraphilia of impersonating a juvenile and being treated as one by the partner. *See also* **infantilism; adolescentilism.**

kleptolagnia: sexuoerotic gratification produced by stealing [from Greek, *kleptein,* to steal + *lagneia,* lust]. *See also* **kleptophilia.**

kleptomania: compulsive stealing, usually of objects that have symbolic significance but not intrinsic value to the thief [from Greek, *kleptein,* to steal + *mania,* madness].

kleptophilia: a paraphilia of the marauding/predatory type in which sexuoerotic arousal and facilitation or attainment of orgasm are responsive to, and dependent upon illicitly entering and stealing from the dwelling of a stranger or potential partner [from Greek, *kleptein,* to steal + -philia]. A kleptophile may or may not also forcefully demand or steal sexual intercourse. There is no techical term for the reciprocal paraphilic condition of setting oneself up as the recipient of kleptophilic robbery by a stranger or an acquaintance. *See also* **kleptolagnia; kleptomania.**

klismaphilia: a paraphilia of the fetishistic/talismanic type in which sexuoerotic arousal and facilitation or attainment of orgasm are responsive to, and dependent upon being given an enema by the partner [from Greek, *klusma,* enema + -philia]. There is no technical term for the reciprocal paraphilic condition, namely of being the enema giver. Klismaphilia may be adjunctive to rubber fetishism or to bondage and discipline.

lust murder: *see* **erotophonophilia.**

marauding/predatory paraphilia: one of a group of paraphilias characterized by triumph wrested developmentally from sexuoerotic tragedy by means of a strategy that incorporates sinful lust into the lovemap on the condition that it be stolen, abducted, or imposed by force, since it irrevocably defiles saintly love.

masochism: a paraphilia of the sacrificial/expiatory type in which sexuoerotic arousal and facilitation or attainment of orgasm are responsive to, and dependent upon being the recipient of abuse, torture, punishment, discipline, humiliation, obedience, and servitude [named after Leopold von Sacher-Masoch, 1836–1895, Austrian author and masochist]. The reciprocal paraphilic condition is **sadism.**

master: sadomasochistic vernacular term for the sadistic partner whose role is one of total domination and disciplinarian. *Antonym,* **slave.** *See also* **dominatrix.**

ménage à trois: *See* **troilism** [French, household of three].

mercantile/venal paraphilia: one of a group of paraphilas characterized by triumph wrested developmentally from sexuoerotic tragedy by means of a strategy that incorporates sinful lust into the lovemap on the condition that it be traded, bartered, or purchased and paid for, not freely exchanged, since it irrevocably defiles saintly love.

mixoscopia: a paraphilia of the solicitational/allurative type in which sexuoerotic arousal and facilitation or attainment of orgasm are responsive to, and dependent upon watching others engaging in sexual intercourse [from Greek, *mixis,* intercourse + *skopein,* to examine]. The reciprocal paraphilic condition is **autagonistophilia.** *Synonyms,* **scoptolagnia; scoptophilia.** *See also* **troilism.**

mysophilia: a paraphilia of the fetishistic/talismanic type in which sexuoerotic arousal and facilitation or attainment of orgasm are responsive to, and dependent upon self-degradation by smelling, chewing or otherwise utilizing sweaty or soiled clothing or articles of menstrual hygiene [from Greek, *mysos,* uncleanness + -philia]. There is overlap between **mysophilia, coprophilia,** and **urophilia.** There is no technical term for the reciprocal paraphilic condition, namely of supplying the mysophilic materials.

narratophilia: a paraphilia of the solicitational/allurative type in which sexuoerotic arousal and facilitation or attainment of orgasm are responsive to, and dependent upon using words and telling stories commonly classified as dirty, pornographic or obscene, in the presence of the sexual partner [from Latin, *narrare,* to narrate + -philia]. The same term is used for the reciprocal paraphilic condition, namely of being dependent on reading or listening to such material for sexuoerotic arousal.

necrophilia: a paraphilia of the stigmatic/eligibilic type in which sexuoerotic arousal and facilitation or attainment of orgasm are responsive to, and dependent upon not a live partner, but a corpse [from Greek, *nekros,* dead + -philia]. There is no reciprocal paraphilic condition except in the make-believe of being dead and copulating in a coffin in preparation for burial—for which there is no technical term.

nepiophilia: a paraphilia of the stigmatic/eligibilic type like **pedophilia** except that the age range is restricted to infancy [from Greek, *nepon,* infant + -philia]. The reciprocal paraphilic condition is **autonepiophilia,** or **paraphilic infantilism,** impersonating a baby. The parallel paraphilias are **ephebophilia,** and **gerontophilia,** as well as **pedophilia.**

normo-: a prefix meaning in conformity with a set of standards [from Latin, *norma,* a carpenter's square, rule, pattern].

normophilia *(adjective,* **normophilic):** a condition of being erotosexually in conformity with the standard as dictated by customary, religious, or legal authority [from Latin, *normo-,* + -philia]. *See also* **paraphilia.**

normophiliac: a person who manifests a normophilia. *Synonym,* **normophile.**

olfactophilia: one of the paraphilias of the fetishistic/talismanic type in which the sexuoerotic stimulus is associated with smell and odors emanating from parts of the body, especially the sexual and adjacent parts [from Latin, *olfacere,* to smell + -philia]. *See also* **osmolagnia.**

ondinisme: [French for undinism] *See* **urophilia.** *See also* **undinism; urolagnia.**

osmolagnia: sexuoerotic stimulation from odors [from Greek, *osme,* smell + *lagneia,* lust]. *See also* **olfactophilia.**

para-: a prefix meaning beside, near, beyond, aside, amiss, and sometimes implying alteration or modification [from Greek, *para,*].

paraphilia: a condition occuring in men and women of being compulsively responsive to and obligatively dependent upon an unusual and personally or socially unacceptable stimulus, perceived or in the imagery of fantasy, for optimal initiation and maintenance of erotosexual arousal and the facilitation or attainment of orgasm [from Greek, *para-* + -philia]. Paraphilic imagery may be replayed in fantasy during solo masturbation or intercourse with a partner. In legal terminology, a paraphilia is a perversion or deviancy; and in the vernacular it is kinky or bizarre sex. *See also* **normophilia.**

paraphiliac: a person who manifests a paraphilia. *Synonym,* **paraphile.** Either of the two endings, -iac and -ile, may be used for each of the -philias.

pederasty: the custom, tracing back to classical Greece, of older men having younger adolescent male lovers as the recipients of anal intercourse [from Greek, *pais,* boy + *erastēs,* lover]. It is not a synonym for **pedophilia,** nor for **ephebophilia.**

pedophilia: a paraphilia of the eligibilic/stigmatic type in which sexuoerotic arousal and the facilitation or attainment of orgasm in a postpubertal adolescent or adult male or female are responsive to, and dependent upon having a juvenile partner of prepubertal or peripubertal developmental status [from Greek, *paidos,* child + -philia]. Pedophile relationships may be heterosexual or homosexual or, more rarely, bisexual. They may take place in imagery or actuality, or both. The technical term for the reciprocal paraphilic condition in which an older person impersonates a juvenile is **paraphilic juvenilism.** The age and developmental status of the partner distinguishes pedophilia from **nepiophilia** and **ephebophilia.** *See also* **gerontophilia.**

Peeping Tom: *see* **voyeurism.**

peodeiktophilia: a paraphilia of the solicitational/allurative type in which sexuoerotic arousal and facilitation or attainment of orgasm are responsive to, and dependent upon evoking surprise, dismay, shock, or panic from a stranger by illicitly exhibiting the penis, either flaccid or erect, with orgasm induced or postponed [from Greek, *peos,* penis + *deiknunain,* to show + -philia]. There is no technical term for the reciprocal paraphilic condition, namely staring at a penis, which is subsumed under the broader concept of **voyeurism.** *See also* **exhibitionism.**

perversion: a vernacular and legal term for **paraphilia,** now outdated in biomedical usage.

petticoat punishment: a vernacular term for a masochistic transvestite practice in which a male, dressed like a school girl or servant girl, gets spanked.

-phile: a word ending, grammatically transformed from -philia, for noun usage. *Example:* one person, a **paraphile.** *Synonym,* **-philiac,** as in one person, a **paraphiliac.**

-philia: a word ending meaning love, or erotic and sexual love of a person, thing, or activity [from Greek, *philos,* loving, dear]. *See also* **normophilia; paraphilia.**

-philiac: a word ending, grammatically transformed from **-philia,** for noun and adjectival usage. *Examples:* one person, a **paraphiliac** (noun); one paraphiliac person (adjective). *See also* **-phile; -philic.**

-philic: a word ending, grammatically transformed from **-philia,** for adjectival usage. *Example:* a **paraphilic** syndrome. *Synonym,* **-philiac,** as in a **paraphiliac** syndrome.

pictophilia: a paraphilia of the solicitational/allurative type in which sexuoerotic arousal and facilitation or attainment of orgasm are not only responsive to, but dependent upon viewing pictures, movies, or video-cassettes of activities commonly classified as dirty, pornographic, or obscene, alone or in the presence of the sexual partner [from Latin, *pictura,* + -philia]. The same term is used for the reciprocal paraphilic condition, namely of having sexuoerotic arousal dependent upon showing visual erotica to the partner.

rape: seizing by force; sexual intercourse with the daughter or wife (conventionally not the son or husband) of someone else without her or his consent [from Latin, *rapere,* to seize]. Rape, as in the pillage and rape of a victorious army is not the same as **biastophilia** or **raptophilia,** and is not a paraphilia.

rapism: *see* **biastophilia; rape.**

raptophilia: *see* **biastophilia [from Latin,** *rapere,* to seize + -philia].

renifleurism: sexuoerotic stimulation from the odor of urine [French, from Latin, *ren,* kidney]. *Synonym,* **urophilia.**

sacrificial/expiatory paraphilia: one of a group of paraphilias characterized by triumph wrested developmentally from sexuoerotic tragedy by means of a strategy that incorporates sinful lust into the lovemap on the condition that it requires reparation or atonement by way of penance and sacrifice, since it irrevocably defiles saintly love.

sadism: a paraphilia of the sacrificial/expiatory type in which sexuoerotic arousal and facilitation or attainment of orgasm are responsive to, and dependent upon being the authority who imposes abuse, torture, punishment, discipline, humiliation, obedience, and servitude [named after the Marquis de Sade, 1740–1814, French author and sadist]. The reciprocal paraphilic condition is **masochism.**

sadomasochism (S/M): sadism and masochism viewed as reciprocals or counterparts of one another, and possibly alternating in the same person.

S and M (S/M): *see* **sadism; masochism; sadomasochism.**

scat: paraphilic vernacular term for **coprophilia [from Greek,** *skatos,* dung].

scopophilia: *see* **scoptophilia.**

scoptolagnia: sexuoerotic gratification produced by watching people engaged in sexual activity [from Greek, *skopein,* to view + *lagneia,* lust]. *See also* **mixoscopia; scoptophilia.**

scoptophilia: a paraphilia of the solicitational/allurative type in which sexuoerotic arousal and facilitation or attainment of orgasm are responsive to, and dependent upon watching others engaging in sexual activity, including sexual intercourse [from Greek, *skopein,* to view + -philia]. The reciprocal paraphilic condition is sometimes also referred to as scoptophilia; or by its own name, **autagonistophilia.** *Synonyms,* **mixoscopia.** *See also* **scoptolagnia; troilism.**

slave: sadomasochistic vernacular term for the masochistic partner whose role is one of total subservience and obedience. *Antonyms,* **master; dominatrix.**

sleeping princess (or prince) syndrome: *see* **somnophilia.**

sodomy: a legally defined term variously applied to zoophilia, and to mouth-genital or anal-genital contact between human beings, especially males [from the Biblical city of *Sodom*]. It is not a paraphilia. *Synonym,* **buggery.**

solicitational/allurative paraphilia: one of a group of paraphilias characterized by triumph wrested developmentally from sexuoerotic tragedy by means of a strategy that incorporates lust into the lovemap on the condition that an invitatory act belonging to the preliminary or proceptive phase be substituted for the copulatory act of the central or acceptive phase, thus ensuring that saintly love be not defiled by sinful lust.

somnophilia: a paraphilia of the marauding/predatory type in which erotic arousal and facilitation or attainment of orgasm are responsive to, and dependent on intruding upon and awakening a sleeping stranger with erotic caresses, including oral sex, not involving force or violence [from Latin, *somnus,* sleep + -philia]. There is no technical term for the reciprocal paraphilic condition of being the recipient, which occurs more readily in fantasy than actuality. *See also* **sleeping princess (or prince) syndrome.**

stigmatic/eligibilic paraphilia: one of a group of paraphilias characterized by triumph wrested developmentally from sexuoerotic tragedy by means of a strategy that incorporates lust into the lovemap on the condition that the partner be, like a pagan infidel, unqualified or ineligible to be a saint defiled.

stigmatophilia: a paraphilia of the stigmatic/eligibilic type in which sexuoerotic arousal and facilitation or attainment of orgasm are responsive to, and dependent upon a partner who has been tattooed, scarified, or pierced for the wearing of gold jewelry (bars or rings), especially in the genital region [from Greek, *stigma*, mark + -philia]. The same term applies to the reciprocal paraphilic condition in which the self is similarly decorated.

symphorophilia: a paraphilia of the sacrificial/expiatory type in which sexuoerotic arousal and facilitation or attainment of orgasm are responsive to, and dependent upon stage-managing the possibility of a disaster, such as a conflagration or traffic accident, and watching for it to happen [from Greek, *symphora*, disaster, + -philia]. The same term is applied to the reciprocal paraphilic condition in which the person arranged to be at risk as a potential victim of arranged disaster.

talisman: something, such as an amulet or charm, that produces extraordinary effects, as in averting evil or danger [from Greek, *telesma*, initiation, incantation].

telephone scatophilia: a paraphilia of the solicitational/allurative type in which sexuoerotic arousal and facilitation or attainment of orgasm are responsive to, and dependent upon deception and ruse in luring or threatening a telephone respondent, known or unknown, into listening to, and making personally explicit conversation in the sexuoerotic vernacular [from telephone + Greek, *skatos*, dung, + -philia]. Typically, the caller is not dangerous, only a nuisance. There is no technical term for the reciprocal paraphilic condition of inviting and possibly charging for such telephone calls. *Synonym,* **telephonicophilia.**

telephonicophilia: *see* **telephone scatophilia.**

top: sadomasochistic vernacular term for the dominant, sadistic partner.

toucheur: one who has the syndrome of **toucheurism.**

toucheurism: a paraphilia of the solicitational/allurative type in which sexuoerotic arousal and facilitation or attainment of orgasm are responsive to, and dependent upon surreptitiously touching a stranger on an erotic part of the body, particularly the breasts, buttocks, or genital area [from French, *toucher*, to touch]. There is no technical name for the reciprocal paraphilic condition, namely being sexuoerotically dependent on being touched by a stranger. *See also* **frotteurism.**

transexualism: the condition of crossing over to live full-time in the role of the other sex, with hormonal and surgical sex reassignment [from Latin, *trans,* across + *sexual*]. The term signifies a method of treatment and rehabilitation rather than a diagnostic entity. There are different biographical antecedents to sex reassignment, one of which may be paraphilic transvestism (transvestophilia). Transexualism itself is not a paraphilia. *See also* **gynemimesis; gynemimetophilia; transvestism.**

transvestism: cross-dressing, either as an act or a syndrome (transvestophilia) of episodic and partial gender transposition. The syndrome of transvestism is also a paraphilia of the fetishistic/talismanic type in which sexuoerotic arousal and facilitation or attainment of orgasm are responsive to, and dependent upon wearing clothing, especially underwear, of the other sex [from Latin, *trans,* across + *vestis,* garment]. The syndrome is believed to occur predominantly in men, and seldom, if ever, in women. There is no technical term for the reciprocal paraphilic condition, namely being sexuoerotically dependent on a cross-dressed partner. *See also* **gynemimesis; gynemimetophila; transexualism; transvestophilia.**

transvestophilia: a paraphilia of the fetishistic/talismanic type in which sexuoerotic arousal and facilitation or attainment of orgasm are responsive to and dependent upon wearing clothing, especially underwear, of the other sex [from Latin, *trans,* across + *vestis,* garment]. *See also* **transvetism.**

troilism: a paraphilia of the mercantile/venal type in which sexuoerotic arousal and facilitation or attainment of orgasm are responsive to, and dependent upon observing one's partner on hire or loan to a third person while engaging in sexual activities, including intercourse, with that person [from French, *trois,* three]. A threesome or group-sex party does not, per se, constitute a paraphilia. There is no technical term for the reciprocal paraphilic condition of being observed by a third party while on hire or loan. *See also* **autagonistophilia.**

undinism: *see* **urophilia** [Undine, a water nymph, from Latin, *unda,* wave]. *See also* **ondinisme; urolagnia.**

urolagnia: *see* **urophilia [from Greek,** *ouron,* urine + *lagneia,* lust]. *See also* **ondinisme; undinism.**

urophilia: a paraphilia of the fetishistic/talismanic type in which sexuo-erotic arousal and facilitation or attainment of orgasm are responsive to, and dependent upon being urinated upon and/or swallowing urine [from Greek, *ouron,* urine + -philia]. There is no technical term for the reciprocal condition of urinating on or in the mouth of the partner. *See also* **coprophilia.**

voyeurism: a paraphilia of the solicitational/allurative type in which sexuoerotic arousal and facilitation or attainment of orgasm are responsive to, and dependent upon the risk of being discovered while covertly or illicitly watching a stranger disrobing or engaging in sexual activity [from French, *voir,* to look at]. The reciprocal paraphilic condition is **exhibitionism.** *See also* **peodeiktophilia.**

water sports: a vernacular term for **urophilia.** *See also* **golden shower.**

zoophilia: a paraphilia of the stigmatic/eligibilic type in which sexuoerotic arousal and facilitation or attainment of orgasm are responsive to, and dependent upon engaging in cross-species sexual activities, that is, with an animal [from Greek, *zoon,* animal + -philia]. There is no technical term for the cross-species reciprocal paraphilic condition in which an animal mates with a member of the human or other species, though the phenomenon does exist.

*   *   *   *   *

Addendum, p.265

morphophilia: one of the stigmatic/eligibilic paraphilias in which one or more of the bodily characteristics of the partner is selectively particularized, prominant, or essential as a prerequisite to sexuoerotic arousal and the facilitation or attainment of orgasm [from Greek, *morphe,* form + −philia].

Glossary of Terms

[See also Chapter 26, Vocabulary of the Paraphilias]

acceptive phase: in a sexuoerotic relationship, the phase, following proception and preceding the possibility of conception, in which the genital organs become mutally involved in bodily contact, typically in genital union. *See also* **proceptive phase; conceptive phase.**

Adam/Eve principle: in embryological development and subsequently, the principle that nature's primary template is that which differentiates a female, and that something must be added to induce the differentiation of a male.

adolescence: the period of development between puberty and young adulthood, equated in the vernacular with teenage.

adulthood: the period of maturity that follows adolescence. There is no fixed age for the onset of young adulthood, except that legally it is for most purposes set at twenty-one.

AIDS: acquired immune deficiency syndrome, caused by a viral infection, and lethal; no cure has been discovered as of 1985.

ambiguous genitalia: a birth defect of the sex organs in which, from their embryonically undifferentiated state, they have failed to become fully differentiated as either male or female, but are unfinished. At birth the baby's sex cannot be declared on the basis of visual inspection. Diagnostically, the term is hermaphroditism or intersexuality. Embryologically, it is not possible to develop a complete penis and scrotum, together with a complete vulva and vagina.

amphoteric: partly one and partly the other [from Greek, *amphoteros,* both].

Androcur: the trade name of the hormone, cyproterone acetate, manufactured by Schering A.G., West Berlin. The hormone resembles progestin and is antiandrogenic. It has various clinical applications, the chief of which is to help sex offenders gain personal governance of their sexuoerotic conduct. *See also* **Depo-Provera.**

androgen: male sex hormone [from Greek, *andros,* man], produced chiefly by the testis, but also by the adrenal cortex and, in small amounts, by the ovary. In biochemical structure, there are several different but related steroid hormones that qualify as androgens. They differ in biological strength and effectiveness.

androgen-insensitivity syndrome *(also called* **testicular-feminizing syndrome):** a congenital condition identified by a 46,XY chromosomal karyotype in girls or women who appear externally to be not sexually different from normal females, except in some cases for a swelling or lump in each groin, or for the absence of pubic hair after puberty. The cells of the body are unable to respond to the male sex hormone, which is made in the testes in normal amounts for a male. They respond instead to the small amount of female sex hormone, estrogen, which is normally made in the testes. The effect before birth is that masculine internal development commences but is not completed. It goes far enough, however, to prevent internal female development. Externally, the genitalia differentiate as female, except for a blind vagina, which is usually not deep enough for satisfactory intercourse and needs either dilation or surgical lengthening in or after middle teenage. There is no menstruation and no fertility. Breasts develop normally.

androgyne: a person who manifests a merging of the roles traditionally stereotyped as belonging to male and female, respectively [from Greek, *andros,* man + *gyne,* woman]. Formerly the term was also used as a synonym for male pseudohermaphrodite, along with gynandroid as a synonym for female pseudohermaphrodite.

Andromeda: in Greek mythology, an Ethiopian princess who was chained to a cliff as a sacrifice to a sea monster, until rescued by Perseus, who married her.

androstenedione: an androgenic hormone, secreted by the adrenocortex, ovary, and testis, less potent than testosterone.

anorexia nervosa: a syndrome of deficient appetite, deficient nutritional intake, and emaciation ending possibly in death from self-starvation. It may alternate with **bulimia.**

anorgasmia: a hypophilic condition or syndrome, variable in etiology, of being unable to attain orgasm under normally conducive modes of stimulation.

Antabuse: a trade name for disulfuram, effective in the treatment of alcoholism as it produces aversive symptoms when combined with alcohol.

antiandrogen: a hormone or other substance that replaces androgen within the nuclei of target cells. It inhibits the secretion of testosterone from the testis and is itself either biologically inert or functionally very weak.

antipode *(plural,* **antipodes;** *adjective,* **antipodean):** the exact opposite or contrary of an idea, thing, or place [pronounce singular to rhyme with ode; plural, an.tip′.od.eez′].

apophasis *(adverb,* **apophasically):** to mention something in disclaiming intention to mention it. *Example:* I dare not mention the abominable practice, the secret vice.

assortative mating: the mating of individuals on the basis of reciprocally matching features, behavior, or mental characteristics.

atonement: an act of reparation or compensation to make amends for an offense or injury.

autoerotic: pertaining to sexuoerotic self-stimulation. The commonest form of autoeroticism is digital, that is, masturbation using the fingers and hands.

autoerotic death: death, typically from asphyxiation or electrocution, as an inadvertent culmination of a paraphilic sexuoerotic ritual involving self-strangulation or self-applied electric current.

bisexualism *(adjective,* **bisexual):** other-sex and same-sex contacts, either concurrently or sequentially in the course of development, and either in genital acts or as a long-term sexuoerotic status [from Latin, *bi,* two + sex]. The distribution of heterophilia and homophilia in bisexualism may be 50:50 or, more likely, in unequal proportions such as 60:40 or 20:80. Bisexualism is not a paraphilia, though paraphilias may exist in association with bisexualism.

blow job: vernacular term for fellatio.

bulimia: a syndrome of increased appetite, excessive nutritional intake typically associated with self-induced vomiting and excessive obesity. It may alternate with **anorexia nervosa.**

canon law: the body of ecclesiastical decrees by which a Christian church is governed and which, in the Roman Catholic church is, the *Corpus Jurio Canonici,* approved by the Pope. *See also* **secular law.**

catatonia *(adjective,* **catatonic):** a psychiatric syndrome of being immobile and unresponsive to sensory stimuli, but not unaware of them.

Cerberus: in Greek and Roman mythology, the three-headed dog that guarded the entrance to the underworld.

cerebral cortex: the external gray layer of the brain, the neocortex. *See also* **limbic system.**

childhood: biomedically, the period of development between infancy and puberty; legally, in the United States, the period of development until the eighteenth birthday (Public Law 98-292, The Child Protection Act of 1984).

chimera: an imaginary monster; in Greek mythology a she-monster that vomits flames and has the head of a lion, the body of a goat, and the tail of a dragon.

chordee: fixed curvature or tying-down of the penis or hypertrophied clitoris as in the hypospadiac birth defect characteristic of various types of hermaphroditism.

chromosome: one of 26 pairs of thread-like structures located within the nucleus of each of the body's cells, the function of which is to transmit genetic information to the cell that governs its growth and biological activity.

chromosomal mosaicism: a chromosomal pattern in which some cells of the body have the standard number of chromosomes (46,XX or 46,XY), and others have more or less, as in 45,X/46,XY (a mosaic variety of Turner's syndrome); or 46,XY/47, XXY (a mosaic variety of Klinefelter's syndrome), and many others.

Clérambault-Kandinsky syndrome: a sexuoerotic pathology in which a person has a limerent fixation on someone unattainable, and an unshaken and false conviction that his/her own life is totally under the control of the reciprocated limerence or love-smittenness of the unattainable one.

clitoris: the small, hooded organ at the top of the cleft of the female sex organs, which is the counterpart of the penis in the male. In the rat, mouse, and hamster, the clitoris is not hooded, but its covering is fused as in the male's penis to form a urinary tube.

coitus or **coition:** the sexual act, specifically the taking of the penis into the vagina, or the penetrating of the vagina with the penis; but more generally the complete interaction between two sexual partners. *See also* **copulate; intercourse.**

collusional marriage: a relationship between married people in which one partner instigates or engages in inordinate, deficient, irregular, or illicit conduct and the other covertly endorses it or covers it up, while ostensibly being in the role of martyr or recipient victim.

complementation: the process of becoming unlike, or reciprocated to someone else, the converse of identification, by reacting to that person's actitivites, behavior and reactions. The term is applied especially to the differentiation of G–I/R (gender-identity/role). *See also* **identification.**

compulsive cruising: *See* **sexual addiction.**

conceptive phase: in a sexuoerotic relationship, the third and the final phase which, if it occurs, is characterized by conception, pregnancy and parenthood. *See also* **proceptive phase; acceptive phase.**

concupiscence: ardent desire, especially as applied to sex or lust.

contusion: a bruise; an injury without breaking the skin.

copulate *(noun,* **copulation):** to couple, join, or unite as in sexual interaction. *See also* **coitus; intercourse.**

copulation fantasy: a fantasy that precedes and/or accompanies loveplay and/or genital union. It may either include or exclude imagery of the actual partner. If the partner is included, fantasy may yield to the total immersion of both in their body sensations. Otherwise, for the partner with the fantasy, its continuance may be necessary, distracting attention away from the other partner, which alone ensues that orgasm does occur. *See also* **masturbation fantasy.**

corpora cavernosa: the two cavernous or spongy bodies of the penis (or clitoris) that traverse the length of the shaft, one on each side, and that erect the organ when they become engorged with blood.

courtship: sexually, the behavior of indicating attraction and of inviting or soliciting attention and a reciprocal response. *See also* **proceptive phase.**

cruising: vernacular term, especially among gay people, for the overt manifestations and responses of the proceptive sexuoerotic phase that indicate one's availability and attractedness toward a potential sexual partner.

cunnilingus: erotic stimulation of the female external sex organs [Latin, *cunnus,* vulva] with the tongue [Latin, *lingere,* to lick], lips, and mouth of a partner of either sex, as a part of normal loveplay, and possibly inducing orgasm. *See also* **fellatio.**

cushingoid facies: a balloon-like swelling of the face characteristic of Cushing's syndrome, in which it is a symptom of a pathological excess of glucocorticoid hormone (cortisol) from the adrenal cortices. It is also a side effect of glucocorticoid therapy if the dosage is high, as is necessary in treating many illnesses.

CVAH (congenital virilizing adrenal hyperplasia): a syndrome produced by a genetically transmitted enzymatic defect in the functioning of the adrenal cortices of males and females, which induces varying degrees of insufficiency of cortisol and aldosterone and excesses of adrenal androgen and pituitary adrenocorticotropin [ACTH]. Abnormal function of the adrenal cortex starts in fetal life and, unless treated, continues chronically after birth. Females born with the syndrome have ambiguous genitalia and, if they survive without salt loss and dehydration, undergo severe virilization. Males are usually not recognized at birth, but if they survive, will prematurely develop sexually during the first years of life. In the severe form of the disease, untreated, mortality rate is almost 100 percent for both sexes. Treatment with glucocorticoids and in some cases also with salt-retaining hormone is life-saving and prevents untimely and, in girls, incongruous postnatal virilization. Plastic surgery is needed to feminize the genitalia. With appropriate therapy, prognosis for survival and good physical and mental health is excellent.

cyproterone acetate: the generic name of Androcur.

cystostomy: surgical implantation of a urinary drainage tube, usually temporarily following a genital operation, directly into the bladder. The suprapubic position is between the navel and the genitals. The perineal position is between the genitals and the anus, in the perineum.

defeminization: the developmental process in which feminization is inhibited or suppressed. The term is used chiefly to refer to defeminization of the brain attributed to a hormonal anomaly in prenatal life.

demasculinization: the developmental process in which masculinization is inhibited or suppressed. The term is used chiefly to refer to demasculinization of the brain attributed to hormonal deficiency in prenatal life.

Depo-Provera: the trade name of the hormone, medroxyprogesterone acetate, manufactured by Upjohn in the U.S. The hormone is progestinic and antiandrogenic. It has many clinical applications, one of which is to help sex offenders gain personal governance of their sexuoerotic conduct. *See also* **Androcur.**

deviant: not in conformity with what is considered ideal, standard, or normal, according to a given criterion standard which may itself be deviantly radical, conventional, despotic, or arbitrary.

diagnosis: the procedure of identifying a disorder or disease and distinguishing it from other similar conditions.

dihydrotestosterone: a powerful androgenic hormone formed from testosterone in peripheral target cells by the action of the enzyme, 5α-reductase.

dissociate *(noun,* **dissociation***)*: to separate or sunder that which is developing as a unity, or has become one, so that it becomes two or more unrelated or partially related entities. In mental life and its expression, these entities are experienced phenomenologically as alternative states of consciousness.

dromomania: compulsive and irrational running away [from Greek, *dromos,* course + *mania,* madness].

dualistic: paired or twofold; not monistic.

dyspareunia: a hypophilic condition or syndrome of difficult or painful coitus, of variable etiology, in men and women [from Greek, *dyspareunos,* badly mated]. The term is used chiefly in reference to women, but applies equally well to men.

ego dystonic: in psychiatry, the term used to apply to a proclivity, for example, toward homosexuality, in a person who seeks to be rid of it.

eidetic: characterized by vivid and precise visualization of objects or events previously seen.

elective mutism: failure to speak, or to speak about certain topics, that is not necessarily permanent, but is reversible under changed circumstances.

embryo: the unborn offspring from conception until, in the human species, the seventh or eighth week of gestation.

endorphin: the general term used to refer to all of the body's own endogenous morphine-like substances which are neuropeptides in chemical structure, and which function as neurotransmitters and neuromodulators.

ephebiatrics: that branch of health care that succeeds pediatrics and serves the age of adolescence and youth, prior to adulthood.

epididymitis: inflammation and pain of the epididymis, the coiled tubular structure immediately adjacent to the testis through which sperms are transported to the vas deferens and the urethra.

eponym *(adjective,* **eponymous***)*: the name of someone so prominently connected with a time, place, group, or event as to become a figurative or symbolic designation for it.

erotic: pertaining to sexual love or, more particularly, to its imagistic expression in daydream, fantasy, or dream, either autonomously or in response to a perceptual stimulus, and either alone or with one or more partners. *See also* **sexual.**

erotic apathy: a hypophilic condition or syndrome, variable in etiology, of defective ability to experience sexuoerotic arousal under normally conducive circumstances; misnamed, **lack of sexual desire.**

erotic inertia: a hypophilic condition or syndrome, variable in etiology, of inability to manifest sexuoerotic initiative or to maintain sexuoerotic activity under normally conducive circumstances.

erotic revulsion: a hypophilic condition or syndrome of variable etiology in which sexuoerotic activity, either in general or with a particular partner, is experienced as aversive and repulsive.

erotography: graphic or written material of an erotic nature, not stigmatized as pornography.

erotomania: morbid exaggeration of, or preoccupation with sexuoerotic imagery and activity [from Greek, *eros,* love + *mania,* madness]. *See also* **Clérambault-Kandisky syndrome.**

erotosexual: the erotic and the sexual experienced as a unity, with more emphasis on erotic imagery than sexual behavior. *See also* **erotic; sexual; sexuoerotic.**

estrogen: female sex hormone, produced chiefly by the ovary, but also in a small amount by the adrenal cortex and the testis, and named for its role in lower animals inducing heat or estrus [Latin, *oestrus,* gadfly; Greek, *oistos,* vehement desire, that which drives one mad]. There are several different estrogens, some more closely chemically related than others, and some more biologically potent.

estradiol: the most biologically potent of the naturally occurring estrogens. It is produced chiefly by the ovary. Commercially it is prepared in various compounds, such as estradiol benzoate and ethinyl estradiol.

estrus *(adjective,* **estrous):** the phenomenon of being sexually receptive, or in heat, as manifested at the ovulatory phase of the sexual cycle of the female, especially in subprimate species.

etiology: the theory of the factors in the genesis, origin, or cause of a disorder or disease.

extravasate: to seep through the skin, like drops of perspiration.

eugenics: the science that deals with breeding to improve the heredity of a species or racial stock.

exocrine: pertaining to a gland with a duct through which its secretion, for example, tears or saliva, passes.

exteroceptive: pertaining to a sensory organ that registers information from outside the body. *Antonym,* **interoceptive.**

5α-reductase: a naturally occurring enzyme necessary for the conversion of testosterone to dihydrotestosterone, the form of the hormone that some androgen-dependent cells require for their activation.

faggie: slang term, diminutive of fag or faggot, for a male who participates in sexual activity with another male and whose sexuoerotic status is homosexual.

falling in love: the personal experience and manifest expression of becoming intensely, and possibly suddenly, attached or bonded to another person. It may be reciprocal and a source of great ecstasy, or one-sided and a source of great agony. Usually it is erotosexual. *See also* **limerence.**

fantasy (*verb,* to **fantasy**): in imagination, a series of mental representations connected by a story line or dramatic plot that may possibly be translated into actuality. *See also* **masturbation fantasy; copulation fantasy.**

fantasize: colloquial modification of the verb, **to fantasy.**

fellatio: erotic stimulation by sucking [Latin, *fellare*] of the penis with the lips, mouth, tongue and throat, by a partner of either sex, as a part of normal loveplay, and possibly inducing orgasm.

fetus: the unborn offspring from the end of the embryonic period of development until birth, which in the human species extends from seven or eight weeks until delivery at thirty-six weeks.

fictive image: an image in the mind that is not perceived through the senses, but construed in the imagination on the basis of past perceptions retrieved from memory and reconstituted. *See also* **perceptual image.**

fisting: a vernacular term for the sexuoerotic practice of inserting the hand and forearm into the rectum or vagina, also known, respectively, as brachiorectal and brachiovaginal insertion.

flagellant: a person who undergoes whipping or scourging, especially as a religious penitent, or as a sexual masochist.

forensic: pertaining to or applied in legal proceedings.

foreplay: the traditional term for erotic/sexual activity during the proceptive phase in which manual, oral, and other skin and body contact ensure erection of the penis, lubrication of the vagina, and an urgency of being ready for orgasm, usually penovaginally induced.

45,X/46,XY syndrome: a chromosomal variant of **Turner's** (typically 45,X) **syndrome** evident neonatally by reason of a birth defect of

the sex organs which look hermaphroditically ambiguous. The gonads are neither ovarian nor testicular, but malformed or dysgenetic
streaks. Short stature is characteristic. At the age of puberty and
thereafter, sex-hormone treatment is necessary. Some babies with
the condition are assigned, reared and clinically habilitated as boys,
some as girls, the latter being more satisfactory.

FSH: follicle stimulating hormone, a gonadotropic secretion of the anterior lobe of the pituitary gland that stimulates sperm formation in
the testis, and the formation of the graafian follicle and the secretion
of estrogen from the ovary.

fuck *(noun; verb):* the Anglo-Saxon synonym for sexual intercourse,
coition or copulation (all Latin-derived). To copulate and to fuck
are the only one-word verbs for mutual genital intercourse. The
former is too stilted for vernacular use. The latter, being tabooed
as dirty, is often replaced by euphemisms like to screw and to ball.

fugue: an altered state of consciousness in which what is happening now
is unrelated to, or dissociated from what had happened then, in
another period of existence, as for example in dual or multiple
personality.

gay: vernacular term for a male with a homoerotic status and lifestyle.

gender: one's personal, social and legal status as male or female, or
mixed, on the basis of somatic and behavioral criteria more inclusive
than the genital criterion and/or erotic criterion alone. *See also* **gen-
der-identity/role.**

gender dysphoria: the state, as subjectively experienced, of incongruity
between the genital anatomy and the gender-identity/role (G-I/R),
particularly in the syndromes of transexualism and transvestism. *See
also* **gender transposition.**

gender identity: *see* **gender-identity/role.**

gender-identity/role (G–I/R): gender identity is the private experience
of gender role, and gender role is public manifestation of gender
identity. Both are like two sides of the same coin, and constitute the
unity of G–I/R. Gender identity is the sameness, unity, and persistence of one's individuality as male, female, or ambivalent, in
greater or lesser degree, especially as it is experienced in self-aware-
ness and behavior. Gender role is everything that a person says and
does to indicate to others or to the self the degree that one is either
male or female or ambivalent; it includes but is not restricted to
sexual and erotic arousal and response (which should never be ex-

cluded from the definition).

gender role: *see* **gender-identity/role.**

gender transposition: the switching or crossing over of attributes, expectancies, or stereotypes, of gender-identity/role (G–I/R) from male to female, or vice versa, either serially or simultaneously, temporarily or persistently, in small or large degree, and with either insignificant or significant repercussions and consequences. *See also* **gender dysphoria.**

genitalia: the sex organs, internal and external. The word is often used to refer to the external organs only. *Synonym,* **genitals.**

genital penetration phobia: a hypophilic condition or syndrome, variable in etiology, of irrational panic and disabling fear that prevents having the vagina entered by something, particularly the penis, or the penis enveloped in something, particularly the vagina. *Synonym,* **aninsertia.**

genitoerotic: erotic feeling and activity specifically involving the genitals in imagery and/or practice.

gestagen: a synthetic type of progesterone. *Synonym,* **progestin; progestogen.**

gestation: the period of bearing a pregnancy from fertilization to delivery.

G–I/R: gender-identity/role.

giving head: vernacular term for performing oral sex.

gonadectomy: surgical removal of a gonad, either an ovary or a testis, on one side or both; castration.

grand mal seizure: an epileptic seizure with convulsing and unconsciousness.

gurney: a wheeled cot or stretcher for ambulance or surgical use, or for use in prisons to restrain a prisoner while killing him/her with a lethal injection.

hallucinosis: a morbid condition, as in acute alcoholic hallucinosis, which is characterized by recurrent acute attacks marked by hallucinated auditory threats of persecution.

haptic: pertaining to the skin feelings and the sense of touch.

hermaphroditism: having genital attributes of both sexes [from Greek, *Hermes* and *Aphrodite,* god and goddess of love]. Some invertebrates are simultaneous hermaphrodites, and some fish are sequential hermaphrodites that change from male to female, or vice versa, once or more often in the course of a lifetime. In the human species, hermaphroditism is a form of birth defect, also known as intersexuality. It is defined as male or female hermaphroditism, if only testes or ovaries are present, respectively; as true hermaphroditism if both tissues are found as in ovotestes, and as gonadally dysgenetic when neither tissue is clearly differentiated. Human hermaphrodites do not have the complete sex organs of both sexes.

heterosexualism: other-sex contact, either as a genital act or as a long-term sexuoerotic status [from Greek, *heteros,* other + sex]. It is analagous to right-handedness in being in conformity with the norm and, therefore, not pathological in itself, though subject to other pathology. A heterosexual person is able to fall in love with, and become the pairbonded sexuoerotic partner of only a person of the other morphologic sex. Paraphilias occur predominantly in association with heterosexual pairing.

heuristic: serving to stimulate investigation; gaining knowledge through discovery.

hijra: in India, the name given to a full-time female impersonator or gynemimetic, in some cases also a eunuch with partial surgical sex reassignment, who is a member of a traditional social organization, part cult and part caste, of hijras whose worship is of the goddess, Bahuchara Mata, and whose sexuoerotic role is as women with men.

Hippocrates: the Greek physician (c. 460–377 B.C.) who is honored as the father of medicine.

homosexualism: same-sex contact, either as a genital act or as a long-term sexuoerotic status [from Greek, *homos,* same + sex]. It is analogous to left-handedness in being not pathological in itself, though not conforming to the statistical nor the ideological norm, and not being exempt from other pathology. A homosexual person is able to fall in love with, and become the pairbonded sexuoerotic partner of only a person of the same morphologic sex. Homosexualism is not a paraphilia but a gender transposition, variable in extent and degree. Paraphilias may occur in association with either homosexual or heterosexual pairing.

hormone: a chemical messenger secreted into the bloodstream from specialized glandular cells, especially those of the endocrine glands. It carries information to other cells and organs of the body. *See also* **pheromone.**

hustler: a person who works with energy and persistence, especially in marketing. As applied to sex, it is a vernacular term especially for males who earn money by servicing women and/or other men of a more effeminate disposition than their own.

hybridization: the mixing of two varieties, races, species, types or subtypes by cross breeding.

hyperorgasmia: the phenomenon of having an inordinate number of orgasms within a given period, as compared with a given criterion standard.

hyperphilia: a condition or syndrome, variable in etiology and diagnosis, of being sexuoerotically above standard or inordinate, particularly with respect to some aspect of genital functioning prior to and at the acceptive phase.

hypophilia: a condition or syndrome, variable in etiology and diagnosis, of being sexuoerotically substandard or deficient, particularly with respect to some aspect of genital functioning at the acceptive phase.

hypospadias: a birth defect in the male in which the urinary opening is on the underside of the shaft of the penis anywhere from the glans (first degree) to the perineum (third degree or penoscrotal hypospadias). Artificial hypospadias may occur as a sequel to injury, as in a circumcision accident.

hypothalamus: a structure of the diencephalic part of the brain of special importance in governing vital functions, including sex, by releasing neurohumoral substances from nerve cells which, in turn, govern the hormones of the nearby pituitary gland, and also the behavior of mating.

ictal *(adjective):* pertaining to the period when an epileptic seizure or seizure-like attack takes place.

identification: the process of becoming like someone as a sequel to assimilating or copying that person's activities, behavior, and reactions. The term is applied especially to the differentiation of G–I/R (gender-identity role). *See also* **complementation.**

imagery: in mental life, the collective representation of mental images or depictions of anything either perceived (perceptual imagery) or, if not actually present as a sensory stimulus, recognized in memory, dream, confabulation, or fantasy (fictive imagery).

impetigo: a streptococcal or staphylococcal infection that erodes the skin and dries to form a yellow-crusted sore.

impotence: a hypophilic condition or syndrome, of variable etiology, in which erection of the penis is lacking or defective under normally conducive conditions.

impregnation: the process of being rendered pregnant by the intromission of sperm into the uterus and the union of egg and sperm.

imprinting: developmental learning of a type first brought to scientific attention in studies of animal behavior by ethologists. Imprinting takes place in a given species when behavior phyletically programed into the nervous system of that species requires a matching social-environmental stimulus to release it, when the matching must take place during a critical or sensitive developmental period (not before or after), and when, having occurred, the resultant behavioral pattern is unusually resistant to extinction. In human beings, native language learning is a manifestation of imprinting.

incest: sexual contact customarily or legally forbidden on the criterion of the close kinship of the two people, variably defined on the basis of genealogical or totemic descent, or by reason of marriage or adoption [from Latin, *incestus,* unchaste].

incubus *(plural* **incubi):** an evil spirit or demon that assumes the form of a male and is supposed to lie upon sleeping people, chiefly women, and to have sexual intercourse with them; a nightmare. *See also* **succubus.**

infancy: babyhood; the period of development between birth and the beginning of early childhood between ages of two and three.

infatuation: foolish and extravagant passion, especially as applied to a love affair that does not meet with family or local community or religious approval, and does not conform to customary criteria of a well arranged marriage.

inguinal: pertaining to the inguen or groin, the region or crease between the abdomen and the thigh.

inguinal hernia: a hernia into the inguinal canal, as for example when an undescended testis protrudes into the canal but fails to reach the scrotum.

interfemoral: between the thighs.

interoceptive: pertaining to a sensory organ that registers information from within the body. *Antonym,* **exteroceptive.**

intercourse: connection or interaction between people. In sexual intercourse, the connection is usually defined as being between two people. It is erroneously restricted to putting the penis into the vagina or the vagina over the penis (penovaginal intercourse), for the entire sexual interaction between the partners constitutes sexual intercourse. *See also* **coitus; copulate.**

interictal *(adjective):* pertaining to the interval between epileptic seizures and seizure-like attacks.

intersexuality: *see* **hermaphroditism.**

keloid: a ridge or lump of progressively enlarging scar tissue due to the accumulation of excessive amounts of collagen during the healing of a wound.

labioscrotal: formed and looking like female labia that, instead of being completely separated are partially fused to resemble a scrotum; or are like a divided scrotum that resembles labia.

lactation: the secretion of milk from the breasts; the period of suckling the young until weaning.

laparotomy: a surgical incision through the flank or loin or, less precisely, the abdominal wall, as for the purpose of exploring the morphology of the internal reproductive organs.

lekking: a mating ritual, relatively rare among species, in which at the beginning of each mating season males assemble on the same site in the same mating ground or lek and wait to be visited by females and possibly selected for copulation.

lesbian *(adjective,* **lesbian):** female homosexual; named after the Aegian island, Lesbos, whence came the homosexual woman poet, Sappho, of ancient Greece. There is no corresponding eponym for a homosexual or gay male.

LH: luteinizing hormone, a gonadotropic secretion of the anterior lobe of the pituitary gland that stimulates testosterone secretion from the testis, in the male, and the formation of the corpus luteum and the secretion of progesterone from the ovary, in the female.

limbic system: the old cortex or paleocortex, as contrasted with the neocortex, of the brain. Its functions pertain to those aspects of the human mind and behavior that are shared by lower, especially mammalian species.

limerence *(adjective,* **limerent):** a recently coined name (Tennov, 1979) for the experience of having fallen in love and being irrationally and fixatedly love-smitten, irrespective of the degree to which one's love is requited or unrequited.

love: the personal experience and manifest expression of being attached or bonded to another person. There is sacred and profane love, and affectional and erotic love. The word is also used in the vernacular as a synonym for like. *See also* **falling in love.**

loveblot: a person (or image) who sufficiently resembles the person or image in someone else's lovemap as to become the recipient onto whom the lovemap is projected in a limerent love affair, regardless of whether the response is one of love requited or, being unrequited, induces a pathological reaction of lovesickness.

lovemap: a developmental representation or template in the mind and in the brain depicting the idealized lover and the idealized program of sexuoerotic activity projected in imagery or actually engaged in with that lover.

lovemap displacement: an intrinsic element that becomes developmentally dislocated from its regular place and repositioned in a lovemap, changing it from normophilic into paraphilic of the displacement type.

lovemap inclusion: an extraneous element that becomes developmentally incorporated into a lovemap, changing it from normophilic into paraphilic of the inclusion type.

lovesickness: the personal experience and manifest expression of agony when the partner with whom one has fallen in love is a total mismatch whose response is indifference, or a partial mismatch whose reciprocity is incomplete, deficient, anomalous, or otherwise unsatisfactory.

lust: longing, eagerness, inclination, or sensuous desire; sexual desire stigmatized as degrading passion.

masculinization: the developmental process of differentiating and/or assimilating masculine features and characteristics.

masturbation: genital self-stimulation by pressure or touch, usually involving the hands, and usually, though not necessarily, culminating in orgasm.

masturbation fantasy: a fantasy of erotosexual content that precedes and/or accompanies masturbation. *See also* **fantasy.**

meatus: an opening or passageway in the body, such as the urinary meatus.

medroxyprogesterone acetate: the generic name of Depo-Provera.

Mayer-Rokitansky-Küster syndrome: a sexual birth defect characterized by impaired differentiation of the müllerian ducts so that the uterus is rudimentary and cordlike. The deep part of the vagina is absent and the outer part is shallow or in the form of a dimple. The fallopian tubes may be defective, and there may be other, sporadic congenital anomalies. The ovaries are normal and induce normal feminizing puberty, except for lack of menstruation secondary to the defective uterus. Psychosexual differentiation is as a female.

micropenis: a birth defect in which the penis is extremely small. The maximum stretched length is no greater than 2.5 standard deviation units (SDU) below the mean for age, and possibly as small as 5.0

SDU below. The diameter is correspondingly small, with extreme hypoplasia of the corpora cavernosa. As compared with a micropenis, the average adult penis's stretched length is 6.6 inches (16.7 cm), with a standard deviation of 0.77 inches (1.95 cm) [Money, Lehne and Pierre-Jerome, 1984].

Minotaur: in Greek mythology, a monster, half man and half bull, confined in the labyrinth built by Daedalus for Minos, where it devoured the periodic tribute of seven youths and seven maidens sent by Athens, until it was slain by Theseus.

miscegenation: interbreeding of races; in U.S. usage, interbreeding of, in particular, white and black.

monistic: single or whole; not dualistic or pluralistic.

morphodite: colloquialism for hermaphrodite.

narcissism: self-love, or self-centeredness.

native lovemap: by analogy with native language, the lovemap that is assimilated as one's own personal, inalienable possession, regardless of how many of its attributes are shared, or not shared by others.

natural law: according to theological doctrine, divine law as revealed in nature. The doctrine of natural sexual law is that the divine purpose is procreation, and that sexual passion is sinful and immoral.

nocturnal penile tumescence (NPT): spontaneous erection of the penis during sleep occurring from birth to advanced old age, typically in three episodes a night for a total of 2-3 hours. It is associated with the REM (rapid eye movement) phase of sleep and with erotosexual dreams. It is measured by harnessing the penis into an expandable ring. Less is known about the corresponding phenomenon in females as there is no fully satisfactory technique for measuring vasocongestion of the female genitals.

nosocomial: belonging to or associated with a hospital, clinic, or other location of the practice of any branch of medicine, surgery, radiology, psychiatry, or pediatrics.

nymph: in Greek and Roman mythology, one of the minor nature goddesses personified as a beautiful maiden of river, mountain or woodland habitat.

nymphomania: in psychiatry, a term, loosely applied to females believed to have an insatiable sexual appetite. *See also* **nymph; satyriasis.**

ontogeny: in biology, the developmental history of the life span of a single individual or organism, as compared with phylogeny, which is the developmental history of all members of the species. *See also* **phylogeny.**

opioid: a peptide, naturally occurring in the brain and elsewhere in the body, the effect of which resembles that of opium or a morphine-like synthetic opiate.

opponent-process theory: a theory, recently proposed by Richard Solomon to augment traditional stimulus-response learning theory, according to which powerful aversion or attraction to a particular activity or experience undergoes reversal, as for example, pain reversing into pleasure, tragedy into triumph, terror into euphoria, or the proscribed into the prescribed.

orgy: vernacular term for sexual sharing of partners at a party, either in pairs, or as a group.

osteoarthritis: noninflammatory degenerative joint disease accompanied by pain, stiffness, and deformity.

pairbond: a strong and long-lasting closeness between two human beings or other creatures, such as exists between parent and child or two lovers.

parthenogenesis: development of an egg without fertilization by a sperm. Parthenogenic species are monochoric, that is, all members of the species are of the same gonadal type; for example, some species of whiptail lizard.

penis: the male urinary and copulatory organ, comprising a root, shaft, and at the extremity, glans penis and foreskin. The shaft or body of the penis consists of two parallel cylindrical bodies, the **corpora cavernosa,** and beneath them, surrounding the urethra, the **corpus spongiosum.** The penis in the male is the homologue of the clitoris in the female.

perceptual image: an image in the mind as presently being perceived through one or more of the senses. *See also* **fictive image.**

perineum: the region between the thighs, bounded by the anus and the scrotum or the vulva.

perversion: the pejorative and also the legal term for paraphilia.

petit mal seizure: an epileptic seizure characterized by lapse of attention and awareness, and failure of subsequent recall, but without convulsing and unconsciousness.

phalangeal: pertaining to any bone of the phalanges, that is the fingers or toes.

pheromone: an odorous substance or smell that acts as a chemical messenger between species and serves as a foe repellant, boundary marker, child-parent bonding agent, or lover-lover attractant. *See also* **hormone.**

phobia *(adjective* **phobic)**: morbid and persistent dread or fear [Greek, *phobos,* fear].

phocomelia: a birth defect of a limb, likened in everyday speech to a seal flipper, the hand or foot being attached to the trunk of the body by a single, small, deformed bone without, respectively, an elbow or knee [Greek, *phoke,* seal + *melos,* limb].

phyletic: of or pertaining to a race. Phyletic components or aspects of behavior in human beings are those shared by all members of the human race, as compared with behavior which is individual and biographically or ontogenetically idiosyncratic. Phyletic behavior is the product of both prenatal and postnatal determinants, as is personal biographic behavior. Each is the end product of both innate and experiential determinants.

phylism: a newly-coined term (Money, 1983) used to refer to an element or unit of response or behavior of an organism that belongs to an individual through its phylogenetic heritage as a member of its species. *Synonym,* **phylon.**

phylogeny: in biology, the developmental history of a species, which is the genealogical history shared by all members of the species. *See also* **ontogeny.**

polymorphism: the quality or character of occurring in several different forms.

pornography: explicit erotic writings and especially graphic depictions of a sexuoerotic nature that are legally or by custom classified as forbidden.

precocious puberty: *see* **premature puberty.**

prednisone: the generic name of one of the synthetic glucocorticoid hormones, used therapeutically as a substitute for cortisol from the adrenal cortices.

premature ejaculation: a hypophilic condition or syndrome, variable in etiology, of being unable to sustain the preorgasmic period of sexuoerotic stimulation, so that ejaculation occurs too soon relative to a self-defined, or partner-defined criterion, for example, at the moment of intromission.

premature puberty: puberty that begins before the normally appointed time and is completed by nine or earlier in girls, and eleven or earlier in boys. In may be an error of timing only, or may be associated with a brain lesion that affects the biological clock of puberty in the brain. *Synonym,* **precocious puberty.**

prenatal masculinization: in embryonic and fetal life, the masculinizing effect on the sexual anatomy and/or the sexual pathways of the brain that is induced by testosterone or other androgenizing sex hormones. The male fetus produces its own androgenic hormones. The female fetus does not need to produce feminizing hormones in order to not masculinize, as nature's basic design is to differentiate a female. Masculinizing is not synonymous with defeminizing. Thus some masculinization and some feminization of the brain and behavior may coexist.

proceptive phase: in a sexuoerotic relationship, the initial phase of reciprocal signaling and responding to attraction and solicitation, in a ritual of wooing or courtship prerequisite to the acceptive (copulatory) phase. Proceptive rituals are species specific, and the signals are variably odors, visual displays, movements, sounds, or mixed. In human beings proceptive rituals are known to be represented in imagery as well as carried out in behavior. *See also* **acceptive phase; conceptive phase.**

progestin: a synthetic type of progesterone. *Synonym,* **gestagen; progestogen.**

progesterone: pregnancy hormone, one of the two sex hormones chiefly characteristic of the female. It is produced by the ovary in the corpus luteum, following ovulation, and also by the placenta during pregnancy. The metabolic pathway of hormone production in the body leads from progesterone to androgen to estrogen.

progestogen: a synthetic type of progesterone. *Synonym,* **gestagen; progestin.**

prognosis: a forecast as to the probable outcome of a disorder or disease, either with or without treatment.

prosthetic testis: an artificial testis made of a soft silicone compound and surgically implanted for cosmetic effect into an empty scrotum.

prurient *(noun,* **prurience):** itching; longing or having a desire, in particular a desire that meets with moral disapproval because of the quality of the lasciviousness or lewdness attributed to it.

pseudohermaphrodite: synonym for hermaphrodite when the gonads are either both testes or both ovaries. *See also* **hermaphroditism.**

psychoendocrinology: the branch of knowledge that deals with the two-way relationship between mental and endocrine or hormonal functioning.

psychohormonal: pertaining to the two-way relationship between mental life and hormones. *Synonym,* **psychoendocrine.**

pubertal delay: failure of puberty to begin until after the normally appointed age for its completion, namely thirteen in girls and fifteen in boys. It may be an error of timing only, or it may be associated with a permanent hormonal deficit in the functioning of the gonads, the pituitary gland, or the hypothalamus in the brain.

puberty: the period between childhood and adolescence when the secondary sexual characteristics have the onset of their development, culminating in procreative maturity. *See also* **premature puberty; pubertal delay.**

pudendum *(plural,* **pudenda):** in human beings, especially females, the external genitals.

pulsatile: pulsating or functioning rhythmically or in cycles.

romantic *(noun,* **romance):** having a wondrous or story-book quality, visionary and idealized. Romantic love belongs to the proceptive phase of a relationship, especially at its onset. Historically, romantic love stopped short of the acceptive phase of sexual intercourse and marriage, but today there is no strict dividing line.

satellite: in genetics, a small mass attached to the end of the short arm of some chromosomes.

satyr: in Greek mythology, a woodland deity, usually depicted as having the hind end of a hairy, hoofed goat and the head end of a horned man, an attendant of Bacchus, fond of merriment and lechery.

satyriasis: in psychiatry, a term loosely applied to a male believed to have an insatiable sexual appetite. *See also* **satyr; nymphomania.**

secret vice: masturbation. *Synonyms,* **self-pollution; solitary vice.** *Antonym,* **social vice.**

secular law: law under the control of the judiciary, not the church. *See also* **canon law.**

self-isolation: phobic withdrawal from social interaction.

sex *(noun):* one's personal and reproductive status as male or female, or uncertain, as declared on the basis of the external genitalia. Also, a vernacular synonym for genital interaction, as in the expression, to have sex.

Sexaholics Anonymous: analogously to Alcoholics Anonymous, a network of self-help therapy groups for people with a particular sexual compulsion or addiction.

sexing-stealing-lying syndrome: a syndrome in which a forbidden or illicit sexual activity coexists with kleptomanic stealing, as in shoplifting, which is not per se erotic, and with confabulatory deception or pseudologia fantastica.

sexology: the body of knowledge that comprises the science of sex, or, more precisely, the science of the differentiation and dimorphism of sex and of the erotic/sexual pairbonding of partners. Its primary data are behavioral-psychological and somatic, and its primary organs are the genitalia, the skin, and the brain. The scientific subdivisions of sexology are: genetic, morphologic, hormonal, neurohormonal, neuroanatomical, neurochemical, pharmacologic, behavioral, sociocultural, conceptive-contraceptive, gestational-parturitional, and parental sexology. The life-span subdivisions of sexology are: embryonal-fetal, infantile, child, pubertal, adolescent, adult, and geriatric sexology. *See also* **sexosophy.**

sexosophy: the body of knowledge that comprises the philosophy, principles, and knowledge that people have about their own personally experienced eroticism and sexuality and that of other people, singly and collectively. It includes values, personal and shared, and it encompasses culturally transmitted value systems. Its subdivisions are historical, regional, ethnic, religious, and developmental or life-span. *See also* **sexology.**

sex roles: patterns of behavior and thought that are traditionally or stereotypically classified or coded as typical of, or especially suited to, either one sex or the other. Some sex roles are related to procreation, and some are not. *See also* **G–I/R**

sexual *(noun,* **sexuality***)*: pertaining to sex or, more particularly, the stimulation, responsiveness and functions of the sex organs either alone or with one or more partners. *See also* **erotic.**

sexual addiction: compulsively frequent reiteration of highly ritualized usage of the sex organs, under conditions of extreme specificity. The addiction is not to sex, generically, but to a particular animate or inanimate sexuoerotic stimulus, or type of stimulus, that is incorporated into the ritual activity. The activity itself may or may not qualify as paraphilic. The analogue of sexual addiction is drinking addiction to alcohol, from which the concept derives. *See also* **Sexaholics Anonymous.**

sexual rehearsal play: motions and positions occurring in infantile and juvenile play, such as pelvic thrusting and presenting, and coital positioning observed in human and other primates, that are components of, and prerequisite to healthy sexuoerotic maturity. *Synonyms,* **sexuoerotic** and **erotosexual rehearsal play.**

sexuoerotic: the sexual and the erotic experienced as a unity, with more emphasis on sexual behavior than erotic imagery. *See also* **erotic; erotosexual; sexual.**

sickle-cell disease: a genetically transmitted form of anemia, characterized by sickle-shaped red blood cells and abnormal hemogoblin.

sinus: a hollow cavity, sac, pouch, or opening, such as a **urogenital**

sinus.

sissy boy: a vernacular term applied to a boy whose developmental differentiation of gender-identity/role (G–I/R) is in variable degree discordant with the evidence of his genital morphology.

Sisyphus: in Greek mythology, a crafty, greedy King of Corinth who was condemned in the underworld to roll uphill a huge stone which constantly rolled back downhill instead of going over the top.

social distancing: absence of sociable approach or response to other people that is phobic rather than depressive, catatonic, or autistic aloneness.

social vice: promiscuous sex, chiefly with prostitutes or hustlers. *Antonym,* **secret vice.**

spermatorrhea: the term medically used for ejaculation while asleep and having an erotosexual dream in the era when this normal occurrence was falsely classified as pathology. *Synonym,* **wet dream.**

steroid hormones: a class of hormone biochemically constructed of the same components of which fats (lipids) are made. They include the hormones of the testis, ovary, and adrenal cortex.

Stockholm syndrome: the name for the bond of attraction that sometimes develops between abuser and abused, molester and molested, captor and captive, and in particular between terrorist and hostage. The term stems from the recent case of a woman held hostage at a bank in Stockholm, Sweden, who became so emotionally attached to one of the robbers that she broke her engagement to her prehostage lover and remained faithful to her captor during his prison term.

succubus *(plural,* **succubi):** an evil spirit or demon that assumes the form of a female and is supposed to lie under sleeping people, chiefly men, and to have sexual intercourse with them. *See also* **incubus.**

taboo (also **tabu,** and in Polynesia, **tapu,** sacred and forbidden): forbidden by tradition or social usage or other authority. A taboo generates fear, shame, and guilt in those who disobey it, thus enabling those in authority to wield power over those under them.

template: a pattern or mold that regulates the shape or appearance of a construction or idea.

territorial marking: in some animals, the marking of the boundary of the home territory with an odorous substance or pheromone secreted from a specialized marking gland, typically near the chin or rump, or secreted in the urine.

testosterone: the biologically most potent of the naturally occurring androgens, measurable in blood plasma and urine. It is produced chiefly by the testis from its precursor hormone, progesterone. In females testosterone is the precursor of estrogen in the ovaries. *See also* **progesterone.**

tomboy: a vernacular term applied to a girl whose developmental differentiation of gender-identity/role (G–I/R) as stereotypically defined is in variable degree discordant with the evidence of her genital morphology.

tonsillitis: inflammation of the tonsils.

Torquemada, Tomás de: 1420–98; Spanish Dominican monk, first Grand Inquisitor of the Spanish Inquisition.

urethroplasty: plastic surgery to construct an artificial urinary canal or urethra in a penis so as to correct a birth defect or an injury.

urinary fistula: an abnormally located opening of the urinary passageway, as when the two edges of a surgical repair fail to join along their full length.

urethral stricture: contraction or closure of the urethra, as when scar tissue contracts following urethral surgery.

urogenital sinus: in embryology, an elongated sac or funnel that precedes the differentiation of the external genitalia. In some types of hermaphroditism its differentiation fails to reach completion so that it constitutes a birth defect of the external genital orifice(s).

vaginismus: a hypophilic condition or syndrome variable in etiology, of premature contraction or spasm of the vaginal musculature in the course of sexuoerotic activity, preventing penile penetration or rendering it intolerably painful.

wet dream: a dream with erotic/sexual content that ends in sexual orgasm. It occurs with greatest frequency in pubertal and adolescent boys. In some instances, the content of the dream is lost or fails to exist, and the ejaculate is the sole sign of the occurrence.

xanith: in Arabic, the term usually translated as male homosexual, but applied only to men who partially impersonate women in clothing, manner, and life style, and in their sexuoerotic role with other men.

youth: the period of development between puberty and maturity; adolescence.

BIBLIOGRAPHY

Ampix. *The Amelotatist: A Statistical Profile.* Lawndale, CA. Author, 1978 (Available from Ampix, Box 864, Lawndale, CA 90260).

Baum, M.J. Differentiation of coital behavior in mammals: A comparative analysis. *Neuroscience and Biobehavioral Reviews,* 3:265–284, 1979.

Baum, M.J., Gallagher, C.A., Martin, J.T. and Damassa, D.A. Effects of testosterone, dihydrotestosterone, or estradiol administered neonatally on sexual behavior of female ferrets. *Endocrinology,* 111:773–780, 1982.

Beach, F.A. Sexual attractivity, proceptivity, and receptivity in female mammals. *Hormones and Behavior,* 7:105–138, 1976.

Belchetz, P.E., Plant, T.M., Nakai, Y., Keogh, E.J. and Knobil, E. Hypophysial responses to continuous and intermittent delivery of hypothalamic gonadotropin-releasing hormone. *Science,* 202:631–633, 1978.

Birkin, A. *J.M. Barrie and the Lost Boys: The Love Story that Gave Birth to Peter Pan.* New York, Clarkson N. Potter, 1979.

Boswell, J. *Christianity, Social Tolerance, and Homosexuality: Gay People in Western Europe from the Beginning of the Christian Era to the Fourteenth Century.* Chicago, University of Chicago Press, 1980.

Breman, J.G. and Arita, I. The confirmation and maintenance of smallpox eradication. *New England Journal of Medicine,* 305:1263–1273, 1980.

Bruno, R.A. *Laws Governing Sexual Behavior in the United States.* San Francisco (824 Corbett Ave., CA 94131), R.A. Bruno, 1984.

Bugliosi, V. and Gentry, C. *Helter Skelter.* New York, Norton, 1974.

Bullough, V.L. *Sexual Variance in Society and History.* New York, Wiley, 1976.

Carnes, P. *The Sexual Addiction.* Minneapolis, CompCare Publications, 1983.

Chan, S.T.H. Spontaneous sex reversal in fishes. In *Handbook of Sexology* (J. Money and H. Musaph, eds.). Amsterdam/London/New York, Excerpta Medica, 1977.

Clarke, I.J. The sexual behaviour of prenatally androgenized ewes observed in the field. *Journal of Reproduction and Fertility,* 49:311–315, 1977.

Cohen, M.N. *Lewis Carroll, Photographer of Children: Four Nude Studies.* The Rosenbach Foundation, Philadelphia, and Clarkson N. Potter, Publishers. Distributed by Crown Publishers, New York, 1978.

Comarr, A.E., Cressy, J.M. and Letch, M. Sleep dreams of sex among traumatic paraplegics and quadriplegics. *Sexuality and Disability*, 6:25–29, 1983.

Commission on Obscenity and Pornography. *Technical Report*, Vol. 2. Washington, U.S. Government Printing Office, 1971.

Comstock, A. *Frauds Exposed*. New York, J.H. Brown, 1880.

Crews, D. On the origin of sexual behavior. *Psychoneuroendocrinology*, 7:259–270, 1982.

Crews, D. Functional associations in behavioral endocrinology. In *The First Kinsey Symposium. Masculinity/Femininity: Concepts and Definitions*. Bloomington, IN, Jan. 26–29th, 1984.

Davies, B.M. and Morgenstern, F.S. A case of cysticerosis, temporal lobe epilepsy, and transvestism. *Journal of Neurological and Neurosurgical Psychiatry*, 23:247–249, 1960.

Dixon, D. An erotic attraction to amputees. *Sexuality and Disability*, 6:3–19, 1983.

Everaerd, W. A case of apotemnophilia: A handicap as sexual preference. *American Journal of Psychotherapy*, 37:285–293, 1983.

Fisher, C., Cohen, H.D., Schiavi, R.C., Davis, D., Furman, B., Ward, K., Edwards, A. and Cunningham, J. Patterns of female sexual arousal during sleep and waking: Vaginal thermo-conductance studies. *Archives of Sexual Behavior*, 12:97–122, 1983.

Gagné, P. Treatment of sex offenders with medroxyprogesterone acetate. *American Journal of Psychiatry*, 138:644–646, 1981.

Getz, L.L. and Carter, C.S. Social organization in *Microtus ochrogaster* populations. *The Biologist*, 62:56–69, 1980.

Getz, L.L., Carter, C.S. and Gavish, L. The mating system of the prairie vole, *Microtus ochrogaster:* Field and laboratory evidence for pair-bonding. *Behavioral Ecology and Sociobiology*, 8:189–194, 1981.

Goldfoot, D.A. Sociosexual behaviors of nonhuman primates during development and maturity: Social and hormonal relationships. In *Behavioral Primatology, Advances in Research and Theory*, Vol. 1 (A.M. Schrier, ed.). Hillsdale, NJ, Lawrence Erlbaum, 1977.

Goldfoot, D.A. and Neff, D.A. On measuring behavioral sex differences in social contexts. In *The First Kinsey Symposium. Masculinity/Femininity: Concepts and Definitions*. Bloomington, IN, Jan. 26–29th, 1984.

Goldfoot, D.A. and Wallen, K. Development of gender role behaviors in heterosexual and isosexual groups of infant rhesus monkeys. In *Recent Advances in Primatology*, Vol. 1., *Behaviour* (D.J. Chivers and J. Herbert, eds.). London, Academic Press, 1978.

Goldfoot, D.A., Wallen, K., Neff, D.A., McBrair, M.C. and Goy, R.W. Social influences upon the display of sexually dimorphic behavior in rhesus monkeys: Isosexual rearing. *Archives of Sexual Behavior*, 13:395–412, 1984.

Gosselin, C. and Wilson, G. *Sexual Variations*. New York, Simon and Schuster, 1980.

Green, R. and Money, J. Stage-acting, role-taking, and effeminate impersonation during boyhood. *Archives of General Psychiatry*, 15:535–538, 1966.

Gurney, M.E. and Konishi, M. Hormone-induced sexual differentiation of brain and behavior in zebra finches. *Science*, 208:1380–1382, 1980.

Hambert, G. *Males with Positive Sex Chromatin: An Epidemiologic Investigation Followed by Psychiatric Study of Seventy-Five Cases.* Göteborg, Elanders Boktryckeri Aktiebolag, 1966.

Hazelwood, R.R., Dietz, P.E. and Burgess, A.W. *Autoerotic Fatalities.* Lexington, Lexington Books, 1983.

Herrmann, W.M. and Beach, R.C. Experimental and clinical data indicating the psychotropic properties of progestogens. *Postgraduate Medical Journal,* 54 (Suppl. 2):82–87, 1978.

Hopp, D.H. A new concept of evolution. Abstract. Presented at the U.S. Army Medical Institute of Infectious Diseases, Fort Detrick, MD, May 2, 1980.

Hunt, M.M. *The Natural History of Love.* New York, Knopf, 1959.

Hunter, R., Logue, V. and McMenemy, W.H. Temporal lobe epilepsy supervening on longstanding transvestism and fetishism. *Epilepsia,* 4:60–65, 1963.

Jordan, H.W. and Howe, G. De Clérambault syndrome (erotomania): A review and case presentation. *Journal of the National Medical Association* 72:979–985, 1980.

Karacan, I., Hursch, C.J., Williams, R.L. and Littell, R.C. Some characteristics of nocturnal penile tumescence during puberty. *Pediatric Research,* 6:529–537, 1972.

Kempe, C.H., Silverman, F.N., Steele, B.F., Droegemueller, W. and Silver, H.K. The battered-child syndrome. *Journal of the American Medical Association,* 181:17–24, 1962.

Kilmann, P.R. Sabalis, R.F., Gearing, M.L., Bukstel, L.H. and Scoverin, A.W. The treatment of sexual paraphilias: A review of the outcome research. *Journal of Sex Research,* 18:193–252, 1982.

Kinsey, A.C., Pomeroy, W.B., Martin, C.E. and Gebhard, P.H. *Sexual Behavior in the Human Female.* Philadelphia, Saunders, 1953.

Kollar, E.J., Beckwith, W.C. and Edgerton, R.B. Sexual behavior of the ARL colony chimpanzees. *Journal of Nervous and Mental Disease,* 147:444–459, 1968.

Lewis, V.G. and Money, J. Gender-identity/role: G–I/R Part A: XY (androgen-insensitivity) syndrome and XX (Rokitansky) syndrome of vaginal atresia compared. In *Handbook of Psychosomatic Obstetrics and Gynecology* (L. Dennerstein and G. Burrows, eds.). Amsterdam/New York/Oxford, Elsevier Biomedical Press, 1983.

Mahood, J. and Wenburg, K. (eds.). *The Mosher Survey: Sexual Attitudes of Forty-Five Victorian Woman.* New York, Arno Press, 1980.

Maple, T. Unusual sexual behavior of nonhuman primates. In *Handbook of Sexology* (J. Money and H. Musaph, eds.). Amsterdam/London/New York, Excerpta Medica, 1977.

Marler, P. and Peters, S. Sparrows learn adult song and more from memory. *Science,* 213:780–782, 1981.

Merryman, W. Progesterone 'anaesthesia' in human subjects. *Journal of Clinical Endocrinology and Metabolism,* 14:1567–1569, 1954.

Migeon, C.J. Diagnosis and treatment of adrenogenital disorders. In *Endocrinology,* Vol. 2 (L.J. DeGroot, G.F. Cahill, Jr., L. Martini, D.H. Nelson, W.D. Odell, J.T. Potts, Jr., E. Steinberger and A.I. Winegrad, eds.). New York, Grune and Stratton, 1979.

Migeon, C.J. and Forest, M.G. Androgens in biological fluids. In *Nuclear Medicine in Vitro*, 2nd ed. (B. Rothfield, ed.). Philadelphia, Lippincott, 1983.

Mitchell, W., Falconer, M.A., and Hill, D. Epilepsy with fetishism relieved by temporal lobectomy. *Lancet*, 2:626–630, 1954.

Moltz, H. Of rats and infants and necrotizing enterocolitis. *Perspectives in Biology and Medicine*, 27:327–335, 1984.

Moltz, H. and Lee, T.M. The coordinate roles of mother and young in establishing and maintaining pheromonal symbiosis in the rat. In *Symbiosis in Parent-Offspring Interactions* (L.A. Rosenblum and H. Moltz, eds.). New York, Plenum, 1983.

Money, J. *Sex Errors of the Body: Dilemmas, Education, Counseling.* Baltimore, Johns Hopkins University Press, 1968.

Money, J. Discussion. In *Endocrinology and Human Behaviour* (R.P. Michael, ed.). London, Oxford University Press, 1968.

Money, J. Matched pairs of hermaphrodites: Behavioral biology of sexual differentiation from chromosomes to gender identity. *Engineering and Science* (California Institute of Technology) Special issue: *Biological Bases of Human Behavior*, 3:34–39, 1970a.

Money, J. Use of an androgen-depleting hormone in the treatment of male sex offenders. *Journal of Sex Research*, 6:165–172, 1970b.

Money, J. Transexualism and the philosophy of healing. *Journal of the American Society of Psychosomatic Dentistry and Medicine*, 18:25–26, 1971.

Money, J. Identification and complementation in the differentiation of gender identity. *Danish Medical Journal*, 19:256–268, 1972.

Money, J. Two names, two wardrobes, and two personalities. *Journal of Homosexuality*, 1:65–70, 1974.

Money, J. Psychologic counseling: Hermaphroditism. In *Endocrine and Genetic Diseases of Childhood and Adolescence*, 2nd ed. (L.I. Gardner, ed.). Philadelphia, Saunders, 1975.

Money, J. Paraphilias. In *Handbook of Sexology* (J. Money and H. Musaph, eds.). Amsterdam/London/New York, Excerpta Medica, 1977.

Money, J. The American heritage of three traditions of pair bonding: Mediterranean, Nordic and Slave. In *Handbook of Sexology* (J. Money and H. Musaph, eds.). Amsterdam/London/New York, Excerpta Medica, 1977a.

Money, J. The syndrome of abuse dwarfism (psychosocial dwarfism or reversible hyposomatotropinism). Behavioral data and case report. *American Journal of Disease of Children.* 131:508–513, 1977b.

Money, J. Sexual dictatorship, dissidence, and democracy. *International Journal of Medicine and Law*, 1:11–20, 1979.

Money, J. *Love and Love Sickness: The Science of Sex, Gender Difference and Pair Bonding.* Baltimore, Johns Hopkins University Press, 1980.

Money, J. Paraphilia and abuse martyrdom: Exhibitionism as a paradigm for reciprocal couple counseling combined with antiandrogen. *Journal of Sex and Marital Therapy*, 7:115–123, 1981a.

Money, J. The development of sexuality and eroticism in humankind. *The Quarterly Review of Biology*, 56:379–404, 1981b.

Money, J. New phylism theory and autism: Pathognomonic impairment of troopbonding. *Medical Hypotheses*, 11:245–250, 1983a.

Money, J. Pairbonding and limerence. *International Encyclopedia of Psychiatry, Psychology, Psychoanalysis and Neurology. Progress Volume I* (B.B. Wolman, ed.). New York, Aesculapius, 1983b.

Money, J. Paraphilias: Phenomenology and classification. *American Journal of Psychotherapy,* 38:164–179, 1984a.

Money, J. Family and gender-identity/role. Part I: Childhood coping and adult follow-up of micropenis syndrome in a case with female sex assignment. *International Journal of Family Psychiatry,* 5:317–339, 1984b.

Money, J. *The Destroying Angel: Sex, Fitness, and Food in the Legacy of Degeneracy Theory, Graham Crackers, Kellogg's Corn Flakes, and American Health History.* Buffalo, Prometheus Books, 1985.

Money, J., Annecillo, C. and Hutchison, J.W. Forensic and family psychiatry in abuse dwarfism: Munchausen's syndrome by proxy, atonement, and addiction to abuse. *Journal of Sex and Marital Therapy,* 11:30–40, 1985.

Money, J. and Bennett, R.G. Postadolescent paraphilic sex offenders: Antiandrogenic and counseling therapy follow-up. *International Journal of Mental Health,* 10:122–133, 1981.

Money, J. and Bohmer, C. Prison sexology: Two personal accounts of masturbation, homosexuality, and rape. *Journal of Sex Research,* 16:258–266, 1980.

Money, J., Cawte, J.E., Bianchi, G.N. and Nurcombe, B. Sex training and traditions in Arnhem Land. *British Journal of Medical Psychology,* 43:383–399, 1970.

Money, J. and Daléry, J. Iatrogenic homosexuality: Gender identity in seven 46,XX chromosomal females with hyperadrenocortical hermaphroditism born with a penis, three reared as boys, four reared as girls. *Journal of Homosexuality,* 1:357–371, 1976.

Money, J. and De Priest, M. Three cases of genital self-surgery and their relationship to transexualism. *Journal of Sex Research,* 12:283–294, 1976.

Money, J. and Ehrhardt, A.A. *Man and Woman, Boy and Girl: The Differentiation and Dimorphism of Gender Identity from Conception to Maturity.* Baltimore, Johns Hopkins University Press, 1972.

Money, J., Jobaris, R. and Furth, G. Apotemnophilia: Two cases of self-demand amputation as a paraphilia. *Journal of Sex Research,* 13:115–125, 1977.

Money, J. and Lamacz, M. Gynemimesis and gynemimetophilia: Individual and cross-cultural manifestations of a gender coping strategy hitherto unnamed. *Comprehensive Psychiatry,* 25:392–403, 1984.

Money, J., Lehne, G.K. and Pierre-Jerome, F. Micropenis: Adult follow-up and comparison of size against new norms. *Journal of Sex and Marital Therapy,* 10:105–116, 1984.

Money, J., Lehne, G.K. and Pierre-Jerome, F. Micropenis: Gender, erotosexual coping strategy, and behavioral health in nine pediatric cases followed to adulthood. *Comprehensive Psychiatry,* 26:29–42, 1985.

Money, J. and Lewis, V.G. Homosexual/heterosexual status in boys at puberty: Idiopathic adolescent gynecomastia and congenital virilizing adrenocorticism compared. *Psychoneuroendocrinology,* 7:339–346, 1982.

Money, J. and Mathews, D. Prenatal exposure to virilizing progestins: An adult follow-up study of twelve women. *Archives of Sexual Behavior,* 11:73–83, 1982.

Money, J., Mazur, T., Abrams, C. and Norman, B.F. Micropenis, family mental health, and neonatal management: A report on 14 patients reared as girls. *Journal of Preventive Psychiatry*, 1:17–27, 1981.

Money, J. and Primrose, C. Sexual dimorphism and dissociation in the psychology of male transsexuals. In *Transsexualism and Sex Reassignment* (R. Green and J. Money, eds.). Baltimore, Johns Hopkins University Press, 1969.

Money, J. and Russo, A.J. Homosexual outcome of discordant gender-identity/role in childhood: Longitudinal follow-up. *Journal of Pediatric Psychology*, 4:29–31, 1979.

Money, J. and Russo, A.J. Homosexual vs. transvestite or transexual gender-identity/role: Outcome study in boys. *International Journal of Family Psychiatry*, 2:139–145, 1981.

Money, J., Schwartz, M. and Lewis, V.G. Adult erotosexual status and fetal hormonal masculinization and demasculinization: 46,XX congenital virilizing adrenal hyperplasia (CVAH) and 46,XY androgen-insensitivity syndrome (AIS) compared. *Psychoneuroendocrinology*, 9:405–414, 1984.

Money, J. and Weinrich, J.D. Juvenile, pedophile, heterophile: Hermeneutics of science, medicine and law in two outcome studies. *Medicine and Law*, 2:39–54, 1983.

Money, J. and Wiedeking, C. Gender-identity/role: Normal differentiation and its transpositions. In *Handbook of Human Sexuality* (B.B. Wolman and J. Money, eds.). Englewood Cliffs, NJ, Prentice Hall, 1980.

Money, J. Wiedeking, C., Walker, P., Migeon, C., Meyer, W., and Borgaonkar, D. 47,XYY and 46,XY males with antisocial and/or sex-offending behavior: Antiandrogen therapy plus counseling. *Psychoneuroendocrinology*, 1:165–178, 1975.

Money, J., Wolff, G. and Annecillo, C. Pain agnosia and self-injury in the syndrome of reversible somatotropin deficiency (psychosocial dwarfism). *Journal of Autism and Childhood Schizophrenia*, 2:127–139, 1972.

Money, J. and Yankowitz, R. The sympathetic-inhibiting effects of the drug Ismelin on human male eroticism, with a note on Mellaril. *Journal of Sex Research*, 3:69–82, 1967.

Nadler, R.D. Sexually dimorphic behavior in the sexual relations of great apes. In *The First Kinsey Symposium. Masculinity/Femininity: Concepts and Definitions*. Bloomington, IN, Jan. 26th–29th, 1984.

Nanda, S. The hijras of India: A preliminary report. *Medicine and Law*, 3:59–75, 1984.

Neuman, D. *Bonnie and Clyde*. Los Angeles, Writers' Guild of America, 1967.

Niedermeyer, E. *Compendium of the Epilepsies*. Springfield, IL, Charles C Thomas, 1974.

Nielsen, J. *Klinefelter's Syndrome and the XYY Syndrome: A Genetical, Endocrinological and Psychiatric-Psychological Study of Thirty-three Severely Hypogonadal Male Patients and Two Patients with Karyotype 47,XYY*. Copenhagen, Munksgaard, 1969.

Nielsen, J., Sørensen, A., Thielgard, A., Frøland, A. and Johnson, S.G. *A Psychiatric-Psychological Study of 50 Severely Hypogonadal Male Patients, Including 34 with Klinefelter's Syndrome, 47,XXY*. Copenhagen, Munksgaard, 1969.

Nordeen, E.J. and Yahr, P. Hemispheric asymmetries in the behavioral and hormonal effects of sexually differentiating mammalian brain. *Science,* 218:391–393, 1982.

Parkes, A.S. and Bruce, H.M. Olfactory stimuli in mammalian reproduction: Odor excites neurohumoral responses affecting oestrus, pseudopregnancy, and pregnancy in the mouse. *Science,* 134:1049–54, 1961.

Parks, G.A., Korth-Schultz, S., Penny, R., Hilding, R.F., Dumars, K.W. Frasier, S.D. and New, M.I. Variation in pituitary-gonadal function in adolescent male homosexuals and heterosexuals. *Journal of Clinical Endocrinology and Metabolism,* 39:796–801, 1974.

Pfäfflin, F. The connections between eugenics, sterilization, and mass murder in Germany, 1933-1945. *Medicine and Law,* in press, 1985.

Reinisch, J.M. and Sanders, S.A. Early barbiturate exposure: The brain, sexually dimorphic behavior and learning. *Neuroscience and Biobehavioral Reviews,* 6:311–319, 1982.

Sanders, R.M., Bain, J., and Langevin, R. Peripheral sex hormones, homosexuality, and gender identity. In *Erotic Preference, Gender Identity, and Aggression in Men: New Research Studies* (R. Langevin, ed.). Hillsdale, NJ, Lawrence Erlbaum, 1985.

Sarrell, P.M. and Sarrell, L.J. Semenarche—Experience of sexually dysfunctional males compared to sexually functional males. *International Academy of Sex Research.* Ninth Annual Meeting, Harriman, NY., Nov. 22–29th, 1983.

Shepher, J. Mate selection among second generation Kibbutz adolescents and adults: Incest avoidance and negative imprinting. *Archives of Sexual Behavior,* 1:293–307, 1971.

Short, R.V. and Clarke, I.J. *Masculinization of the Female Sheep.* Distributed by MRC Reproductive Biology Unit, 2 Forrest Road, Edinburgh, EHI 2QW, U.K. Undated.

Shuster, R.H. Lekking behavior in Kafue lechwe. *Science,* 192:1240–1242, 1976.

Silver, R. *Biparental Care in Birds: Mechanisms Controlling Incubation Bout Duration* (J. Balthazart, E. Pröve, and R. Gilles, eds.). Berlin/Heidelberg, Springer Verlag, 1983.

Silverstein, C. *Man to Man: Gay Couples in America.* New York, Morrow, 1981.

Solomon, R.L. The opponent-process theory of acquired motivation. *American Psychologist,* 35:691–712, 1980.

Tennov, D. *Love and Limerence: The Experience of Being in Love.* New York, Stein and Day, 1979.

Tissot, S.A. *A Treatise on the Diseases Produced by Onanism.* Translated from a New Edition of the French, with Notes and Appendix by an American Physician. New York, 1832. Facsimile reprint edition in *The Secret Vice Exposed! Some Arguments Against Masturbation* (C. Rosenberg and C. Smith-Rosenberg, advisory eds.). New York, Arno Press, 1974.

Trall, R.T. *Sexual Physiology: A Scientific and Popular Exposition of the Fundamental Problems in Sociology* (29th ed.). New York, M.L. Holbrook, 1881. Facsimile reprint edition. New York, Arno Press, 1974.

Wallman, J., Grabon, M. and Silver, R. What determines the pattern of sharing in incubation and brooding in ringdoves? *Journal of Comparative and Physiological Psychology*, 93:481–492, 1979.

Walker, P.A. and Meyer, W.J. III Medroxyprogesterone acetate treatment for paraphiliac sex offenders. In *Violence and the Violent Individual* (J.R. Hayes, T.K. Roberts and K.S. Solway, eds.). New York, SP Medical and Scientific Books, 1981.

Ward, I.L. Prenatal stress feminizes and demasculinizes the behavior of males. *Science*, 175:82–84, 1972.

Ward, I.L. The prenatal stress syndrome: Current status. *Psychoneuroendocrinology*, 9:3–11, 1984.

Ward, I.L. and Weisz, J. Maternal stress alters plasma testosterone in fetal males. *Science*, 207:328–329, 1980.

Waters, J. Next stop: The electric chair. John Waters interviews Arthur Goode. Baltimore, *City Paper*, 8:8–10, March, 9–15, 1984.

Weis, D.L. Affective reactions of woman to their initial experience of coitus. *Journal of Sex Research*, 19:209–237, 1983.

Wikan, U. Man becomes woman: Transexualism in Oman as a key to gender roles. *Man (N.S.)*, 12:304–319, 1977.

Wildt, L., Marshall, G. and Knobil, E. Experimental induction of puberty in the infantile female rhesus monkey. *Science*, 207:1373–1375, 1980.

Williams, G.J. Cruelty and kindness to children: Documentary of a century, 1874–1974. In *Traumatic Abuse and Neglect of Children at Home* (G.J. Williams and J. Money, eds.). Baltimore, Johns Hopkins University Press, 1980.

Name Index

Subject Index

Also available from Prometheus Books . . .

VANDALIZED LOVEMAPS
Paraphilic Outcome of Seven Cases in Pediatric Sexology
by John Money and Margaret Lamacz

Vandalized lovemaps: In science and medicine they are called paraphilic. In the criminal justice system they are called perverted. On the street they are called kinky and bizarre.

A lovemap has a developmental history, beginning prenatally. This book traces that history, year by year, in seven cases in which the outcome has been a lovemap that is vandalized, or paraphilic. It is the first study to chronicle lovemaps in progress rather than reconstructing them after the fact.

The seven sets of biographical findings are sorted and sifted in the final three chapters, where the principles of paraphilic lovemap formation are examined. These principles are synthesized into a theory of biographical determinism, which makes special use of the ethological principle of critical-period effects, and of Solomon's principle of opponent-process. The book concludes with a scholarly review of the five grand principles of determinism that have been used to explain paraphilia for a century or more. Sexologists from Krafft-Ebing to Freud are placed in historical perspective, according to the criterion of which deterministic principles they adhere to.

John Money is Professor of Medical Psychology and Professor of Pediatrics, emeritus, at The Johns Hopkins University and Hospital, where he is director of the Psychohormonal Research Unit. He is internationally known for his clinical and research work in gender identity, and the new and growing science of developmental sexology.

Margaret Lamacz is a Ph.D. candidate at The Johns Hopkins University and Hospital, where she is a Research Associate in the Psychohormonal Research Unit.

ISBN 0-87975-513-X Cloth

Prometheus Books
700 E. Amherst Street, Buffalo, New York 14215
Call toll-free: (800) 421-0351. In N.Y. State: (716) 837-2475

AMPUTEES AND DEVOTEES
By Grant C. Riddle
Introduction by John Money

Forthcoming from Irvington—1989

This is the first book to deal with the personal, psychological, and sociological realities of this little understood romantic and sexual world.

> *"Amputees and Devotees is of utmost importance in creating both a public and a professional awareness of what paraphilic amputeeism is really like."*
>
> —*John Money, Ph.D.*

Table of Contents
Why all the fuss, anyway?
Once upon a time...
Amputees in Literature
Profiles in Courage
Sociology for the Amputee
Love, Sex, and the Disabled
Psychology for the Amputee
Lovemap Development
Lovemaps and Eligibility
Fantasyland
Hobbyists, Devotees, et. al.
Psychology of the Devotee
The Woman's Viewpoint
A Woman's Opinion
A Statistical Survey of Devotees
An Active Investigation
Additional Viewpoints
Recent Evaluations
Lovemaps and the World of Amputees

Cloth   Price: $24.95 tentative

Irvington Publishers, Inc.
740 Broadway, Suite 905, New York, New York 10003